Globalization and Emerging Societies

D1741921

Frontiers of Globalization Series

Series Editor: **Jan Nederveen Pieterse**, Professor of Sociology, University of California, Santa Barbara, US.

Titles Include

Jan Neverdeen Pieterse and Boike Rehbein (*editors*)
GLOBALIZATION AND EMERGING SOCIETIES
Development and Inequality

Boike Rehbein (*editor*)
GLOBALIZATION AND INEQUALITY IN EMERGING SOCIETIES

Frontiers of Globalization Series
Series Standing Order: HBK: 9780230284326 PBK: 9780230284333
(*outside North America only*)

You can receive future titles in this series as they are published by placing a standing order. Please contact your bookseller or, in case of difficulty, write to us at the address below with your name and address, the title of the series and the ISBN quoted above.

Customer Services Department, Macmillan Distribution Ltd, Houndmills, Basingstoke, Hampshire RG21 6XS, England

Globalization and Emerging Societies

Development and Inequality

Edited by

Jan Nederveen Pieterse
University of California, Santa Barbara

Boike Rehbein
University of Freiburg, Germany

First published in hardback 2009
This paperback edition published 2011 by
PALGRAVE MACMILLAN

Palgrave Macmillan in the UK is an imprint of Macmillan Publishers Limited,
registered in England, company number 785998, of Houndmills, Basingstoke,
Hampshire RG21 6XS.

Palgrave Macmillan in the US is a division of St Martin's Press LLC,
175 Fifth Avenue, New York, NY 10010.

Palgrave Macmillan is the global academic imprint of the above companies
and has companies and representatives throughout the world.

Palgrave® and Macmillan® are registered trademarks in the United States,
the United Kingdom, Europe and other countries.

ISBN 978–0–230–22405–6   hardback
ISBN 978–0–230–35449–4   paperback

This book is printed on paper suitable for recycling and made from fully
managed and sustained forest sources. Logging, pulping and manufacturing
processes are expected to conform to the environmental regulations of the
country of origin.

A catalogue record for this book is available from the British Library.

A catalog record for this book is available from the Library of Congress.

10   9   8   7   6   5   4   3   2   1
20   19   18   17   16   15   14   13   12   11

Printed and bound in Great Britain by
CPI Antony Rowe, Chippenham and Eastbourne

Contents

Contributors

Joanildo A. Burity is Senior Researcher, Fundação Joaquim Nabuco, and Lecturer in Sociology and Political Science, Federal University of Pernambuco, Recife, Brazil. His research interests include religion and politics, collective action and participatory politics, culture and identity, and contemporary political theory. Recent books are *Redes, parcerias e participação religiosa nas políticas sociais no Brasil* (2006), and, as editor, with Maria D. C. Machado, *Os votos de Deus: evangélicos, política e eleições no Brasil* (2007) (joanildo@fundaj.gov.br).

Johanna Jansson is a Senior Analyst at the Centre for Chinese Studies, Stellenbosch University, South Africa. Her areas of interest are South Africa and China. Her latest publication is a volume edited with H. Edinger and H. Herman, *New Impulses from the South: China's Engagement of Africa* (Stellenbosch University 2008).

Anirudh Krishna is Associate Professor of Public Policy and Political Science at the Sanford Institute of Public Policy, Duke University. His research interests are poverty dynamics and community development. Before turning to academia, Dr Krishna worked for 14 years in the Indian Administrative Service, where he managed diverse initiatives in rural and urban development. Publications include *Active Social Capital: Tracing the Roots of Development and Democracy* (Columbia University Press 2002), *Changing Policy and Practice From Below: Community Experiences in Poverty Reduction* (United Nations Press 2000) and *Reasons for Hope: Instructive Experiences in Rural Development* (Kumarian Press 1997) (ak30@duke.edu).

Anand Kumar is Professor of Sociology and chair of the Department of Sociology at Jawaharlal Nehru University, New Delhi, Secretary of the Indian Association of Sociology, and Coordinator of the Global Studies Programme. His research interests include poverty, India and nation-building. Recent books include *Quest for Participatory Democracy* (Rawat Publications 2007) and *Political Sociology of Poverty In India* (IIPA 2004) (anandkumar1@hotmail.com).

James H. Mittelman is University Professor of International Affairs at American University, Washington, DC. His research interests are East Asia and globalization. His recent books include *The Globalization Syndrome: Transformation and Resistance* (Princeton University Press 2000) and *Whither Globalization? The Vortex of Knowledge and Ideology* (Routledge 2004) (jmittelman@american.edu).

Sanusha Naidu is Research Director of the China in Africa programme based at FAHAMU in South Africa. Her areas of interest include China and Asia-Africa relations. Recent edited books are *Crouching Tiger, Hidden Dragon? Africa and China* (with Kweku Ampiah, University of KwaZulu Natal Press 2008), and *The New Face of China-Africa Co-operation*, Special Issue *Review of African Political Economy* (with Marcus Power and Giles Mohan, 2008) (sanusha@fahamu.org).

Jan Nederveen Pieterse is Mellichamp Professor of Global Studies and Sociology, University of California-Santa Barbara. Areas of interest are new globalization, global political economy and Asia. Recent books are *Is There Hope for Uncle Sam? Beyond the American Bubble* (Zed 2008), *Ethnicities and Global Multiculture: Pants for an Octopus* (Rowman & Littlefield 2007) and *Globalization or Empire?* (Routledge 2004) (jnp@global.ucsb.edu).

Ravi A. Palat is Associate Professor of Sociology at Binghamton University, New York. His research interests include global political economy, inequality and the rise of Asia. Important books are *Capitalist Restructuring and the Pacific Rim* (Routledge Curzon 2007) (ed.) and *Pacific-Asia and the Future of the World-System* (Greenwood Press 1993) (palat@binghamton.edu).

Boike Rehbein is Director of the Global Studies Programme, University of Freiburg, Germany. His research interests include social structure, globalization and Southeast Asia. Recent books are *Theorien der Globalisierung* (with Hermann Schwengel, UTB 2008) and *Globalization, Culture and Society in Laos* (Routledge 2007) (brehbein@gmx.de).

Hermann Schwengel is Professor and Chair of Sociology, University of Freiburg, Germany. His research interests are globalization, labour and political sociology. Recent publications include *Theorien der Globalisierung* (with Boike Rehbein, UTB 2008) and *Optimismus im Konjunktiv*, e-book (www.freidok.uni-freiburg.de/volltexte/2008) (hermann.schwengel@soziologie.uni-freiburg.de).

Ganesh K. Trichur teaches global political economy and Asian political economy in the Global Studies department at St Lawrence University, New York. Areas of interest include globalization, the new imperial conjuncture, political Islam and political Hinduism, and the relationship between the privatization of warfare and the privatization of disaster. Some of his work is published in *Globalizations, Journal of World Systems Research*. He is currently working on an edited volume on *New Perspectives on Asia and the World System in the New Century* (tganesh@stlawu.edu).

Figures and Tables

Acknowledgements

Chapter 4, by James Mittelman, 'Globalization and Development: Learning from Debates in China', originally appeared in the journal *Globalizations*, 3 (3), September 2006, pp. 377–91. Reprinted by permission of the publisher, Taylor & Francis Ltd; www.informaworld.com.

Chapter 7, by Anirudh Krishna and Jan Nederveen Pieterse, 'Hierarchical Integration: The Dollar Economy and the Rupee Economy', originally appeared in the journal *Development and Change*, 39 (2), 2008, pp. 219–37. Reprinted by permission.

Introduction 1: Development and Inequality

Jan Nederveen Pieterse

When the term 'emerging markets' arose in the 1970s it referred to the tiger economies of South Korea, Taiwan, Singapore and Hong Kong. In time its use extended to Southeast Asian countries such as Malaysia and Thailand. In the 1990s it applied to all newly industrializing countries, from Turkey to Latin American states. The term represented a portfolio category for investors. A parallel term in global political economy and development studies is newly industrializing countries or economies (NICs or NIEs). More recently the investment bank Goldman Sachs coined the term *BRIC* or Brazil Russia India China to denote a special category of large, strategic, highly promising economies.

Another term that gained currency in recent years is 'emerging powers' in view of the growing political and geopolitical influence of several large developing countries. The term first referred to Japan but now includes China and Russia as members of the UN Security Council, India and Brazil as aspirant members and as regional powers, South Africa as a force in Africa, Turkey as a member of NATO, and several countries as leading forces in G-77, G-21 and other international forums.

Look up 'emerging markets' and 'emerging powers' in Google and a multitude of references turn up. Both terms are successors to the conventional terminology of 'developing countries' and to UN classifications such as high, middle and low-income developing countries. These countries have emerged from the waiting room of history and earned a different classification. Yet both terms reflect a limited remit –'emerging markets' refers to business and finance and 'emerging powers' refers to international politics. So of the big three in social science – state, market, society – only two are represented.

In opting for the term 'emerging societies' – in a sense introducing it for it is rarely used – this volume seeks to address this gap. This reflects several moves. We intend this as a comprehensive terminology that encompasses state and market dynamics, which is not usually the case the other way around; emerging markets or emerging powers do not per se include interest in social forces (except as variables in risk analysis). We are interested in the dynamics of emerging economies and new power equations, but view this, above all, in a social context, framed by and in light of the interests, sensibilities and debates *within* these societies. Thus we opt for a view of emerging societies that is sociologically rich and is embedded in social reflexivity. From emerging societies it is a small step to another innovative terminology, that of multiple modernities (Eisenstadt 2002, Gaonkar 2001), which goes beyond the scope of this introduction.

This avoids the pitfalls of other terms. 'Emerging powers' creates the impression of a political-science, international-relations treatment and prompts the question: Why not focus primarily on the large emerging societies such as Russia and China? This is interesting but a more limited remit than we have in mind. Emerging markets and emerging powers represent mainly external interests and perspectives on the part of financial markets, investors and power politics. In contrast, 'emerging societies' reckons as much with internal perspectives. Social reflexivity matters as an expression of social vitality and active democracy and, of course, in the sense of Ulrich Beck's new modernity (1992). The litmus test of emerging societies is, after all, whether and how their emergence serves the emancipation of the majority, which is taken up below.

'Emerging societies' carries a drawback if it privileges and reifies 'society' as the unit of analysis. These are times of cross-border economies, new regionalism, transnational corporations, offshoring and outsourcing, a transnational capitalist class and a capitalism that is in significant respects transnational, rather than national. Global political economy, global sociology and world-systems theory assume this as a starting point. A counterpoint to this perspective is that differences between national institutions and regulations matter. Nation states remain strategic forces, a little more so the larger the nation state. Thus, according to Dani Rodrik (2000), we have globalization but not global capitalism. As several scholars note, the conventional notion of 'society' as a homogeneous unit is outdated (Mann 1986, Urry 2000), yet, of course, to ignore states and social institutions is no alternative. Vital decision-making runs through nation states and nation states remain the forums for democratic decision-making, no matter how imperfect. Even so, the notion of society does not have to be confined to nation states (the 'container model' of society) but increasingly extends to transnational configurations and is used in wider meanings as in social networks, network society, transnational societies (in migration literature) and 'world society'.

Development and inequality

For quite some time growth rates in the global South have substantially exceeded those in the North, new industrializing countries are booming, Asia is rising, and the spotlight is on the BRIC and China and India. New workers join the global workforce by the millions and sprawling new middle classes open vast new consumer markets. Transnational corporations take up new opportunities for offshoring and outsourcing and banks, stock exchanges and hedge funds roll out new rounds of financial expansion. The new industrialization boosts demand for commodities and the commodities boom changes transnational networks of trade and flows of finance.

Business optimism and corporate perspectives loom large in reports of the brave new world in the making. Crossborder economies and financial links emerge at the confluence of technological changes (which lower wages for unskilled labour), liberalization (which reduces state capacities and oversight) and globalization. Sidebars report on looming risks, ecological constraints, corruption and political uncertainty. They point to slow growth or stagnation in advanced countries – even though familiar mantras hold that 'The World is Flat' and outsourcing is beneficial in the end.

There is no question that in 21st-century globalization sea changes are underway (see Nederveen Pieterse, Chapter 1 this volume). Structurally, the world economy at the turn of the millennium resembles the postwar boom and the 'golden years of capitalism' – the current period is again driven by industrialization, but now centred in the new industrializing economies.

Emergence denotes rising levels of development and gradually rising influence in the vicissitudes of globalization, for instance, in international trade policy and the WTO. These changes are part of 'the crazy vitality of capitalism' (Thrift 2004, p. 1), but surely the 'crazy vitality of capitalism' carries different meanings in different settings, such as societies where the majority of the population are peasants or are illiterate, as in, say, Pakistan or Afghanistan. If globally the rise of emerging societies is a major frontier, *in* the emerging societies inequality is the major frontier. In the decades to come much depends on how emerging societies address inequality.

Practically without exception, the emerging societies face major social crises in rural areas and urban poverty. Thus, the flipside of cutting-edge globalization is that across the world multi-speed societies are taking shape. In the emerging societies, a new middle class, educated, technologically savvy and increasingly influential, coexists side by side with a peasant hinterland. Reports of 'two Egypts' or 'two Perus' have been increasingly common.

The key question this volume poses is how the development path of emerging societies relates to social inequality; what is the relationship between economic vitality in emerging economies and social inequality? Are social inequality and multi-speed economies built into the pattern of accumulation such that if inequality recedes accumulation declines, or is the development path geared towards reducing inequality? Where do the emerging societies lay their growing weight – growth without equity or growth with equity? This is meaningful, of course, beyond these societies themselves. At issue is whether the ongoing transformations represent the annexation of emerging economies into global neoliberal capitalism, or alternatively, whether they hold an emancipatory potential for the majority of the world population.

Social inequality has myriad dimensions and meanings. In social terms it carries implications for social protest and social movements; it holds ramifications for families, reproduction and demography. From a cultural angle, the phenomenology of inequality or what inequality means and represents is radically different between and within societies. Caste in India, race in the United States and South Africa, colour in Brazil, and ethnicity in other societies are familiar examples of cultural inequality complexes. Cultural heterogeneity intersects with inequality and various intersections of gender, race, ethnicity, national origin or citizenship status shape constructions of inequality. Along the ideological spectrum, social Darwinism (revived and rearticulated in the ethos of neoliberalism) and egalitarian social democracy are two extremes on the continuum of class ideology. Is poverty accepted ('the poor will always be with us') or is it viewed as a social sore whose elimination is a yardstick of social and cultural progress? Inequality holds different political meanings, as a source of political stability (it provides economic opportunities by maintaining a reserve army of labour and establishes cohesion across ruling-class factions) or as a threat to political stability (in view of rising levels of social and political organization).

Polarizing growth has been a classic trend. The notion of pauperizing, immiserizing growth goes back to, among others, Brazil in the 1970s. Since then neoliberalism has added its path of growth-without-equity, the path of Anglo-American capitalism and the structural adjustment policies implemented under its auspices. Other variants are being and may yet be added, as this volume discusses.

A framework that seeks to come to terms with these trends is hierarchical integration (see Krishna and Nederveen Pieterse, Chapter 7 this volume). Hierarchical integration may be a description of 21st century accelerated globalization in which people interact more closely worldwide, yet are also more separated, in various kinds of local-global 'upstairs downstairs' relationships.

The human development approach has argued all along that what matters is not growth but the *quality* of growth (Haq 1995). Thus, a contrasting case is growth with equity as represented by social market capitalism in Scandinavian and Rhineland versions, the East Asian developmental states and Japan's bureaucratically coordinated capitalism (until the fin de millennium turn to market forces). In this view, growth premised on inequality is not sustainable. With social polarization comes crime, lack of accountability and corruption, hence economic and political instability. Unequal societies cannot regulate markets and permissive, unregulated markets are unstable and crisis-prone.

Another major vortex of inequality is the relationship between emerging societies and commodity-exporting societies (for instance, between China and African countries). Here a key question is whether the ongoing commodities boom will yield a bust so that this relationship is part of an unsustainable development path, or are gains from commodities exports converted into human capital? Oil-rich countries leasing fertile agricultural land pose further risks.

An implication of multi-speed societies is that there is no single development path but there may be different paths for different sectors, regions, ethnicities, genders. 'Development', of course, must be disaggregated, just as aggregate figures such as growth, GDP and per capita income must be unpacked to make sense. Besides, the units of analysis are not necessarily countries; they may be cross-border economies, economic sectors, or migratory flows. While all this is true, nevertheless the public sector exercises a special responsibility in relation to the development path.

Reflecting on the growth paths of new industrializing countries, the Growth Commission Report (2008) notes that there is no single formula for growth because historical circumstances and contexts matter; a view that breaks with the Washington-consensus one-size-fits-all approach. The report devotes special attention to the role of the public sector – which includes building a coalition around a growth path, mitigating the social impact of a growth path, and steering towards inclusive development. Present trends are quite diverse. As a macroeconomic approach neoliberalism has lost ground, yet the impact of neoliberal policies is still being felt across sectors and societies. Keynotes are spikes and valleys, competitiveness and flexibility. The growing role of sovereign wealth funds, based on the surpluses of export-oriented economies and of energy exporters from the Persian Gulf to Norway, suggests a return of state capitalism. It suggests a revindication and comeback of developmental states, in contrast to the claims and policies of neoliberal ideology. Yet, of course, this involves very different states, so state capitalism itself is a glyph to decipher.

After the crisis

How are the trends sketched in this book holding up in the wake of the economic crisis? The first major test of the decoupling thesis shows that Asia and other emerging societies are not able to take up the slack if slowdown affects not just the US but Europe as well. The decoupling thesis is passé. Arun Kumar, an economist at Jawaharlal Nehru University, notes:

> The year [2008] began with policy makers and experts suggesting a decoupling between the Asian and the US and European economies. They suggested that the rapidly growing economies of Asia will provide the boost to the advanced economies so that there would be a soft landing for the world. This was based more on hope and hype rather than on analysis. These economies were already at their peak growth rates and could not double them, which was required to compensate for a decline in the rates of growth in the OECD economies. Further, since China is heavily dependent on exports to these economies and India is much more open than earlier, if anything, their rates of growth were bound to fall. These two economies could not move in a direction opposite to that of the bigger economies, as events have borne out. Clearly, all along, the policy makers and experts have been hoodwinking by denying the reality (Kumar 2009).

Commodity prices – high from 2002 to 2008 – have come tumbling down; with petrol prices coming down as well it is a mixed message for developing countries. But since growth in leading emerging societies remains strong, demand for commodities will swing back to some extent. Migration to the North has slowed and will not easily recover, which in turn affects remittances. The slump enables the IMF and World Bank to make a comeback, but with a different script – a tad more self-critical, less confident about their prescriptions, refraining from economic micromanagement while looking over their shoulders for funds. The IMF's capital base has eroded and to resume its financial role its capital stock should include significant participation of sovereign wealth funds from the global South. This is possible only on the basis of financial power sharing with emerging economies, which, in turn, signals the passing of the Washington era, not immediately but in time.

In the wake of crisis, financial institutions in the global South have become more careful about acquiring Western assets. From South Korea to the Middle East, everyone is cutting back on US-dollar assets. Temasek Holdings, Singapore's main sovereign wealth fund, suffered significant losses on its investments in Merrill Lynch early in 2008. China is cutting back on acquiring US Treasury bonds as part of what looks to be a fundamental realignment.[1] The message of crisis is that global capital will stay home rather than migrate to American assets and Treasuries. This bodes ill for the US-government repair plan of deficit financing.

The economic weakness of the United States is structural and, unlike in the 1990s, not amenable to financial fixes. The financial overhang in debts, derivatives and hedge funds is too large (for instance, outstanding hedge funds' capital amounts to $71 trillion) and economic foundations are too weak. As the Chinese premier pointed out at the 2009 World Economic Forum in Davos, high consumption and prolonged low savings is not a sustainable development path. A related problem of the American economy is decades' long underinvestment in the private sector, in new technologies generally and in manufacturing. The industrialization in emerging societies is, in part, a counterpart to deindustrialization in the US. Financialization of the economy, coinciding with increasing deregulation, has deepened American economic troubles.[2]

The rise of emerging societies is structural, too, and outlasts the crisis. Although the short-term picture has changed, medium and long-term trends have not. According to Goldman Sachs's forecasts, 'the Bric countries will be the only source of domestic demand growth globally in 2009'. Thus, 'coming on top of 2008, we project that for three consecutive years we will have seen global demand expansion led by the Bric economies'. A question is 'are we going to discover that not only can these nations cope better than people in the west think, but that some of their own forms of economic model will be mimicked by developed countries to help them cope with the decline of private sector market systems?'[3]

Crisis may be an opportunity for 'redoing globalization' and global social policy emerges on the agenda. This is unlikely to materialize also because major players are occupied by their own problems. The main portée of crisis is that neoliberalism is past, Keynesianism is back in, financialization will have to be brought under control, rating agencies must be 'rated', and the American lead of the world economy has faded. Clearly, the current era signals a new epoch, more multipolar, with a much greater role of emerging societies and a greater importance of South-South relations.

Introduction 2: Chapters

Boike Rehbein

The chapters in this volume add socio-cultural perspectives to the dominant perception of emergence as an economic and political phenomenon. Inequality is not only looked at in conventional terms of income distribution but also from a cultural and qualitative perspective, and emergence is primarily conceived as a transformation of social relations. There are several levels of the transformation of social relations and of ensuing new patterns of inequality. Several chapters map emerging patterns of *global* interaction (Nederveen Pieterse, Palat, Naidu and Mbazima, Schwengel), several address specific *national* frameworks, namely China (Mittelman, Trichur), India (Kumar, Krishna), Brazil (Burity) plus Uganda, Peru and Kenya (Krishna), while some focus on local and transnational aspects (Burity, Krishna, Trichur). One chapter develops an overarching perspective of hierarchical integration with reference to the relation between the dollar and the rupee economies in India (Krishna and Nederveen Pieterse). A sobering awareness that runs throughout the book is that the patterns of accumulation that are driving the new round of globalization have profound inequality built in and trends in contemporary globalization sustain this inequality.

According to the opening chapter by Jan Nederveen Pieterse, the 21st-century momentum of globalization is markedly different from 20th-century globalization and involves a new geography of trade, weaker hegemony and growing multipolarity. This presents major questions. Is the rise of East Asia, China and India just another episode in the rise and decline of nations, another reshuffling of capitalism, a relocation of accumulation centres without affecting the logics of accumulation? Does it advance, sustain or halt neoliberalism? The rise of Asia is co-dependent with neoliberal globalization and yet unfolds outside the neoliberal mould. What is the relationship between zones of accumulation and modes of regulation? What are the ramifications for global inequality? The first part of this chapter discusses trends in trade, finance, international institutions, hegemony and inequality and social struggle. The second part discusses what the new trends mean for the emerging 21st-century international division of labour.

While Ravi Palat in Chapter 2 also acknowledges the rise of the global South as a major transformation in world history and a new phase of globalization, he goes on to ask whether China, India, Brazil and South Africa actually challenge the Euro-North American domination of world affairs, and answers in the negative. The reluctance of the large states in the global South to challenge the contemporary world order suggests that they are increasingly complicit in this new world order. However, as growing income and wealth inequalities within the emerging states lead to political instability, the global South increasingly has to find new ways of cooperation and political intervention.

In Chapter 3, Anirudh Krishna looks at the marginalization of poorer social groups in a comparative perspective. He agrees that inequality in emerging countries has grown in the wake of globalization and liberalization but seeks to probe more specifically the dynamics of poverty. Disaggregated studies show that descents into poverty have occurred alongside escapes from poverty. On the basis of these, Krishna studies upward and downward movements of 25,000 households in Uganda, Kenya, Peru, India and the United States. In every region studied, upward and downward movements have occurred in parallel. Poverty has been created anew even as some existing poverty was overcome. Vulnerability is ever-present and is a larger problem in some contexts than in others. However, *increasing* vulnerability and *growing* volatility were found within communities of all five countries studied. Krishna's study shows that ill-health and high health costs play a major role in increasing vulnerability.

In Chapter 4, James Mittelman picks up on the notion of increasing internal tensions in emerging societies with reference to China. China's development path does not offer a model for the rest of the world but it is a compelling case of a deliberate strategy of transformation and self-determination. Mittelman points to debates in China that could be interpreted as alternatives to the paradigms of developmentalism and neoliberalism.

In Chapter 5, Ganesh Trichur focuses on inequality in China's development. He highlights the huge internal migration due to Chinese economic expansion, export-orientation and regional integration. Widening rural-urban and inter-provincial income gaps encourage more than 150 million rural labourers to look for work in the prospering coastal zones. However, exploitation and lay-offs cause migrants to protest or seek work closer to their homes. For the time being, Chinese social policies and the constant economic growth may have stabilized the situation but according to Trichur's analysis, 'subaltern groups' that are excluded from the benefits of economic prosperity will sooner or later react with more intense social unrest and create labour shortage in the growth areas.

Chapter 6 by Anand Kumar deals with the consequences of India's growth. India is regarded as one of the most important emerging powers. It has impressive growth rates, which seem to have their basis in the recent policies of liberalization, privatization and globalization. In spite of apparent success, a number of problems are associated with India's emergence. For supporters, there are four structural bottlenecks in the fields of energy, employment, education and environment. Critics, on the other hand, point to increasing disparities and divides due to the uneven impact of growth and to the marginalization of the rural population.

In Chapter 7, Anirudh Krishna and Jan Nederveen Pieterse examine the relationship between the dollar economy and the rupee economy in India and find that while contemporary globalization makes the world more interconnected, it also reworks and builds on existing cleavages and uneven development. This is an under-researched dimension of the emerging 21st-century international division of labour. The core question is whether new developments (associated with exports, offshoring and outsourcing) spin off to the majority in the countryside and to the urban poor. The chapter documents the various ways in which inequality is built into and sustains India's development. The authors discuss other instances of multi-speed economies and analytics that seek to come to grips with these relations, from combined and uneven development to global value chains. They present three ways of capturing contemporary inequality: asymmetric inclusion, enlargement-and-containment, and hierarchical integration, each of which captures different dimensions of inequality.

In Chapter 8, Joanildo Burity takes a closer look at the relation between globalization, social forces, culture and inequality in Brazil. He finds that transnational economic powers and forces cutting across social domains, national borders, and social groups seek to reinforce or to overturn inequalities. The rising global players both represent particular historical courses toward modern capitalism and express in their contradictory outlook the very trends that inform hegemonic globalization. Emerging societies are characterized by deep contradictions with regard to economic and socio-cultural dynamics. In the case of Brazil, its capitalist modernization has been rooted in inequality, connected to the legacy of slavery, and recent globalization has both deepened inequality and opened chances of countering it.

In Chapter 9, Sanusha Naidu and Johanna Jansson study the impact of an emerging power, China, on the unevenly developed societies of Africa. They pose the key question of whether China's impact is mainly extractive or developmental. Critics view China's engagement as a terrifying threat while for optimists it is a tantalizing opportunity. The findings of this study are partly encouraging. China's role gives Africa more leverage in its relations with the global North, it compels African governments to reflect on and adopt initiatives that address the challenges of globalization and compels them to adopt nuanced understandings of the varied impacts that China can have on Africa's development path.

In the final chapter, Hermann Schwengel adopts a wider perspective by applying the term of emergence to a variety of social phenomena: countries or regions, social scapes and flows, economic networks, or global cities. He argues that the new globalization has to be understood and mediated and links emerging societies to the experience of established states. European cultural memories of conflict, mediation and negotiation may enable Europe to go beyond the fading stages of empires, nation states and the global capitalist economy. In this setting and on the basis of reflexivity and complexity, the social sciences, if they understand the present 'Machiavellian moment', can play a more important public role than they have done for decades.

Notes

1. Bradsher (2009).
2. On deindustrialization in the US see Zysman and Cohen (1987); on the US economy see Nederveen Pieterse (2008b).
3. O'Neill (2009). See ongoing discussions, such as Hutton (2008).

Part I
Twenty-first Century
Globalization

1
Twenty-first Century Globalization: Global Sociology

Jan Nederveen Pieterse[1]

With 4 per cent of the world population the United States absorbs 25 per cent of world energy supplies, 40 per cent of world consumption and spends 50 per cent of world military spending and 50 per cent of world health care spending (at $1.3 trillion a year). US borrowing of $700 billion per year or $2.6 billion per day absorbs 70 to 80 per cent of net world savings. Meanwhile the US share of world manufacturing output has steadily declined and the share of manufacturing in US GDP at 12.7 per cent is now smaller than that of the health-care sector at 14 per cent and financial services at 20 per cent. This shrinking of the physical economy makes it unlikely that the massive American external debt can ever be repaid (Prestowitz 2005).

According to IMF estimates, China and India are expected to overtake the GDP of the world's leading economies in the coming decades. China is expected to pass the GDP of Japan in 2016 and of the US by 2025. In 2005 China surpassed the US as Japan's biggest trading partner, surpassed Canada as the biggest trading partner of the US and surpassed the US as the world's top choice of foreign direct investment. If current trends continue China will become the biggest trading partner of practically every nation. By 2025 the combined GDP of the BRIC – Brazil, Russia, India and China – would grow to one-half the combined GDP of the G-6 countries (the US, Japan, Germany, France, Italy, Britain). By 2050, according to a Goldman Sachs report, the combined BRIC economies will surpass that group and 'China, India, Brazil and Russia will be the first-, third-, fifth- and sixth-biggest economies by 2050, with the United States and Japan in second and fourth place, respectively'. BRIC spending growth measured in dollars could surpass the G-6 countries' levels as early as 2009 (Whelan 2004).

Both these data sets are uncontroversial, almost commonplace, yet combining them raises major questions. How do we get from here to there and what does this mean for the course and shape of globalization? The United States, Europe and Japan rode the previous wave of globalization, notably during 1980–2000, but in recent years their lead in manufacturing, trade, finance and international politics has been gradually slipping. The United States set the rules, in economics through the Washington consensus, in trade through the WTO, in finance through the dollar standard and the IMF, and in security through its hegemony and formidable military. Each of these dimensions is now out of whack. The old winners are still winning but the *terms* on which they are winning cedes more and more to emerging forces. In production and services, education and demography, the advantages are no longer squarely with the old winners. In several respects in the maelstrom of globalization, the old winners have become conservative forces.

The 21st-century momentum of globalization is markedly different from 20th-century globalization. Slowly, like a giant oil tanker, the axis of globalization is turning from North-South to East-South relations. This presents major questions. Is the rise of Asia and the newly industrialized economies (NIEs) just another episode in the rise and decline of nations, another reshuffling of capitalism, a relocation of accumulation centres without affecting the *logics* of accumulation? Does it advance, sustain or halt neoliberalism? Is it just another shift in national economic fortunes, or is it an alternative political economy with different institutions, class relations, energy use and transnational politics? What is the relationship between zones of accumulation and modes of regulation and what are the ramifications for global inequality?

Examining this poses methodological problems. Extrapolating trends is risky. The units of analysis are not what they used to be or seem to be. Statistics measure countries but economies are crossborder. The story, of course, is not merely one of change but also continuity, and in some respects, merely apparent continuity.

Glyn Ford, a member of the European parliament, notes, 'The EU has more votes in the International Monetary Fund than the US, but has not yet used them to challenge the current neoliberal orthodoxy [...] With support from Latin America, in the World Trade Organization, at UN conferences in Tokyo as well as from the Santiago-plus-five and Durban-plus-five groupings, an alternative world could emerge' (Ford 2005).

It could, but, so far, it hasn't. There is a certain stickiness and stodginess to social change. Power plays continue as long as they can. Policies continue in the old style until a policy paradigm change is inevitable, not unlike Thomas Kuhn's revolutions in science. There is a sleepwalking choreography to social existence, never quite in sync with actual trends; or rather, trends are only trends when they enter discourse. (In a similar way what we teach in universities is often years behind what we know or what we're thinking about because there is no convenient structure or heading yet under which to place and communicate it.) Changes become manifest after certain time lags – an institutional lag, discursive lag, policy lag; yet changes are underway even if the language to signal them isn't quite there yet. Some changes we can name, some we can surmise and some escape detection and will catch up with us. So at times it feels much like business as usual. Thus we should identify structural trends and discursive changes as well as tipping points that would tilt the pattern and the paradigm.

According to Kemal Dervis, director of the UN Development Program, globalization in the past was a profoundly 'unequalising process', yet 'today, the process is rapidly turning on its head. The south is growing faster than the north. Southern companies are more competitive than their northern counterparts. [...] Leading the charge is a new generation of southern multinationals, from China, Korea, India, Latin America and even the odd one from Africa, aggressively seeking investments in both the northern and southern hemispheres, competing head-to-head with their northern counterparts to win market share and buy undervalued assets' (quoted in Peel 2005). This optimistic assessment counts economic changes – which this paper also highlights – but it doesn't address social questions.

About cutting-edge globalization there are two big stories to tell. One is the rise of Asia and the accompanying growth of East-South trade, energy, financial and political relations. Part of this story is being covered in general media, often with brio (Marber 1998; Agtmael 2007). In the words of Paul Kennedy, 'we can no more stop the rise of Asia than we can stop the winter snows and the summer heat' (2001, p. 78). The other story, which receives mention only in patchy ways, is that the emerging societies face major social crises in agriculture and urban poverty.

The first section of this paper discusses the main trends in 21st-century globalization by comparing trends during 1980–2000 and 2000–present under the headings of trade, finance, international institutions, hegemony, and inequality and social struggle. I preface each trend report with a brief proposition. I don't discuss cultural changes in this treatment because they generally follow slower timelines than trends in political economy. In the second part I seek to understand what the new trends mean for the emerging 21st-century international division of labour.

Trade

Growing East-South trade leads to a 'new geography of trade' and new trade pacts.

Through the postwar period North-South trade relations were dominant. In recent years East-South trade has been growing, driven by the rise of Asian economies and the accompanying commodities boom (particularly since 2003) and high petrol prices (since 2004). According to the UN Conference on Trade and Development, a 'new geography of trade' is taking shape: 'The new axis stretches from the manufacturing might and emerging middle classes of China, and from the software powerhouse of India in the south, to the mineral riches of South Africa, a beachhead to the rest of the African continent, and across the Indian and Pacific oceans to South America which is oil-rich and mineral- and agriculture-laden' (Whelan 2004).

Brazil opened new trade links with the Middle East and Asia. Chile and Peru are negotiating trade agreements with China (Weitzman 2005). 'The Middle East has started looking to Asia for trade and expertise'; trade has expanded threefold in the past years and the fastest growing markets for oil are in China and India (Vatikiotis 2005). Growing Sino-Indian trade combines countries with 1.3 and 1.2 billion people each (Dawar 2005).

During 1980–2000, American-led trade pacts such as NAFTA, APEC and the WTO played a dominant role. In the 2000s these trade pacts are in impasse or passé. Dissatisfaction with NAFTA is commonplace, also in the US. In Latin America, Mercosur, enlarged with Venezuela and with Cuba as associate member, undercuts the Free Trade Association of the Americas (FTAA). The association of Southeast Asian nations, ASEAN, in combination with Japan, South Korea and China (ASEAN+3) sidelines APEC, which is increasingly on the backburner, and reduces Asian dependence on the American market. As Michael Lind (2005) notes, 'This group has the potential to be the world's largest trade bloc, dwarfing the European Union and North American Free Trade Association'.

During 1980–2000, the overall trend was toward regional and global trade pacts. The G-22 walkout in Cancún in November 2003 upped the ante in subsequent negotiations. Advanced countries that previously pushed trade liberalization now resist liberalizing trade and retreat to 'economic patriotism'. The United States has been zigzagging in relation to the WTO (with steel tariffs and agriculture and cotton subsidies). Given the WTO gridlock in the Doha development round and blocked regional trade talks (the Cancún walkout was followed by the failure of the FTAA talks in Miami) the US has increasingly opted for free-trade agreements, which further erode the WTO (Nederveen Pieterse 2004b). Thus there has been a marked shift toward bilateral free-trade agreements (FTAs) in North-South trade. American terms in free-trade agreements typically include cooperation in the war on terror, exempting American forces from the International Criminal Court, accepting genetically modified food, and preferential terms for American multinationals and financial institutions. FTAs include Chile, Colombia, Central America, Jordan, Morocco, Oman and Singapore and are under negotiation with South Korea, Thailand, Australia, Peru and Panama.

In South-South trade, however, the trend is toward regional and interregional combinations such as Mercosur and ASEAN. China has established a free-trade zone with ASEAN. In the future India may join ASEAN+3. Since 2003 there have been talks to establish a free-trade zone encompassing India, Brazil and South Africa (IBSA).

So the old 'core-periphery' relations no longer hold. The South no longer looks just north but also sideways. In development policies East and Southeast Asian models have long overtaken Western development examples. South-South cooperation, heralded as an alternative to dependence on the West ever since the Bandung meeting of the Nonaligned Movement in 1955, is now taking shape. 'Already 43 per cent of the South's global trade is accounted for by intra-South trade' (Gosh 2006, p. 7).

The downside is that much of this growth is sparked by a commodities boom that will not last. Note for instance the rollercoaster experience of the Zambian copper belt (Ferguson 1999) which now is experiencing another upturn, spurred by Chinese investments, which will be as precarious as the previous round. Only countries that convert commodity surpluses into productive investments and 'intellectual capital' will outlast the current commodities cycle.

Finance

The current imbalances in the world economy (American overconsumption and deficits and Asian surpluses) are unsustainable and are producing a gradual reorganization of global finance and trade.

During 1980–2000 finance capital played a key role in restructuring global capitalism. The financialization of economies (or the growing preponderance of financial instruments) and the hegemony of finance capital reflects the maturation of advanced economies, the role of finance as a key force in globalization, financialization as the final stage of American hegemony, and growth of financial innovations such as hedge funds and derivatives. The return to hegemony of finance capital ranks as one of the defining features of neoliberal globalization (Duménil and Lévy 2001).

The role of speculative capital led to the diagnoses such as casino capitalism and Las Vegas capitalism. International finance capital has been crisis-prone and financial crises have hit Mexico, Asia, Russia, Latin America and Argentina. Attempts to reform the architecture of international finance have come to little more than one-sided pleas for transparency. The trend since 2000 is that NIEs hold vast foreign reserves to safeguard against financial turbulence; 'the South holds more than $2 trillion as foreign exchange reserves' (Gosh 2006, p. 7). As many historians note, the final stage of hegemony is financialization. Accordingly, emerging economies view competition in financial markets as the next strategic arena – beyond competition in manufacturing, resources and services.

During 1980–2000 the IMF was the hard taskmaster of developing economies; now year after year the IMF warns that US deficits threaten global economic stability (Becker and Andrews 2004; Guha 2007).

Through the postwar period the US dollar led as the world reserve currency, but since 2001 there has been a gradual shift from the dollar to other currencies. After the decoupling of the dollar from gold in 1971, OPEC in 1975 agreed to sell oil for dollars and established a de facto oil-dollar standard. Now Venezuela, Iran and Russia price their oil in other currencies. In 2001–5 the dollar declined by 28 per cent against the euro and a further 12 per cent in 2006. In 2002 the leading central banks held on average 73 per cent world reserves in dollars; by 2005 this was 66 per cent (Johnson 2005) and the trend for 2006 was towards 60 per cent. China and Japan, with 70 to 80 per cent of their foreign reserves in US dollars, reflecting their close ties to the American market, deviate markedly from the world average. Of China's $1.3 trillion in foreign reserves up to $1 trillion is in dollars. The current trend is for China to diversify its foreign reserves towards a target of 65 per cent in dollars (McGregor 2006). For obvious reasons this diversification must be gradual.

In the wake of the 1997 Asian financial crisis the IMF vetoed Japan's initiative for an Asian monetary fund. Subsequently, Thailand's Chiang Mai Initiative established an Asian Bond Fund. Venezuela, backed by petroleum funds, withdrew from the IMF and World Bank and established an alternative Bank of the South. In time Japan, China and

South Korea – *if* they would settle their differences – may develop a yen-yuan-won Asian reserve, or an 'Asian dollar'.

Western financial markets have been dominant since the 17th century. In the 2000s, however, financial sources outside the West have played an increasingly important role, reflecting the rise of Asia, the global commodities boom and high petroleum prices. The accumulation of petro-money during 2005–7 was three times the annual Asian surpluses from exports (Magnus 2006). A new East-East financial network is emerging. China's initial public offerings are increasingly no longer routed via New York and London, but via Saudi Arabia (Timmons 2006) and Borse Dubai. Wall Street is losing its primacy as the centre of world finance to London with Shanghai and Hong Kong as runners-up (Tucker 2007).

East Asian countries are active investors in Latin America and Africa. Thirty seven per cent of FDI in developing countries now comes from other developing countries. China emerges as a new lender to developing countries, at lower rates and without the conditions of the Washington institutions (Parker and Beattie 2006). China's foreign aid competes with Western donors and Venezuela plays this role in Latin America.

Hedge funds have become more active international players than investment banks. In 2006 there were 10,000 hedge funds with $1.5 trillion in assets, the daily global turnover in derivatives was $6 trillion and the credit derivative market was worth $26 trillion. Financialization has increased the risk of financial instability (Glyn 2006) and new financial instruments such as derivatives are increasingly opaque and out-of-control. This underlies the financial instability that increasingly affects institutions in the West, such as the collapse of LTCM in 1998, the Enron episode along with WorldCom, HealthSouth and other corporations in 2001, Parmalat in 2003 and Amaranth in 2006. The crisis of the US subprime mortgage lenders such as New Century in 2007 has had ripple effects throughout the international financial system. It indicates the deeper problem that many of the American economic successes have been enabled by the Greenspan regime of easy money. An analyst comments, 'This confusion of talent with temporary favourable conditions has combined to make clients willing to pay disproportionate fees' (Grantham 2007).

In the Davos meetings of the World Economic Forum the American economy and the unstable dollar have been a major cause of concern. US Treasury debt at $7.6 trillion and net external debt at $4 trillion add up to an annual borrowing need of $1 trillion, or 10 per cent of GDP (Buckler 2005) and interest payments of $300 billion a year and rising.

The United States is deeply in the red to Asian central banks and relies on inflows of Asian capital and recycled oil dollars, and 'what flows in could just as easily flow out' (Williams 2004). The dollar is now upheld more by fear of turbulence than by confidence and appeal.

For all these changes, the net financial drain from the global South is still ongoing. Poorer nations sustain American overconsumption and the overvalued dollar. The world economy increasingly resembles a giant Ponzi scheme with massive debt that is sustained by dollar surpluses and vendor financing in China, Japan and East Asia. The tipping points are that financialization backfires when it turns out that financial successes (leveraged buyouts, mergers and acquisitions and the rise in stock ratings) have been based on easy credit, and secondly, when finance follows the 'new money'.

Institutions

The 1990s architecture of globalization is fragile and the clout of emerging economies is growing.

The 1990s institutional architecture of globalization was built around the convergence of the IMF, World Bank and WTO and is increasingly fragile. Since its handling of the Asian crisis in 1997–8 and Argentina's crisis in 2001, the IMF has earned the nickname 'the master of disaster'. Argentina, Brazil, Venezuela, South Africa, Russia and other countries have repaid their debt to the IMF early, so the IMF has less financial leverage, also in view of the new flows of petro-money. IMF lending went down from $70 billion in 2003 to $20 billion in 2006. The IMF has adopted marginal reforms (it now accepts capital controls and has increased the vote quota of four emerging economies) but faces financial constraints.

The World Bank has lost standing as well. In the 1990s the Bank shifted gear from neoliberalism to social liberalism and structural adjustment 'with a human face' and an emphasis on poverty reduction and social-risk mitigation. But the poverty reduction targets of the Bank and the Millennium Development Goals are, as usual, not being met. Paul Wolfowitz's attempts as World Bank president (2005–7) to merge neoliberalism and neoconservatism were counterproductive, with an internally divisive anti-corruption campaign and a focus on Iraq.

The infrastructure of power has changed as well. The 'Wall Street-Treasury-IMF complex' of the 1990s weakened because the Treasury played a weak and minor role in the George W. Bush administration, until Henry Paulson's appointment in 2006, which brought Wall Street back into the cockpit.

The 1990s architecture of globalization has become fragile for several reasons. The disciplinary regime of the Washington consensus has been slipping away. Structural adjustment has shown a consistently high failure rate, with casualties in sub-Saharan Africa, most of Latin America, and the 1997 Asian crisis and how it was handled by the IMF. Research indicates a correlation between IMF and World Bank involvement and negative economic performance, arguably for political reasons: since IMF involvement signals economic troubles it attracts further troubles (McKenna 2005). Zigzag behaviour by the hegemon – flaunting WTO rules, an utter lack of fiscal discipline and building massive deficits – has further weakened the international institutions. Following the spate of financial crises in the 1990s, crisis mismanagement and growing American deficits, the macroeconomic dogmas of the Washington consensus have given way to a post-Washington no-consensus. Meanwhile increasing pressure from the global South is backed by greater economic weight and bargaining power.

Hegemony

Rather than hegemonic rivalry, what is taking place is global repositioning and realignments toward growing multipolarity.

In general terms, the main possibilities in relation to hegemony are continued American hegemony, hegemonic rivalry, hegemonic transition and multipolarity. The previous episode of hegemonic decline at the turn of the 19th century took the form of wars of hegemonic rivalry, culminating in the transition of the United States into the new hegemon. But the current transition looks to be structurally different from previous episodes. Economic and technological interdependence and cultural interplay are now far greater than at the *fin de siècle*. What is emerging is not simply a decline of (American) hegemony and rise of (Asian) hegemony but a more complex multipolar field.

During the 1990s American hegemony was solvent, showed high growth and seemed to be dynamic at the throttle of the new-economy boom. The United States followed a mixed uni-multipolar approach with cooperative security (as in the Gulf War) and 'humanitarian intervention' (as in Bosnia, Kosovo and Kurdistan) as leitmotivs. Unilateralism with a multilateral face during the 1990s gave way to unilateralism with a unilateral face under the Bush administration, a high-risk and high-cost approach that flaunted its weaknesses (Nederveen Pieterse 2004a). By opting for unilateral 'preventive war' the Bush administration abandoned international law. After declaring an 'axis of evil', the US had few tools left. The US is now caught up in its new wars. In going to war in Iraq the US overplayed its hand. In its first out-of-area operation in Afghanistan NATO met fierce resistance, and the US was forced to give up its access to a base in Uzbekistan.

During the cold war Muslims were cultivated as allies and partners on many fronts. Thus in the 1980s Ronald Reagan lauded the Mujahideen in the Afghan war as 'the moral equivalent of our founding fathers'. As the cold war waned these allies were sidelined. Samuel Huntington's 'clash of civilizations' article in 1993 signalled a major turn by shifting the target from ideology to culture and from communism to the Islamic world. (In fact, he warned against a Confucian-Islamic alliance and specifically military cooperation between China and Pakistan.) Thus erstwhile allies and partners were redefined as enemies and yesterday's freedom fighters were reclassified as today's terrorists.

In response to this policy shift and the continuing Israeli and American politics of tension in the Middle East, a militant Muslim backlash took shape, of which the attacks of 11 September 2001 were part. The cold war 'green belt' and 'arc of crisis' has become an 'arc of extremism' with flashpoints from the Middle East to Central Asia. Satellite TV channels in the Arab world contribute to awareness among Muslims. Muslim organizations increasingly demonstrate high militancy and swift responses, for instance to the cartoons lampooning Muslims in a Danish newspaper in 2006 and statements perceived as anti-Muslim made by Pope Benedict in the same year. The Lebanon war in 2006 showed Israel's weakness and Hezbollah's strength as part of a regional realignment away from the American-supported Sunni governments to Iran, Syria and Shiites. The United States siding with Israel's insular stance in the region continues to contribute to its self-isolation (Mearsheimer and Walt 2005; Petras 2006).

New security axes and poles have emerged, notably the Shanghai Cooperation Organization (deemed a 'counterweight to NATO') and the triangular cooperation of China, Russia and Iran. Other emerging poles of influence are India, Brazil, Venezuela and South Africa. The G-77 has made its influence felt in international trade and diplomacy. For instance, it blocked intervention in Darfur on the grounds of state sovereignty involving an Islamic government in a strategic part of the world, in part as a response to American expansion in the Middle East and Africa. China has generally backed G-77 positions in UN Security Council negotiations (Traub 2006), a position that is now gradually changing.

On the military frontiers of hegemony, although the United States accounts for 48 per cent of world military spending (in 2005) and maintains a formidable 'empire of bases', the wars in Iraq and Afghanistan have demonstrated the limits of American military power. As a traditional maritime and air power, the United States has traditionally been unable to win ground wars (Reifer 2005). 'Globalization from the barrel of a gun' is a costly proposition, also because of the growing hiatus between American military and economic power (Nederveen Pieterse 2007a).

On the economic front the US is import-dependent and 'Brand America' is losing points. In business circles the Bush presidency is viewed as a massive failure of American brand management. The aura of American power is fading. Rising anti-Americanism affects the status of American products, and American pop culture is no longer the edge of cool. An advertising executive notes growing resentment of American-led globalization.

> We know that in the Group of 8 countries, 18 per cent of the population claim they avoid American brands, with the top brand being Marlboro in terms of avoidance. Barbie is another one. McDonald's is another. There is a cooling towards American culture generally across the globe (Holstein 2005).

The main tipping points of American hegemony are domestic and external. *Domestic* tipping points are the inflated housing market and high levels of debt. Not only are US levels of debt high, but manufacturing capacity is eroded, there are no cash reserves and the domestic savings rate turned negative for the first time in 2005, so an adjustment seems inevitable. If interest rates remain low it will undermine the appeal of dollar assets for foreign investors. If interest rates rise it will increase the pressure on domestic debt and the highly leveraged financial and corporate system. The main *external* tipping points are fading dollar loyalty, financial markets following new money, the growing American legitimacy crisis and the strategic debacles in Iraq and the Middle East.

There are generally three different responses to American hegemony. The first is *continued support* – which is adopted for a variety of reasons, including the appeal of the American market, the role of the dollar, the shelter of the American military umbrella, and lingering hope in the possibility of American self-correction. The second option is *soft balancing* – which ranges from tacit non-cooperation (such as most European countries staying out of the Iraq war and declining genetically modified food) to establishing alternative institutions without US participation (such as the Kyoto Protocol and the International Criminal Court). And the third response is *hard balancing* – which only few countries can afford either because they have been branded as enemies of the US already so they have little to lose (Cuba, Venezuela, Iran, Sudan) or because their bargaining power allows them manoeuvring room (as in the case of China and Russia and the Shanghai Cooperation Organization – SCO). An intriguing trend is that the number of countries that *combine* these different responses to American hegemony in different policy domains is increasing. Thus China displays all three responses in different spheres – economic cooperation (WTO, trade), non-cooperation in diplomacy (UN Security Council) and finance (valuation of renminbi), and overt resistance in Central Asia (Wolfe 2005) and in support for Iran.

American unilateralism and preventive war are gradually giving way to multipolarity if only because unilateralism is becoming too costly, militarily, politically and economically. New clusters and alignments are gradually taking shape around trade, energy and security. Sprawling and cross-zone global realignments point to growing multipolarity rather than hegemonic rivalry.

Inequality and social struggle

The flashpoints of global inequality are rural crises and urban poverty in emerging economies and chronic poverty in the least developed countries. International migration is a worldwide flashpoint of inequality.

Let us review these trends in a wider time frame. Postwar capitalism from 1950 to the 1970s combined growth and equity. Although overall North-South inequality widened, economic growth went together with growing equality among and within countries. Neoliberal 'free-market' economies during 1980–2000 produced a sharp trend break: now economic growth came with sharply increasing inequality within and among countries. The main exceptions to the trend were the East Asian tiger economies.

The trend in the 2000s has been that overall inequality between advanced economies and emerging economies is narrowing while inequality in emerging societies is increasing. Overall global inequality is staggering, with 1 per cent of the world population owning 40 per cent of the world's assets. The pattern of rising inequality in neoliberal economies (the US, the UK and New Zealand) continues and has begun to extend to Australia, Japan and South Korea (Lim and Jang 2006). International migration has become a major flashpoint of global inequality and produces growing conflicts and dilemmas around migration and multiculturalism in many countries (Nederveen Pieterse 2007b).

James Rosenau has offered an optimistic assessment of global trends according to which rising human development indices, urbanization and growing social and communication densities are producing a general 'skills revolution' (1999). However, the flipside of technological change and knowledge economies is that with rising skill levels come widening skills differentials and urban-rural disparities. The second general cause of growing inequality is unfettered market forces promoted by multinational corporations, international institutions and business media. Familiar shorthand terms include 'shareholder capitalism' (in contrast to stakeholder capitalism), 'Wal-Mart capitalism' (low wages, low benefits and temporary workers) and 'Las Vegas capitalism' (speculative capital). The third general cause of inequality is financialization because its employment base is much narrower than in manufacturing and income differentials are much steeper. A fourth cause of inequality in developing countries are fast-growth policies that reflect middle-class and urban bias and aggravate rich-poor and urban-rural gaps.

Practically all emerging economies face major rural and agricultural crises. In China this takes the form of pressure on land, deepening rural poverty, pollution, village-level corruption and urban migration. In Brazil and the Philippines, land reform drags because the political coalition for confronting landholding oligarchies is too weak. In South Africa, the apartheid legacy and the poor soil and weak agricultural base in the former Bantustans contribute to rural crisis.

These are classic problems of modernization. In the past, failure to bring the peasant hinterland into modernity gave rise to fascism. A major failing of communism in Russia was the collectivization of agriculture. Emerging economies need balanced development and 'walking on two legs', yet urban bias (low agriculture prices, inadequate support for agriculture) and the intrusion of transnational market forces in agriculture (land appropriations, multinational agribusiness) are crisis-prone.

Yet the *impact* of poor peoples' movements and social struggles in the 2000s has been greater than during 1980–2000, notably in China and Latin America. In China, where 'a social protest erupts every five minutes', social crises are widely recognized and led to the 'harmonious society' policies adopted in 2005. In Latin America poor peoples' movements have contributed to the election of left-wing governments in Venezuela, Bolivia, Ecuador and Nicaragua and to policy adjustments in Argentina and Chile.

Whereas the 'Shanghai model' of fast-growth policies geared towards attracting foreign investment has been abandoned in China, it is being pursued with fervour in India. A case in point is the 'Shanghaing of

Mumbai' (Mahadevia 2006) and the growing role of special economic zones.

What is the relationship between the India of Thomas Friedman (*The World is Flat*, 2005) and P. Sainath (*Everybody Loves a Good Drought*, 1996), between celebrating growth and deepening poverty, between Gurgaon's Millennium City of Malls and abject poverty kilometres away, between dynamic 'Cyberabad' and rising farmer suicides nearby in the same state of Andhra Pradesh? According to official figures, 100,248 farmers committed suicide between 1993 and 2003. Armed Maoist struggles have spread to 170 rural districts, affecting 16 states and 43 per cent of the country's territory (Johnson 2006) and are now the country's top security problem.

> For every swank mall that will spring up in a booming Indian city, a neglected village will explode in Naxalite [an informal name given to communist groups] rage; for every child who will take wings to study in a foreign university there will be 10 who fall off the map without even the raft of a basic alphabet to keep them afloat; for every new Italian eatery that will serve up fettuccine there will be a debt-ridden farmer hanging himself and his hopes by a rope (Tejpal 2006).

India's economic growth benefits a top stratum of 4 per cent in the urban areas with little or negative spin-off for 80 per cent of the population in the countryside. The software sector rewards the well-educated middle class. The IT sector has an upper-caste aura – brainy, requiring good education, English language – and extends upper-caste privileges to the knowledge economy, with low-cost services from the majority population in the informal sector (Krishna and Nederveen Pieterse 2008). Public awareness in India is split between middle-class hype and recognition of social problems, but there are no major policies in place to address the problems of rural majorities and the urban poor.

In addition to rural crisis, the emerging powers face profound *urban poverty*, as part of the 'planet of slums' (Davis 2005). The rural crisis feeds into the sprawling world of the favelas, bidonvilles, shanty towns and shacks. Urban policies are at best ambivalent towards the poor and often negligent. Thus Bangkok's glitzy monorail mass transit system connects different shopping areas, but not the outlying suburbs. As India's rural poor are driven out of agriculture, they flock to the cities, while land appropriations and clampdowns on informal settlements, hawking and unlicensed stores squeeze the urban poor out of the cities, creating a scissor operation which leaves the poor with nowhere to go.

Trends in 21st-century globalization

Now let us review these trends. Is the cusp of the millennium, 1980–2000 and 2000–present, a significant enough period to monitor significant changes in globalization? Why in a short period of decades would be there be significant trend breaks? My argument is essentially that two projects that defined the 1980–2000 period, American hegemony and neoliberalism – which are of course the culminating expressions of longer trends – are now over their peak. They are not gone from the stage but they gather no new adherents and face mounting problems (indebtedness, military overstretch, legitimacy crises, rising inequality), and new forces are rising. The new forces stand in an ambiguous relationship to neoliberalism and American hegemony.

In sum, the overall picture shows distinct new trends in trade, institutions, finance and hegemony and to some extent in social inequality. Table 1.1 reviews the main trends in current globalization. The trend break with the old patterns is undeniable, yet it is too early to speak of a new pattern.

Reorienting globalization: back to normal?

We can also reflect on these changes in a longer time frame. According to the thesis of Oriental globalization (Hobson 2004; Nederveen Pieterse 2006), early globalization was centred in the Middle East (500–1100 CE) and between 1100 and 1800 was centred in China, India and Southeast Asia. Now, as a Shanghai economist remarks, after 'a few hundred bad years' China and India are back as the world's leading manufacturing centre and information-processing centre, respectively (Prestowitz 2005).

Thus in a historical sense 21st-century globalization is reverting to normal if we consider that Asia has been at the centre of the world economy through most of the course of long-term globalization. In this light, 200 years of Western hegemony have been a historical interlude.

Note, for instance, that it is not the first time that China has been in the position of having accumulated the lion's share of the world's financial reserves. During 'several periods of rapid growth in international commerce – from AD600 to 750, from 1000 to 1300 and from 1500 to 1800 – China again tended to run very large trade surpluses'. Between 1500 and 1800 China accumulated most of the world's silver and gold (Bradsher 2006; Frank 1998). So it is not the first time in history that China faces the 'trillion dollar question' of holding the world's largest financial surplus.

Table 1.1   Trends in 21st-century globalization

Pattern 1990s	Pattern 2000s
	Trade
North-South trade dominates	Growing East-South trade
US-led trade pacts dominate	FTAA, APEC, WTO: passé or in impasse
Trend to regional/global trade pacts	Shift to bilateral FTAs (in North-South trade)
	Finance
Finance capital leads, crisis-prone	Emerging economies hold dollar surpluses
IMF and World Bank discipline developing economies	IMF warns US its policies threaten economic stability
US dollar leads	Decline of dollar as world reserve currency
US top destination of FDI	China top destination of FDI
IMF blocks Asian monetary fund	Thai Asian Bond Fund; Bank of the South
Western financial markets dominate	New financial flows outside the West
Investment banks	Hedge funds, new financial instruments
	Institutions
Convergence IMF-WB-WTO	IMF lending down ($70bn 2003,
Social liberalism, poverty reduction	$20bn 2006)
'Wall Street-Treasury-IMF complex'	World Bank lost standing
Washington consensus	Weak Treasury
	(Post)Washington no-consensus
	Hegemony
US hegemony solvent and dynamic 'clash of civilizations'	US in deficit and cornered in new wars
	Muslim backlash
US-led security	New security axes and poles
	Inequality
Growth & increasing inequality (except East Asia)	Inequality between North and NIEs decreases while inequality in NIEs increases
Deepening rural and urban poverty	Deepening rural and urban poverty
	International migration as flashpoint of global inequality

Now, however, Asia resumes its normal role in a world that is imprinted and shaped by 200 years of Western hegemony – in politics, military affairs, corporate networks, intellectual property rights and patents, institutions, styles and images. Asia is making its comeback in a world that, unlike that of 1800, is deeply interconnected socially, politically and culturally, a world that is undergoing rapid technological change, more rapid than in 1800.

The West followed Asia and transcended it by introducing new modes of production (industrialism, mass production, Fordism), and now Asia is following the West and transcending it. Japan pioneered flexible accumulation and the East Asian development states and the 'Beijing consensus' represent other modes of regulation; the question is which of the modes of regulation that Asia introduces will be sustainable.

Global sociology

The perplexities of globalization are, so to speak, the demand side. Now consider the supply side: what does sociology contribute to this question? Among social sciences, sociology, more than others, plays a double role as a discipline and meeting place of social sciences. Arguably sociology is more open than other social sciences and better positioned to develop a social science synthesis. Addressing globalization requires an interdisciplinary rendezvous of sociology, global political economy, development studies, geography, history, anthropology and cultural studies.

'Society' as the conventional unit of analysis, shaping the legacy of sociology, is gradually being surpassed in comparative, regional and transnational studies. Historians (Mazlish 2006) and sociologists (Beck 2005) claim that we have entered a 'global age' and that a global sociology is taking shape (for example, Cohen and Kennedy 2007). In global sociology the main theoretical synthesis and comprehensive assessment remains world-system theory (WST). Even so, the limitations of WST are familiar: WST is Eurocentric, preoccupied with the long 16th century as the genesis of the modern world-system and with capitalism in the singular. For instance, if the rise of Asia is a comeback that builds on and in some respects resumes the experience of prior oriental globalization, WST precludes this option and we must look for guidance outside to the historical work of Andre Gunder Frank (1998) and others. Some variants of WST point to deeper historical lineages, yet the question of the analytics remains.

In effect, WST replicates on a global canvas the two main analytics and limitations of sociology: modernity and capitalism. *Modernity* remains wedded to a Eurocentric legacy. Its variants – new, reflexive, liquid modernity, postmodernism – retain an occidental cast as well. Capitalism likewise is a powerful problematic, but *capitalism in the singular* remains implicitly embedded in 19th-century stages theory with its unilinear cast.

To go beyond Eurocentric and historically fixed and biased conceptualizations we must opt for the plural: modernities and capitalisms. The idea of multiple *modernities* has the potential to transcend Eurocentrism and accommodate the 'new modernities' that are taking shape. It raises fundamental questions: which patterns of relations are structural invariables (yielding modernity) and which vary according to history, geography, culture (yielding modernities)?

The modernities approach abandons linear history and the idea of advanced societies as models. This means that the most important variables are the domestic balance of forces and debates; it means not simply applying models but giving priority to the domestic balance of forces and local debates and expecting local (national, regional) adaptations of transnational influences. This approach also has downsides. As an approach, *modernities* is descriptive, interpretative and open-ended, rather than critical, normative and programmatic. Critical theory may fall by the wayside and the critical edge may be blunted to make way for bland pluralism. An immanent critique becomes difficult, for what are the criteria of judgment? Cultural relativism is the strength and weakness of this approach.

Implicitly the modernities approach may follow the 'national' paradigm of sociology with accounts of different Thai, Indonesian, Chinese, Brazilian etc. modernities, so 'society' returns via a side door. Work on regional modernities (Latin American, Southeast Asian, East Asian, and so on) opens this window wider, yet leans towards a civilizational approach. A further concern is that what matters are not just modernities but also the *interaction of modernities*.

Capitalisms

Another major analytical tool is the variety of capitalism, or *capitalisms*, which is ordinary in global political economy but rare and under-researched in sociology. Conventional approaches mainly accommodate stages of capitalism (early, late, advanced) and modes of regulation (Fordism, flexible production) and retain a unilinear bias. In contrast, *capitalisms* reckons with the actual variety of capitalist institutional practices. Just as the sociology of modernity gives rise to modernities (the variety of real existing modernities), the political economy of capitalism yields capitalisms. Let's consider the limitations of capitalism singular.

First, the orthodox approach frames the problematic as capitalism *or* socialism ('barbarism or civilization', in some accounts). This echoes 19th-century evolutionism and implicitly reiterates the Marxist 'gospel of crisis' according to which capitalism has no other script than its inevitable undoing. Crisis has been pending since 1848. The gospel of crisis underestimates the ingenuity of capitalism: capitalism survives crises due to the biodiversity of capitalism; *capitalisms uphold capitalism* (Nederveen Pieterse 2004a, p. 146). Rather than ignoring or bemoaning this we should recognize and analyse it and examine what potential it holds as a diagnostic and for an emancipatory approach.

Second, capitalism singular tends to downplay variations in capitalism over time and by region. Capitalism's 'golden years', 1950–73, combined growth with equity; inequality between and within countries decreased. Neoliberal capitalism, 1980–2000, produced radically different effects: growth with growing inequality or polarizing growth.

Third, capitalism singular reinforces the cliché that 'there is no alternative'. It upholds the *idée fixe* that neoliberalism is 'real capitalism', rather than a rightwing utopia. As Dani Rodrik and many others note, we have globalization but not global capitalism (2000). Variations in national institutions matter and the contest between capitalisms, between Anglo-American capitalism and other variants, is at issue worldwide and reverberates in development policies, business decisions, finance and geopolitics. Capitalism singular leads to a binary, polarizing approach that reproduces the old disputes between revolution and reform (revisiting Kautsky and Bernstein vs. Lenin, Luxemburg and Trotsky). Today this takes the form of a false choice between neoliberalism and socialism. Anyone who works in development studies knows that these options are unreal. Neoliberalism is unworkable and socialism, in general, is not a realistic programme.

Kenichi Ohmae rejects the notion of an Asian model and argues that the characteristics of Asian companies reflect a stage of development rather than a geography (Pilling and Guerrera 2003). However, the idea of stages of development implies understanding capitalism in the singular; presumably in a more advanced stage Asian capitalism would resemble American capitalism.

According to Wallerstein (2005), the three main cleavages in 21st-century globalization are rivalry within the triad (US, EU, Japan), the North-South divide in global inequality, and the divide between the World Economic Forum and the World Social Forum, or between Davos and Porto Alegre. In part this can be understood as the interaction and contestation of different capitalisms. The latter rift is often interpreted as a choice between capitalism and socialism. I question this: the main divide now runs not between capitalism and socialism, but between capitalism and capitalism, or what kind of capitalism?

Fourth, capitalisms pose the question: *which capitalism* – American, Rhineland, Scandinavian, Japanese, Chinese, etc.? This has the advantage of clearly posing the problem of future directions within societies rather than implicitly upholding American capitalism as the standard (in relation to which only socialism is an alternative).

Fifth, capitalisms pose the question of *the interaction of capitalisms* as a core problem of globalization. The various capitalisms are intertwined through technology, finance, investments, trade, international institutions and knowledge and ideology. Capitalisms plural draws attention to the *terms* of this interaction without posing one form of capitalism as the norm. Indeed it has become difficult to uphold American capitalism as the standard because it is dependent on cheap Asian imports, Asian labour and Asian vendor financing.

> The calls for structural reform in Japan and Europe stem from the belief that the Americans and the other 'Anglo-Saxon' economies have the sort of flexibility that breeds success. Yet that hardly squares with the IMF's notion that the US economy could be going down the pan at any moment (Elliott 2005).

Sixth, capitalisms and modernities also point to *globalizations*: each capitalism and each modernity pursues its preferred mode of globalization. Capitalisms and modernities concern different ways of analyzing and navigating different modes of regulation and social organization. Beyond the 'rise of Asia' they pose the questions of what kind of Asia, what kind of capitalism, what kind of modernity? Growth-obsessed, consumerist, authoritarian, polluting? Fast-track tycoon capitalism or development that combines and balances growth, equity and sustainability? Social struggles, people's movements, trade unions, feminist and ecological movements, struggles for democracy and new regionalism inflect modernities in different ways. A sociological approach means placing the analysis of the balance of forces centre-stage.

The spectrum of political and ideological positions that exists in each society cannot be captured in simple binary positions. However, this discussion takes place in a battlefield of paradigms, an arena in which few statistics, diagnoses and policies are ideologically neutral. Economic success and failure don't come with radio silence but are immersed in ideological noise and filtered through representations. The World Bank posited the 'East Asian miracle' as evidence of the wisdom of its policies of liberalization and export-led growth, whereas according to Japan it showed the virtues of capable government intervention (Wade 1996). According to Alan Greenspan, the Asian crisis of 1997 demonstrated that Anglo-American capitalism was the only viable economic model. Most others have drawn the opposite conclusion, that American-led finance capital is crisis prone, and this has been one of the spurs of the turn-of-the-millennium trend break in globalization patterns. The subprime mortgage crisis in the American housing market prompted a 'liquidity crisis' (because banks reassessed credit risks) which is really a confidence crisis that signals deeper weaknesses of Anglo-American financialized capitalism.

If the Washington institutions have lost clout, the knowledge grid of financial markets remains intact, with ideological ratings such as the Economic Freedom Index and the Competitiveness Index. Business media (such as the *Wall Street Journal* and the *The Economist*) and the media big six (such as Time Warner and Rupert Murdoch's News Corporation) echo the ideological impression management of conservative think-tanks and corporate interests. In the game of perceptions, Western media reports often blame social unrest in emerging societies on state authoritarianism (and emphasize 'human rights'), pro-market economists blame government inefficiency and corruption, whereas state and social forces focus on capitalist excesses (and local government incompetence). International institutions and free-trade agreements, multinationals, financial markets and World Bank economists weigh in on the debates. Meanwhile neoliberalism remains a prevailing adapt-or-die ideology whose influence is transmitted via financial markets, international institutions and free-trade agreements. Does, then, the rise of China, India and other emerging economies validate or invalidate neoliberalism?

According to American conventional wisdom and authors such as Thomas Friedman (2005), China's economic rise follows Deng Xiaoping's four modernizations and the subsequent liberalization, and India's economic rise dates from its 1991 liberalization. These views are ideologically rather than research-based because research indicates different explanations. Rodrik's work on the 'Hindu rate of growth' argues that the foundations of India's economic resurgence were laid during the 1970s and 1980s (2004). Recent studies of China break the mould of Mao-stigmatization and find that improvements in industrial production, rural modernization, literacy and health care during Mao's time laid the groundwork for the post-1978 transformation (Gittings 2005; Guthrie 2006).

Liberalization and export orientation – the Washington consensus and World Bank formula – contributed to the rise of Asia. American offshoring and outsourcing spurred rapid growth (Wal-Mart's imports alone represent 15 per cent of the US trade deficit with China; Prestowitz 2005, p. 68). But this would not have been possible or produced sustainable growth without Asia's developmental states. Their development policies enabled Asian societies and producers to upgrade technologically and to foster domestic, regional and alternative markets. China's spending on high-tech research and development now ranks third after the US and Japan.

If we consider the *cultural politics* of neoliberalism, emerging economies surely match neoliberal trends. Middle-class consumerism and its attendant features – marketing, commercial media, malls, shopping culture – are a leading trend throughout emerging societies. It is developing countries that now underpin the 'boom in advertising spending': 'Advertising spending is soaring in the developing world, suggesting that US-style consumerism is alive and well from Brazil and Russia to Saudi Arabia and Indonesia' (Silverman 2005).

If we consider *economic doctrine*, market fundamentalism is widely rejected. If we focus on neoliberal *economics*, the picture is less clear. If neoliberalism refers to *monetarism* and fiscal conservatism (which is doubtful), many developing countries are *more* neoliberal than the fiscally profligate US. Monetarism and fiscal conservatism aim to counteract inflation and avoid a deficit and the risk of financial turbulence.

Emerging societies must strike a cautious balance. While throughout the global South it is a cliché that neoliberalism doesn't work, the international financial markets continue business as usual, so for developing countries diplomacy is in order. Deficit countries cannot afford to offend the hegemonic institutions and credit regimes. Most countries must walk the tightrope and remain on reasonably good terms with financial markets and credit-rating agencies in case their costs of borrowing and doing business rise.

This is a different situation from that of the 1990s. Then the main considerations were debt and dependence on Washington institutions – which now applies to fewer countries – and a default belief in free-market policies as the most dynamic and pro-growth, which has lost adherents since the crises of the 1990s and the economic and financial disarray in the United States. If the deficit-dominated American economy is crisis-prone and inequality in the US is growing sharply, why follow this model? Now emerging economies follow neoliberal policies (in the sense of fiscal conservatism) to *escape* from neoliberalism (in the sense of the vagaries of the 'free market').

If neoliberalism refers to *high-exploitation capitalism*, again the picture is mixed. It does not generally apply to the tiger economies, South Korea, Taiwan or Singapore, at least in the sense that they all have sizeable public sectors. It does apply to China where migrants from the impoverished countryside have been an essential component in the razor sharp 'China price' and to India where the low-wage rural economy and the urban poor support the modern sector with cheap labour, services and produce. Inequality has not been a just-so circumstance or a minor quirk en route to growth but a fundamental factor in production and in establishing the international competitiveness of several emerging economies. In China this has begun to change since the adoption of the 'harmonious society' policy in 2005. In India high-exploitation capitalism, buttressed by caste in the countryside, continues unabated without major changes in government policy.

'Beating them at their own game' and using market forces to push development while keeping one's identity is a difficult balancing act because competitiveness means conforming to business standards where, so far, neoliberalism remains the default policy. In effect this means that existing structures of inequality, such as caste or ethnicity, are reworked. Besides, domestic politics are influential in areas such as 'governability' in Brazil where the Workers' Party (PT) governs with a slim margin and must make coalitions with conservative parties in parliament.

Of the two major trends in 21st-century globalization, the gradual East-South turn is widely recognized, but the deepening rural and urban poverty in emerging societies is not. Business media engage in emerging-markets boosterism. Meanwhile, for emerging societies the key to sustainable development is to take the peasantry and the urban poor along. Discussions in emerging societies are about rehabilitating the developmental state (where it has been away), not into an authoritarian developmental state but into one that is democratic, inclusive and innovative.

Throughout the world, in a 'structure of common differences', interests affiliated with state, market or society interests shape policy debates (for instance, for China see Kang 1998; Hui 2003; Xin 2003; Mittelman 2006). This 'structure of common differences' is crosscut by the varieties of capitalism and the transnational interaction of capitalisms (often referred to as 'globalization'). Capitalisms are different ways of distributing risk and of understanding and negotiating inequality, evolving from historical and cultural legacies, such as caste and communalism in India and race in South Africa and Brazil.

The East-South turn introduces a different vortex of capitalisms. China as the workshop of the world competes with other developing countries; not just the US, Europe and Japan see manufacturing jobs go to China but so do Mexico, Kenya and Bangladesh. Garment workers from Bangladesh to South Africa are under pressure from Chinese textile exports. In 2005 trade unions in Africa issued a call for action against

China, noting '250,000 jobs lost in African clothing, textile and leather industries' (ITGLWF press release 2005).

A budding debate in China concerns the 'harmonious world' or the idea that China's rise should not come at the expense of other developing countries and the world's poor. This is new on the agenda and not nearly as well developed as the 'harmonious society' and is yet to find a balance with China's other pressing priorities.

Alternatives that were sidelined during the epoch of neoliberal hegemony have taken on new influence and legitimacy since the turn of the millennium. The Beijing consensus – 'a model for global development that is attracting adherents at almost the same speed that the US model is repelling them' (Ramo 2004) is an emerging alternative in Asia and the Bolivarian alternative (ALBA) in Latin America. Countries that are financially independent and have relative room for manoeuvre, such as China because of its size and Venezuela because of its oil wealth, are in a strong position to articulate alternatives to neoliberalism.

If we look at the world as a whole, the majority economic form is the mixed economy with the social market in the EU, bureaucratically coordinated market economies (Japan) and developmental states (with different leanings in Asia, Latin America and Africa). On balance, mixed economies are doing better and several are more sustainable in terms of their growth paths and energy use. Social-market and human-development approaches have generally come back on the agenda. Global emancipation hinges on rebalancing the state, market and society and introducing social cohesion and sustainability into the growth equation. This means that each component changes: the state becomes a civic state, the market a social market, and growth turns green.

Note

1. I presented versions of this paper at several institutions in autumn 2006 (Korean Sociological Association conference, Seoul; Chulalongkorn University, Bangkok; Yunnan University, Kunming; the Chinese Academy of Social Sciences, Beijing; Globalism Institute, Royal Melbourne Institute of Technology; Jawaharlal Nehru University, New Delhi) and 2007 (Global Studies Association, UC Irvine) and am indebted to participants' feedback and the advice of many colleagues.

2

Rise of the Global South and the Emerging Contours of a New World Order[1]

Ravi Arvind Palat

The steady, relentless growth of manufacturing in China and the consequent hollowing out of the old industrial heartlands in North America, Western Europe and elsewhere, combined with the expansion of information technology and knowledge-intensive sectors in India, have begun to rapidly transform geopolitical relations on a global scale. Economic growth in China and India has fuelled a boom in commodity prices to the benefit of resource-rich states in Africa, Latin America and the Middle East as well as Russia. The resulting growth of South-South trade and the accumulation of large foreign-exchange surpluses have widely been taken to undermine the global dominance of Euro-North American economies. As China has emerged as the third largest trading partner of Africa after the United States and France, Sanusha Naidu and Johanna Jansson (Chapter 9 in this volume) among others have argued that it has given African states increased leverage in their dealings with the North.

Such a rosy view is unwarranted, as several African scholars and activists have argued, because neither the Chinese corporations nor the Chinese government has done anything to benefit trade unions or social justice movements in Africa, Latin America, or anywhere else (see Martin 2008). Despite all the talk of the rise of the global South and the decline of Euro-North American domination of the world, as Table 2.1 indicates, if India and China are excluded from the Third World, other states of the global South have declined relative to the First World. Furthermore, while the per capita GNP of states in the Third World as a percentage of the GNP per capita of states in the First World indicates that the command over goods and services traded in the global market of the citizens of the former states has declined over the last half-century relative to the citizens of the

Table 2.1   GNP per capita as percentage of the GNP per capita of the First World

Region	1960	1970	1980	1985	1990	1995	2000	2005
Sub-Saharan Africa	5.6	4.7	3.9	3.1	2.7	2.5	2.0	2.3
Latin America	19.7	16.4	17.6	14.4	12.3	12.9	13.4	11.2
West Asia and North Africa	8.7	7.8	8.7	7.9	7.4	7.2	7.7	8.4
South Asia (w/o India)	1.9	1.7	1.3	1.4	1.4	1.5	1.6	1.6
East Asia (w/o China & Japan)	6.0	6.1	8.0	8.6	11.0	13.8	11.5	11.8
China	0.9	0.7	0.8	1.2	1.3	2.1	3.2	4.6
India	1.5	1.3	1.1	1.2	1.2	1.4	1.6	1.9
Third World*	**4.5**	**4.0**	**4.3**	**4.1**	**4.1**	**4.7**	**4.9**	**5.2**
Third World (w/o China)	**6.5**	**5.7**	**6.1**	**5.5**	**5.3**	**5.9**	**5.6**	**5.5**
Third World (w/o China & India)	**9.3**	**8.1**	**8.8**	**7.7**	**7.5**	**8.2**	**7.7**	**7.3**
North America	123.7	105.0	100.7	101.6	98.2	98.9	116.4	112.5
Western Europe	111.1	104.6	104.6	101.5	100.5	98.5	92.0	99.7
Southern Europe	51.9	58.2	60.0	57.6	58.6	59.2	61.5	70.2
Australia & New Zealand	94.8	83.5	74.7	73.3	66.4	70.6	68.6	84.5
Japan	78.7	126.4	134.4	140.8	149.8	151.9	121.0	103.1
First World	**100**	**100**	**100**	**100**	**100**	**100**	**100**	**100**

*Third World includes: **Sub-Saharan Africa:** Benin, Botswana, Burkina Faso, Burundi, Cameroon, Central African Republic, Chad, Republic of Congo, Congo Democratic Republic, Côte d'Ivoire, Gabon, Ghana, Kenya, Lesotho, Madagascar, Malawi, Mauritania, Mauritius, Niger, Nigeria, Rwanda, Senegal, South Africa, Tanzania, Togo, Uganda, Zambia, Zimbabwe; **Latin America:** Argentina, Bolivia, Brazil, Chile, Colombia, Costa Rica, Dominican Republic, Ecuador, El Salvador, Guatemala, Haiti, Honduras, Jamaica, Mexico, Nicaragua, Panama, Paraguay, Peru, Trinidad & Tobago, Uruguay, Venezuela; **West Asia & North Africa:** Algeria, Egypt, Morocco, Saudi Arabia, Sudan, Syria, Tunisia, and Turkey; **South Asia:** Bangladesh, India, Nepal, Pakistan, Sri Lanka; **East Asia:** China, Hong Kong, Indonesia, South Korea, Malaysia, Philippines, Singapore, Taiwan, Thailand.
Source: Adapted from Arrighi and Zhang (2007), Table 1.

latter states, it says nothing of the distribution of income within these states.

If the inclusion of India and especially China shows that the GNP per capita of the Third World has marginally improved relative to the First World over its level in 1960, it should be noted that inequalities in income grew rapidly in China after the adoption of market-oriented reforms, as indicated by Figure 2.1. Income inequalities in China today

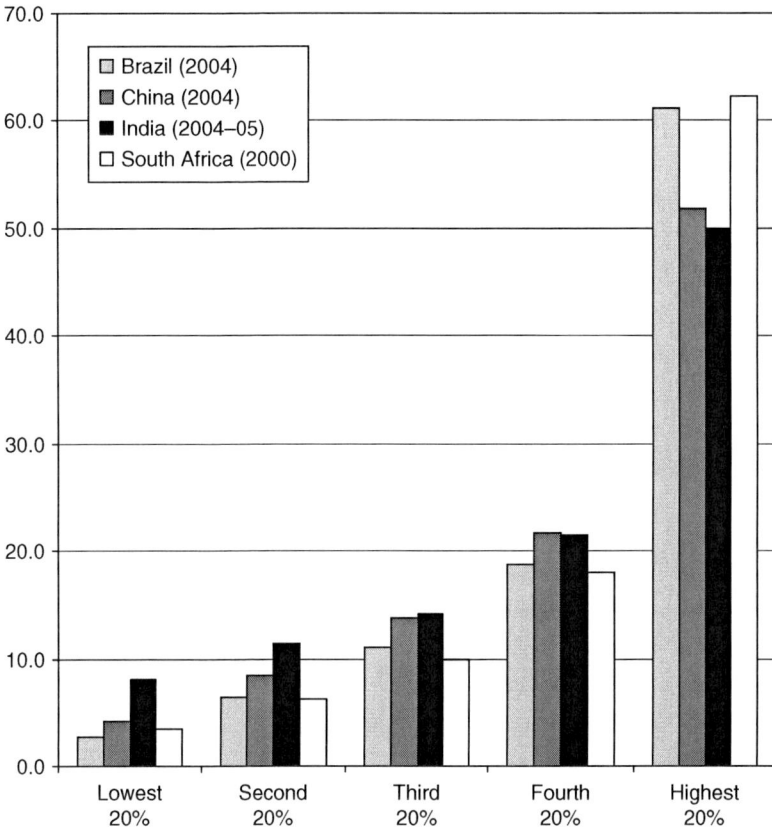

Figure 2.1 Inequality: percentage share of income or consumption by population quintile

are even more pronounced than in India though the levels of absolute deprivation remain higher in the latter, as demonstrated by Figure 2.1. The higher levels of absolute deprivation in India, moreover, emphasize the fact that despite registering high rates of economic growth since the deregulation of the economy in 1991, rates of growth for industrial and agricultural production in the 1990s were no higher than in the previous decade (Balakrishnan 2005; Nayyar 2006).

Looked at another way, though the United States, with a per capita income of $38,000 and China with $1,700, are virtually at opposite ends of the spectrum, their Gini coefficients are now virtually identical – 0.41 for the US and 0.47 for China. The shift from the egalitarianism of the

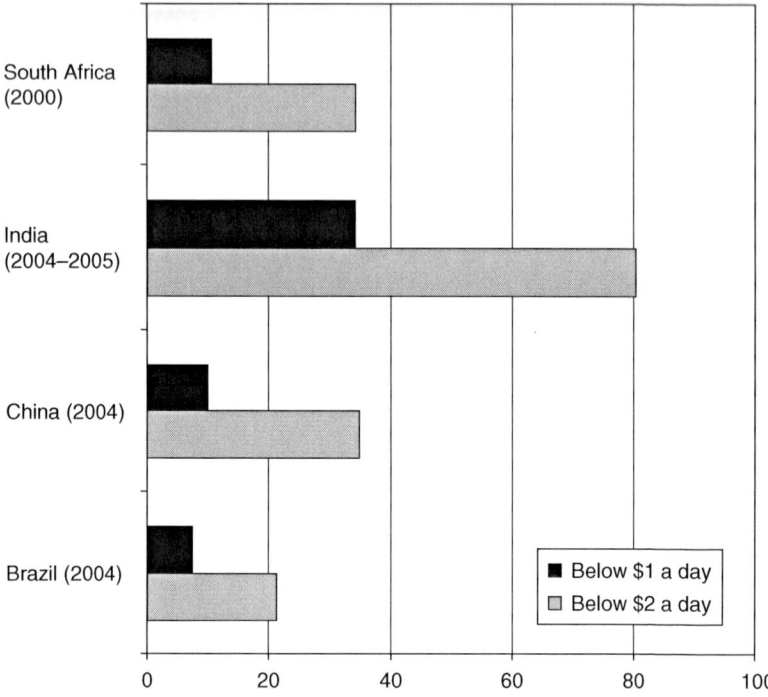

Figure 2.2   Poverty: percentage of population below $1 and $2 a day

Mao era is even more marked when the more skewed Gini coefficient for China is placed in the context of a worsening Gini coefficient for the United States, from 0.35 in 1970 to 0.41 today. Moreover, the rising rate of rural-to-urban migration in China has had little impact on rural-urban inequalities, as the per capita incomes of the top 35 cities in 2004 were more than three times the level of those in rural areas. Finally, the Chinese Academy of Social Sciences noted in a recent report that average incomes of the lowest quintile of urban workers was less than 5 per cent of the average income of the highest quintile (Roach 2006; Weil 2006).

As these figures indicate, elites in the global South – and particularly in India and China – have benefited enormously from economic deregulation and what has been called 'accumulation by dispossession' (Harvey 2003) or 'accumulation through encroachment' (Patnaik 2005) – the expropriation or purchase at throwaway prices of assets, including privatized state assets. Given high levels of absolute and relative depri-vation in their domestic markets, the economic growth on which the prosperity of the elites is based relies on exports to high-income mar-kets and to the recycling of their trade surpluses to the United States to compensate for the declining hegemonic power's continually worsening balance of payments deficit. Hence, despite greater economic clout and an incomparably stronger domestic institutional structure, leaders of the 'emerging powers' of the global South are reluctant to challenge the Euro-North American domination of world affairs. Unlike their predecessors who loudly condemned imperialism, the contemporary leaders of Brazil, China, India and South Africa have been timid in challenging the US-led invasions of Afghanistan and Iraq, or the continuing Israeli occupation of Palestine and its brutal blockade of the Gaza strip. Even in the run-up to the US invasion of Iraq in 2003, it was the 'old' Great Powers – France and Germany – rather than the leaders of the 'emerging powers' who spearheaded the successful drive to block a United Nations Secu-rity Council resolution to legitimate an illegal invasion. In the global South, opposition to the Euro-North American domination has come, instead, from Venezuela's Hugo Chavez, Bolivia's Evo Morales, and Iran's Mahmoud Ahmedinejad. Wang Hui (2003, pp. 74–5) and Han Yuhai (2006, p. 2207) have even argued that Deng Xiaoping's policy of open-ing China to the world market and the setting up of Special Economic Zones along its southeastern coasts represented a shift in its relations with the global South and was akin to attempts by the Japanese state since 1898 of 'shedding Asia and entering Europe'.

Nevertheless, the sheer demographic mass of China and India and the scale and magnitude of their economic growth over the past few decades have had massive repercussions across the globe. The greater density of inter-relations between the 'emerging economies', fuelled in large part by the voracious demand for energy, raw materials, and intermediate and capital inputs by Chinese and Indian industries, have enabled them to thwart, or at least blunt, the thrust of some changes to interstate economic relations sought by the high-income states, as indicated by the leadership exercised by Brazil, India and South Africa in world trade negotiations, and by the massive foreign exchange reserves commanded by China. In this context, though the United States has toned down its rhetoric against China after the events of 11 September 2001, it has courted India, and encouraged the ambitions of the South Asian state to become a world power by offering it a special deal that undercuts the nuclear Non-Proliferation Treaty and recognizing India as a 'responsible' nuclear weapons state. This is part of a worldwide US strategy to enlist regional powers including South Africa and Brazil in a global hub-and-spoke arrangement so that their relationship to the US is more important than their relationships to each other (Alden and Vieira 2005). Despite all this, and the US using the cover of its 'war against terrorism' to re-animate defence agreements with the Philippines and Indonesia and to initiate defence agreements and install military bases in Central Asian states to encircle China, the Chinese leadership has been reluctant to challenge US policies even with regards to its attempts to impose sanctions on Iran for allegedly seeking to develop nuclear weapons, and on North Korea for conducting a nuclear test. The second section of this chapter locates this reluctance in the social bases of these elites and the changes in the geopolitical ecology of capitalist production that underlay the re-emergence of these economies.

Great Leap Forward

The dramatic rise of China to become the 'workshop of the world' and India's attempts to be the 'world's back office' has once again turned the spotlight on these two Asian giants just as their emergence from colonialism and foreign occupation in the late 1940s also thrust them into the limelight when they were hailed as models of centrally planned and mixed economies respectively and both experienced massive social transformations.[2] Yet, despite achieving significant gains, their performance was surpassed by Italy, Japan and Israel in the 1950s and 1960s, by the Latin American 'miracles' in the 1970s, by the Asian 'miracle economies' in the 1980s and early 1990s, and by the dotcom bubble in the US in the late 1990s.

If economic models have a short shelf-life, the contemporary rise of China and India is different because the scale and magnitude of their economic growth and their demographic weight radically transforms the global ecology of production, investment and trade – 'the world begins to feel the dragon's breath on its back,' as Martin Wolf (2005) once put it. In the first instance, the opening of China and India to the world market and the entry of some 20 to 25 million workers from these economies into the labour market each year has led to a relentless haemorrhaging of jobs to these two Asian giants. What is more, an estimated 200 to 300 million workers from these economies, or the equivalent of the entire labour force of North America or the European Union, will enter the world market over the next 20 years. While China's population will age rapidly in the next 10 to 15 years, half of India's population of over 1.1 billion is under the age of 20 and its demographic weight will only increase: in the next five years alone it is estimated that 71 million will be added to India's labour force which will then have a working-age population of 762 million (Johnson 2006).

Equally important are estimates that wage disparities between China and India and the high-income states are likely to increase in the next few years. Given that average hourly wage rates in manufacturing in the United States or Western Europe range between $15 and $30 compared to average hourly wages of less than a dollar in China, a study by the Boston Consulting Group suggests these disparities will increase even if Chinese wages rise sharply. If Chinese wages increase by an annual average of 15 per cent over the next five years and wages in Western Europe and the US by only by three to four per cent, the typical hourly wage in China in 2009 will be $2 as opposed to between $18 and $35 in the United States and Western Europe (Stalk and Young 2004). Similarly, Ashok Deo Bardhan and Cynthia Kroll estimate that in 2002–2003, the average wages of white-collar employees like telephone operators, medical transcriptionists and payroll clerks averaged between $13–15 in the US and ranged from less than a dollar to $2 in India (Bardhan and Kroll 2003, Table 5). No amount of tinkering with exchange rates will resolve this situation in favour of core states.

The spectacular expansion of production and exports from China and India are not limited to low-value bulk goods but are increasingly in high-value goods. In many industrial sectors – most notably in electronics and motor vehicles – while the Chinese government welcomed foreign investors, it fashioned an industrial strategy that ensured technology transfer by requiring foreign investors to enter into joint ventures with domestic firms, often state-owned enterprises, insisting on foreign investors achieving a high level of domestic content rapidly, and not enforcing intellectual protection laws to enable local manufacturers to reverse-engineer products whenever it was feasible. The fact that foreign investors have not resorted to higher imports of inputs when domestic content requirements were eased as a precondition to China's admission to the World Trade Organization (WTO) is testimony to the success of these policies; Dani Rodrik (2006, p. 4) has calculated that China's export profile matches that of an economy with a per capita income level three times that of China. India is also an outlier and, as Rodrik only tracks commodity exports and does not include software exports, it could be expected to occupy a similar position. Indeed, after the first wave of outsourcing brought an estimated 348,000 jobs in call centres and associated back-office operations to India since the late 1990s, a second wave of outsourcing is transferring more sophisticated jobs ranging from processing student applications for universities and editing legal and professional documents to architectural and visual design of offices and buildings, three-dimensional modelling in aerospace, automotive and industrial machinery, and medical diagnostics (Minwala 2005). In turn, the US trade balance in high-technology goods turned from a surplus of $33 billion in 1990 to a deficit of $24 million in 2003 (Augustine 2005).

The increased technological quality of products from the large states in the global South is paralleled by a decline in science and education in the high-income states, especially in the US. According to one estimate, compared to the 70,000 engineers who graduate in the US each year, India and China graduate a collective total of 950,000 engineers and that due to wage disparities, a company can hire five chemists in China or 11 engineers in India for the price of one in the US.[3] Put differently, of the 120 large chemical plants, each costing more than a billion dollars, being built across the world, only one is in the United States and 50 are in China (Zakaria 2006). Infosys, the Indian software firm, invests $65 of every $1,000 it earns in training its workers compared to IBM which spends a mere $6.56 (Giridharadas 2007).

To take advantage of these massive reservoirs of cheap scientific and engineering talent, large corporations are increasingly relocating their research and development (R&D) facilities to China and India. In just two years, from 2002 to 2004, the number of foreign R&D centres in China shot up from 200 to 600 and the number of IBM employees in India rose from 9,000 in 2004 to 43,000 in early June 2006 when the company announced a tripling of its investment in India over the next three years. As the information-technology sector in India grew by 30 per cent in 2005 over the previous year, other companies have similarly raised their investments in the country (Rai 2006; Ross 2006, p. 4). India already enjoys 12 per cent of the engineering services outsourcing market and its share is widely predicted to grow substantially in the next few years when it is also expected to corner two-thirds of the global knowledge process outsourcing market (Bharadwaj 2006). Reflecting these realities, Samuel Palmisano (2006), the Chairman and CEO of IBM, claimed that the 'emerging business model' for the present century is not a 'multinational' but a 'globally integrated enterprise' – that rather than shifting production operations to take advantage of wage and cost differentials, 'shared technologies and shared business standards' would permit companies to 'treat their functions and operations as component pieces' which can be put together in different combinations depending on local circumstances.

If the emergence of China – and of India to a lesser extent – as low-cost manufacturers has led to an evisceration of manufacturing sectors, especially in high-income states, it has also been a major factor in curbing inflationary tendencies on a global scale. In the United States, for instance, Wal-Mart has been able to hold down prices by expanding its procurement from China-based factories. Between 1996 and 2003, the share of imports in the merchandise sold by the discount chain increased from 6 per cent to 60 per cent, and 80 per cent of the 6,000 factories supplying products to the chain are located in China. If Wal-Mart were a nation, it would be China's eighth-largest trade partner! The decline of manufacturing was also accelerated by the increasing organic composition of capital – the mechanization, automation and computerization of operations – and especially the greater resort to informalization so that some 22 million manufacturing jobs were lost worldwide between 1995 and 2002 including a 15 per cent fall in manufacturing employment in China (Palat 2004; Zoubir 2004).

More notably, China's transformation into the world's workshop has also not come at the expense of its neighbouring states. The Malaysian Prime Minister, Abdullah Ahmad Badawi, even noted in 2004, 'China is today a creator of prosperity of the highest order' (quoted in Economy 2005, pp. 313–14). The expanded scale of manufacturing in China from 2.4 per cent of global industrial production to 4.7 per cent in 2002 triggered a sharp escalation in Chinese imports of raw materials and sophisticated components and capital goods. Industrialization on a massive scale and at an historically unprecedented pace has pushed China and India towards forging agreements with governments in Africa, Latin America and the Middle East to secure for themselves sources of strategic raw materials and fossil fuels. In 2004, China alone consumed 33 per cent of the world's steel, 31 per cent of its coal, 20 per cent of its copper, 19 per cent of its aluminum, 10 per cent of its electricity, and more than 8 per cent of its petroleum (Ross 2006, p. 9).

In turn, the voracious demand for raw materials and energy has pushed up commodity prices. The International Energy Agency estimates that between 2002 and 2005, 43 per cent of the increased demand for oil came from Asia – 26 per cent from China alone – and that, deflated by the export prices of high-income countries, oil prices are now as high as they were during the second 'oil shock' of 1979. Almost 50 per cent of China's foreign direct investments have been in Latin America to obtain raw materials, and Chinese trade with that continent grew four-fold in the first five years of the present decade. The prices of metals have similarly increased to levels unmatched since 1989 and, after years of decline, even the real price of foodstuffs has begun to rise sharply due to the higher cost of inputs, including petroleum (Wolf 2005; Harris 2005, p. 11; Magnier 2006). This pattern of trade meant that China's trade surplus with the US of $103 billion in 2002 was accompanied by a $68 billion deficit in its trade with the rest of Asia. Bilateral trade between China and Southeast Asia has grown at an annual rate of almost 20 per cent since 1991 while China (including Hong Kong) became Japan's most important two-way trade partner and South Korea's largest export market. China has also pushed to create a free-trade agreement with ASEAN between 2010 and 2015 and committed itself to aid Myanmar to the tune of $100 million, develop natural gas reserves in Indonesia, infrastructure in the Philippines, establish highway links to Cambodia, Singapore and Thailand, and make the Mekong river more suited to commercial navigation by dredging it along parts of Laos and Myanmar (Palat 2004, pp. 3623–4; Economy 2005, pp. 414–15; Marshall 2006). Even though China had a $124 billion trade surplus with the US in 2003, in its overall trade it had a $5 billion deficit.

Since Chinese wages are about 20 per cent of the rates in Malaysia and Taiwan and about 10 per cent of the rate in Singapore, many corporations in these countries ship products for final processing in China – making it the favorite villain for the loss of jobs in the US. Increasing economic integration within the region is not limited to merchandise trade: Singapore, Hong Kong and even Thailand have been focusing on banking, education, healthcare and tourism to compensate for the loss of low-wage manufacturing jobs to China. Recognizing the importance of reorienting the Japanese economy towards new growth sectors, the Ministry of Economy, Trade and Industry also proposes to spend ¥24,000 billion over the next five years on information technology, environment, biotechnology and nanotechnology. Similarly, unemployment in South Korea has held steady at 3.3 per cent despite the increasing migration of manufacturing jobs to China, suggesting that the disappearing factory jobs were being replaced by other employment opportunities.

The greater density of economic networks in East Asia has been complemented by better political relations. During the economic and financial crisis of 1997–8, although China opposed a Japanese proposal to create an AMF that would have significantly cushioned the adverse impact of the meltdown, its decision not to devalue its currency was greatly appreciated. At the same time, the economies suffering the most were resentful that the US did not argue for more favorable terms for IMF loans to help them ride out the storm. This has led to greater inter-governmental attempts to create closer regional ties, ranging from bilateral trade agreements and economic cooperation to currency swaps. In the past few years, China has also peacefully resolved its territorial disputes with all its neighbours except India and even there considerable progress has been made; the two states have even started holding joint military exercises. Since 1999–2000, China has increasingly participated in regional associations like ASEAN, the ASEAN Regional Forum (ARF), and the Council on Security Cooperation in the Asia-Pacific (CSCAP). China has also launched the Shanghai Cooperation Organization with Russia and Central Asian states. Putting its bitter border skirmish with Vietnam in 1979 behind, China has begun to aid its southern neighbour to the tune of $1 billion as well as to conduct joint military exercises. And it has started convening a regional equivalent to the Davos meeting of business and government leaders in Hainan Island called the Boao Forum. ASEAN has also begun to hold expanded meetings with Australia, China, India, Japan, New Zealand and South Korea – pointedly excluding the United States!

Likewise, in its search for raw materials – oil from Angola, Nigeria and the Sudan; tropical timber from Congo-Brazzaville; iron ore from South Africa, copper from Zambia; and platinum from Zimbabwe – Chinese investment quadrupled in the first five years of the present decade and some 800 Chinese-funded companies have begun operations in Africa over the past 10 years. These include not only companies to extract raw materials, but also those seeking to avail themselves of opportunities for duty-free export to the United States and the European Union granted to some of the Least Developed Countries (White et al. 2006). Chinese corporations and state agencies have been especially involved in oil exploration in West Africa because Nigeria is the only state in the region to be a member of OPEC and the other states are not subject to the cartel's export and production caps (Naidu and Mbazima 2008). Trade between India and African states has also increased substantially over the last two decades – from $967 million in 1991 to more than $30 billion in 2007–8 (Bajpaee 2008) – though this is substantially smaller than the China-Africa trade, as was illustrated by the 44 African heads of state who attended the first China-Africa summit in 2007 compared to the 14 heads of state who went to New Delhi for the first India-Africa summit the following year.

These developments imply that the material conditions for South-South cooperation and for the subversion of the Euro-North American world order has never been better. Unlike the earlier attempt by leaders of newly independent states in Asia and Africa to forge a united front in Bandung, when they had moral authority due to their leadership of independence movements but little room to manoeuvre because of the structural fragility of their economies, leaders of several large states in the 'global South' now have much greater latitude to act because their economies are stronger. India, Brazil and South Africa – a trilateral IBSA partnership was formalized in July 2003 through the Declaration of Brasilia – have taken the lead in forging joint positions in international fora on world trade and emerged as strong power brokers by leading variously constituted groups of low- and middle-income countries: the Group of 20,[4] the Group of 33,[5] the Group of 110,[6] and the 79-member grouping of Africa Caribbean Pacific countries (ACP). More recently, in May 2008, at a meeting in Yekaterinburg, the foreign ministers of Russia, India, China and Brazil institutionalized annual meetings to forge a common front to reform global political financial institutions, promote food and energy security, and to fight terrorism (Radyuhin 2008).

To undercut Euro-North American influence in setting international commodity prices, the Chinese government is attempting to set up an alternate mechanism for commodity prices by instituting a diamond exchange in Shanghai (Naidu and Mbazima 2008). In a similar move, Russia, the world's second-largest oil exporter, began to price Russian Ural Blend oil, its primary petroleum export, in roubles rather than in the greenback. On another register, Chinese companies are increasingly making their initial public offerings of shares through Saudi Arabia rather than through the stock exchanges of London and New York (Nederveen Pieterse 2008; Timmons 2006).

Culturally, the existence of large diasporas, the Internet, the circulation of video and audio cassettes, cheap international flights, and international phone calls are also bridging distances like never before. The transnational expansion of businesses has also led to cultural exchanges on several levels – Korean restaurants following Korean investments, the popularity of Indian movies across the Middle East and Asia, the spread of Ethiopian and Thai restaurants, Japanese karaoke bars, and Latin music and dance. Increased trade with China has led to greater prominence for local Chinese communities in Southeast Asia – symbolized by the opening of a new museum devoted to Chinese-Filipino heritage and by pilgrimages made by the former Philippine President Corazon Aquino and the former Thai Prime Minister Thaksin Shinawatra to their ancestral homes during state visits to China (Marshall 2006). Fifty years ago, as states in Asia and Africa were emerging from colonialism, cultural ties among these states were virtually non-existent (except for some diasporas which were created by colonial labour exchanges, and by subordinate financial and business communities like the Indians in East Africa and the Chinese in Southeast Asia).

The elimination of tariffs and subsidies, and the greater commodification of resources, has also led to movements for better social protection and as the integration of the world economy proceeds apace, these movements have also become increasingly transnational – as manifested by Porto Alegre, the World Social Forum, and a slew of anti-globalization movements. Indigenous peoples everywhere are uniting to resist their marginalization, most notably in recent days in Bolivia. But these movements also address issues of ecological degradation, poverty and more inclusive modes of political action. Concern with environmental degradation also ties in with feminist movements across the world.

In marked contrast, governments of the larger states in the global South have offered little support to anti-systemic movements in a range of countries from Zimbabwe to Myanmar and their investments in these states and sales of military equipment have bolstered repressive military juntas and authoritarian governments. In their drive to secure strategic raw materials and fossil fuels, they have been eager to sign deals with Sudan and other countries where governments have been involved in brutal ethnic conflicts. The Chinese government has consistently blocked attempts to impose sanctions on Sudan and has in fact increased sales of fighter aircraft and set up facilities to manufacture weapons and ammunition, which undercuts embargos on military supplies to the rebels in Darfur (White et al. 2006). Chinese appetite for aluminum, nickel, copper and steel has led to a project to construct the world's second largest dam to provide electricity to the mines in the Amazon basin on the Xingu River which is predicted to cause extensive environmental damage and displace many indigenous peoples (Rohter 2005).

Elsewhere, there have been allegations that cheap Chinese imports have displaced local production as garment factories have closed in Lesotho and other states in Africa. Chinese companies have also been chastised for preferring to employ Chinese workers in Africa, and to provide poor working conditions when they employ Africans (White et al. 2006). Similarly, the expansion of Johannesburg-based businesses in the construction, financial services, mining, mobile phone, retail, television and tourism sectors in Africa has raised the charge of South African subimperialism (Alden and Vieira 2005, p. 1084; Bond 2004, p. 231; Bond 2006a; Bond 2006b). The growth of Chinese – and less significantly, Indian – investments and trade with African states may, of course, undermine South Africa's dominance in the continent as

Asian imports undercut South African industrial exports and even under-mine the regional economic formation in which South Africa occupies a privileged position (Martin 2008).

In China, a report by the International Confederation on Free Trade Unions indicates that while WTO membership has boosted incomes of owners of private enterprises and skilled white-collar workers, it has had an extremely adverse impact on blue-collar workers, farmers and unskilled office workers. Imports of subsidized US cotton, for instance, have been estimated to have resulted in a loss of 720,000 jobs, mostly in two of China's poorest regions – Gansu and Xinjiang. To compensate for similar job losses over the next decade in agriculture and state-owned enterprises, it is estimated that China needs to create 300 million new jobs over the next five years.

Furthermore, 47 per cent of the population live on less than $2 a day – and 250 million on less than a dollar a day. The people who provide everything from T-shirts to DVD players to the world's consumers have 60- to 70-hour working weeks, live in dormitories with eight to 16 people in each room, earn less than the minimum wage, that go as low as $44 per month, and have unemployment as the only prospect if they should get injured in the factories (Taylor 2005).

Just as subsidized imports of cotton caused distress in Chinese provinces, cheap imports of subsidized cotton and other agricultural crops have caused agrarian distress in India – most evident by a spurt of suicides by farmers, some 8,900 cases between 2000 and 2005 accord-ing to official sources. It is significant that the incidence of suicides come from states with the most diversified agriculture – Andhra Pradesh, Gujarat, Karnataka, Kerala, Maharashtra, Punjab and Tamil Nadu – where the political leadership is drawn from farming communities. As for the reason why agrarian distress manifests itself in suicides rather than rebellions or flight from the land, it has plausibly been suggested it is due to the impact of the green revolution which – by the greater use of farm machinery, monoculture under market pressure, and increased numbers of smallholdings – has rendered cooperation anachronistic, and to the import of subsidized agricultural products, the high cost of seeds, fertil-izers and other inputs, and the parallel rise of expenditures, especially in education in the drive to send children to private schools. Moreover, although two-thirds of the population of India live in rural areas, they share less than a quarter of the national income (Suri 2006).[7]

In short, the rapid resurgence of China and India – due to their demo-graphic weight – has radically altered the global geopolitical ecology of investment, production and trade. Their vastly expanded scale of

operations has generated a tidal wave of demand for capital and intermediate goods, raw materials and energy that, by pushing up commodity
prices, has lifted many other low- and middle-income economies as well.
Intensifying economic relations have been accompanied by closer political, diplomatic and cultural relations. However, this has often meant that
the larger states of the global South, with their virtually unquenchable
thirst for raw materials and energy, have tended to prop up authoritarian regimes and military juntas across the world. In part, I have also
suggested, their support for these regimes stems from their inability to
address deepening inequalities in income and wealth within their own
jurisdictions – a factor that also underpins their reluctance to frontally
challenge the Euro-North American domination of the world, as we see
in the next section.

One step forward, two steps back

The reluctance of the governments of the major states of the global
South, despite their far more favourable position compared to 1955, to
challenge the Euro-North American domination of the world order is
attributable not only to the collapse of the Soviet Union and thus to
the possibility of playing off the two superpowers against each other,
but also to the wide-ranging transformations in the geopolitical ecology of production, trade and investment that have underlain their rise.
In particular, they can be traced to the recurrent proclivity of capitalist production to generate capital above and beyond that which can be
invested profitably in the production and circulation of commodities.
Rosa Luxemburg and Hannah Arendt both underscored that the emergence of such tendencies in the second half of the 19th century had not
only led to the export of capital to areas forcibly incorporated into the
capitalist world-economy, but also to the human debris that every crisis,
following invariably upon each period of industrial growth, eliminated
permanently from productive society. 'Men who had become permanently idle were as superfluous to the community as were the owners
of superfluous wealth [...] The new fact in the imperialist era is that
these two superfluous forces, superfluous capital and superfluous working power, joined hands and left the country together' (Arendt 1958,
p. 150).

While the present epoch has several parallels to this, as David Harvey
(2003) has emphasized, there are several clear differences as well; formal
colonization and the division of the planet into competing imperial formations as in the late 19th century is unimaginable. The largest military

power in human history – the United States – despite some 12 years of crippling sanctions and the dropping of more bombs than on Vietnam, has been unable to pacify Iraq after three years of occupation, and no other high-income state can even envisage militarily subjugating a large low- or middle-income state. This suggests that inter-state capitalist rivalry no longer implies the carving of the world into distinct 'spheres of influence'. In fact, Palmisano's notion of a 'globally integrated enterprise' model suggests more the cooptation of government and business elites from different jurisdictions for their mutual benefit at the expense of the large majority of their domestic populations. Moreover, unlike in the 19th century, which was marked by massive emigration of the 'human debris' from Europe to the 'countries of recent European settlement', even the possibility of such migration cannot be entertained today – when in fact migrants from low- and middle-income states continue to arrive in high-income states in record numbers.

In these conditions, 'accumulation by dispossession' takes place through the privatization of state assets and the expropriation of the commons – both of which suited business and state elites in the major states of the global South. As the victims of the Chinese Cultural Revolution were gradually rehabilitated in the 1970s, Deng Xiaoping began to implement measures to give greater autonomy to enterprises in 1975 and, three years after the end of the Vietnam War, to open 'special economic zones' to attract Japanese and other overseas investments. After deregulating agricultural prices and disbanding rural collectives, a move that rapidly increased rural incomes in coastal areas, the Chinese government began to deregulate industries. In this process, former state managers and sons and relatives of party officials emerged as a new stratum of 'new rich' as they used their connections to acquire assets at bargain prices (Wang Hui 2003). The collapse of guaranteed employment and the social welfare system meant that market-oriented reforms failed to generate sufficient domestic demand and the economy was increasingly dependent on exports. Thus, as China increasingly becomes the world's industrial workshop, income and wealth inequalities are widening rapidly.

Though the immediate trigger for liberalization of the economy in India was the collapse of the Soviet Union, which was its major trading partner in 1991, and a consequent foreign exchange crisis the following year when there were hard currency reserves to pay for only two weeks' worth of imports, a strong lobby for change had gradually been slowly consolidating among the middle classes. The Indian bourgeoisie, which had already been the most class-conscious capitalist class during

Table 2.2   Growth rates compared (per cent)

	1950–64	1965–79	1980–90	1991–2004	1980–2004
GDP growth	3.7	2.9	5.8	5.6	5.7
Industrial growth	7.4	3.8	6.5	5.8	6.1
Agricultural growth	3.1	2.3	3.9	3	3.4
Gross Investment/GDP	13	18	22.8	22.3	22.5

the late colonial period, had successfully used industrial regulations under the import-substitution model to capture market segments and keep potential new entrants – with a few notable exceptions like the Reliance group – out of lucrative production lines. As the size of the market increased, the pressure from new aspirants to enter these lucrative segments mounted and barriers to entry for domestic firms began to be relaxed by diluting provisions of the Monopolies and Restrictive Trade Practices Act, beginning in 1980. Shielded for decades from foreign competition, domestic firms were not at all confident of their chances against foreign transnational corporations and as late as 1995 the Confederation of Indian Industries chastised the government for not adequately protecting domestic firms from foreign competition (Chibber 2006; Kohli 2006a; Kohli 2006b). Hence, unlike the case of China, there was significant opposition to foreign investment – and the Indian reforms can be more accurately characterized as 'business-friendly' rather than 'market-friendly'. This explains largely why industrial growth in the first decade of reforms in the 1990s was no higher, and perhaps marginally lower, than in the 1980s, as indicated by Table 2.2. Notably, too, when the reforms in industrial policy were announced in 1991, they were embodied in a government 'statement' rather than a 'resolution', to sidestep a parliamentary discussion and vote (Kohli 2006b, p. 1363). Rather than industrial or agricultural production, the main engine of growth was the information-technology sector and the growth of call centres and other back-office operations.

Likewise in Latin America, under the banner of increasing competitiveness, between the assumption of office as President of Chile by Patricio Aylwin on 11 March 1990 and of Luiz Inácio 'Lula' da Silva as President of Brazil on 1 January 2003, 'democratization' was followed by the privatization of state assets. Modelled on General Augusto Pinochet's 1973 'Law for the Defence of Free Competition', a series of measures were implemented to de-nationalize state assets and curb the power of labour: the 'Law to Promote and Protect Free Competition' in Venezuela and the Peruvian Institute for the Defence of Competition and Protection of Intellectual Property Commission in 1992; the creation of the Mexican Federal Competition Commission the following year; Brazil's 'Law for the Defence of Economic Order' in 1994; a series of measures in Central America designed to be pro-market and facilitate privatization; and the creation in Argentina of the National Tribunal for the Defence of Competition in 1999 (Cammack 2004).

The United States has also played on the aspirations of the elites of the large states of the global South, except of course China, by recognizing them as regional leaders in a hub-and-spokes approach. This was evidenced in the designation of South Africa as the lead state in dealing with Zimbabwe, recruiting Brazil for peacekeeping missions in Haiti, and above all in sponsoring an India-specific exception to the nuclear Non-Proliferation Treaty while pointedly refusing a similar arrangement for Pakistan (see Alden and Vieira 2005, p. 1091; Bond 2004; Bond 2006a; Bond 2006b). The then US Secretary of State, Condoleezza Rice, even announced in March 2005 that Washington was determined to 'make India a global power' and if this catered to the ambitions of Indian elites, they did not pause to wonder what substance 'a global power' status could have if it could be conferred by a United States administration at its will! How could India project its military power across the globe without aerial reconnaissance and refuelling capabilities, long-range aircraft, attack helicopters, and aircraft carrier groups, especially when even the much better-equipped states of the European Union had to depend on the United States military to intervene in the Balkans (Research Unit for Political Economy 2006)?

To fulfill their aspirations to be global players, and to show that they were responsible powers, Brazil and India were instrumental in getting states of the global South to accept a loophole-ridden agreement in favour of high-income states at the Hong Kong ministerial meeting that saved the World Trade Organization (WTO) after the failed meetings at Seattle and Cancún. In return, these two states, along with the European Union and the United States, came to form an informal grouping called the New Quad to set the agenda for global trade talks.[8]

Though the US-led alliances are increasingly directed against China, the Chinese leadership has been reluctant to challenge US domination in world politics, and indeed the repatriation of Chinese – and other East Asian – trade surpluses to the United States in a bid to maintain favourable exchange rates for their currencies in fact allowed the George W. Bush administration to conduct an expensive occupation in Iraq and maintain military spending at a level higher than all other states combined while actually cutting US taxes! In February 2006, China surpassed Japan as the largest holder of foreign exchange reserves – by May 2007, Chinese foreign exchange reserves stood at a staggering $1.3 trillion and were growing at the rate of $1 million a minute – and China typically maintains three-quarters of its reserves in dollar-dominated sources such as US Treasury bills (Bradsher 2006; Goodman 2006; Watts and Clark 2007). Peter Garber, a Deutsche Bank economist, has argued that the repatriation of current-account surpluses to the United States to help it fund its trade deficits and maintain low domestic interest rates is essential to absorbing the millions of Indian and Chinese low-wage labourers entering the world market (Palat 2004, pp. 3624–5).

Looked at another way, however, the repatriation of trade surpluses is vital to propping up US dominance in the world. The greenback's role as the world's currency since the end of the Second World War meant that the US was committed to running consistent current-account deficits with its major partners. This allowed its rivals to exploit the production frontier and install the latest technologies as they rebuilt their economies. While this is a common pattern for hegemonic powers, unlike previous hegemons, which had balanced their deficits with expropriations from their colonies – most notably the 'Home Charges' levied on India by the British government – the United States could not similarly compensate for capital outflows; attempts to turn Iraq into America's India seems doomed to failure (Patnaik 2005). In this context, the willingness of East Asian states, particularly China, to buy US Treasury notes and provide the more than $2 billion a day that is required to balance the US current-account deficit is vital to the preservation of US dominance.

Indeed, because US assets are denominated in foreign currencies and its liabilities in dollars, the US is well-placed to reap substantial gains in its gross positions if the dollar was to fall due to a withdrawal or substantial decline of capital inflows. Consequently, while a fall in the value of the dollar may reduce private capital inflows to the US, it is often compensated by foreign central banks increasing their holdings of US Treasury bonds. Hence when the dollar fell by some 20 per cent between 2000 and 2003, and net capital inflows by private overseas investors began to decline in 2004, the US Treasury Department reported that intervention by foreign central banks prevented a massive economic contraction (Dwyer 2004; Porter 2004).

The cost of repatriating surpluses to the United States, however, is a dampening of domestic consumption and widening income and wealth differentials in Asia, especially in China and India. Inadequate domestic demand makes them reliant on the US as a market of last resort and though there has been increasing consumer credit in countries like South Korea and Thailand and there is considerable potential for further growth, as credit card usage is in its infancy in India, China and Japan which collectively account for 70 per cent of consumer expenditure in Asia (Palat 2005). When the euro represents an alternative world currency to the dollar, a falling dollar and growing Asian-EU trade means that Asian central banks have less incentive to prop up the greenback, as private investors have already realized. Thus, while the foreign net purchases of long-term US securities averaged $70 billion a month in 2005, in July 2007 it dropped to $19.9 billion and to minus $70.6 billion in August before rising to $26.4 billion in September (Munchau 2007). A drying-up of cash inflows, in conditions of high current-account deficits, would lead to a sharp rise in domestic US interest rates, the effects of which would be catastrophic as low interest rates led to household debt rising twice as fast as household income between 2000 and 2003 (Palat 2004, p. 3624).

In this context, the surge in commodity prices as a result of expanded production in the global South means that the real challenge to the Euro-North American domination of world politics has emerged from resource-rich states, most notably Venezuela and Bolivia, and less significantly from Iran. By placing nationalization of resources and expropriation of land back on the agenda Hugo Chavez and Evo Morales – reflecting their social bases in the urban poor and indigenous communities – have been at the forefront of reversing the neoliberal tendency. Unlike some other OPEC countries, which have also repatriated the profits they have gained from the spurt in oil prices,[9] Venezuela has used its oil revenues to purchase $2.5 billion in Argentine debt, selling oil at below-market prices to 13 Caribbean states, financing better healthcare for Latin American states through Cuban doctors, providing aid to African states, and even subsidizing heating to some poor neighbourhoods in the United States (Chomsky 2006; Fernandes 2006; Forero 2006).

To recapitulate, reopening of China and India – and the consequent entry of hundreds of millions of cheap labourers into the world market – has the potential to reshape the world economy fundamentally. With improvements in communications and transport, virtually no job other than those occupations that by their very nature have to be performed on site is immune to being transferred to these locations. The scale and magnitude of these nations' expansions have not only exerted massive deflationary pressure but have also led to a rise in the prices of strategic raw materials and energy, thus providing already richly endowed economies with substantial cash infusions. While it is possible that the search for new sources of supplies and the development of substitutes could lower prices, for now greater South-South links have bolstered many authoritarian regimes and military juntas, though they have also enabled progressive governments such as those in Venezuela and Bolivia to challenge the neoliberal world order and bring nationalization of mineral resources and land appropriations back on to the agenda. The opening to the market in most countries has, however, only benefited narrow elites – the creation of 'globally integrated enterprises' symbolizes more of an inter-state alliance of business and government elites – and has widened inequalities in income and wealth within almost every state. It is this inter-elite alliance that has stymied leaders of the large states of the global South in any challenge to Euro-North American domination. However, since increased income and wealth inequalities trigger widespread unrest and rebellion, political leaderships in these states will be compelled to address the root causes of distress. In this context, the resurgence of the Maoists in Nepal is a welcome sign.

Notes

1. Earlier incarnations of this chapter appeared in *Futures*, XL (8), October 2008, and in M. Petrusewicz et al. (2008).
2. Freed from colonial conditions, growth rates in India increased substantially from the early 1950s as five-year plans were implemented: between 1900–1 and 1946–7, the average growth of GDP in real terms was 1.15 per cent a year and during this period, per capita GDP increased from Rs 224 to Rs 233 (in 1948–9 prices). From 1951 to 1980, the annual average growth of GDP was 3.6 per cent, and the annual average per capita GDP growth was 1.6 per cent (Hatekar and Dongre 2005, pp. 1432–3).
3. In 2005, India graduated 200,000 engineers – about three times as many as the US – and had 450,000 students enrolled in four-year engineering colleges, implying that the numbers of engineers it graduates would double by 2009. However, the rapid growth of private engineering colleges to cater to this demand – between 2003 and 2004, the numbers of applicants to a relatively mediocre engineering school rose from 7,000 to 44,000 – means that the quality of education varies widely (Mallaby 2006).
4. The group of countries with special interests in agriculture: Argentina, Bolivia, Brazil, Chile, China, Cuba, Egypt, Guatemala, India, Indonesia, Mexico, Nigeria, Pakistan, Paraguay, the Philippines, South Africa, Tanzania, Thailand, Uruguay, Venezuela and Zimbabwe.
5. The group currently has 40 members, some of which, like Indonesia, Nigeria and the Philippines, are also part of the G-20, while other states, including some Central American states which have free-trade agreements with the United States, have not joined the G-20 for fear of US retaliation. It lobbies for special and differential treatment for specific commodities of importance to its member states.

6. Consists of the 50 Least Developed Countries plus other members of the ACP.
7. With the lowering of tariffs, between 1996–7 and 2003–4, agricultural imports increased by 270 per cent by volume and by 300 per cent by value (Suri 2006, p. 1526).
8. The deal accepted the so-called Swiss formula for Non-Agricultural Market Access which disproportionately trims higher tariffs rather than lower ones. This affects poorer states more adversely as they tend to have higher tariffs to protect their domestic industries – and may in fact help India and Brazil because of their more advanced industrial structures but not the smaller countries which aspire to be represented in international fora. Similarly, while the agreement called for an end to formally defined export subsidies in agriculture by 2013, it allowed for other forms of export subsidies. It is estimated that this loophole will allow the European Union to subsidize exports to as much as €55 billion after 2013. In turn the low-income states made an 'aid-for-trade' deal which ignored the demands of West African cotton producers for compensation for US export subsidies and permitted the US to continue the subsidies for an extra year after they had been found inconsistent with WTO agreements, and to accept aid to make their economic regulations consistent with the new WTO requirements (Bello 2005).
9. While it is difficult to determine the extent of OPEC purchases of US Treasury bills, because some of them channel their investments through banks in London and the Caribbean, it is estimated that they must have bought at least $21.2 billion worth between the end of 2003 and the end of 2005 (Fitzgerald 2006).

3
Are More People Becoming Vulnerable to Poverty? Evidence from Grassroots Investigations in Five Countries

Anirudh Krishna

Evidence is mounting that inequality in developing countries has grown in the wake of globalization and liberalization (for example, Milanovic 2005; Wade 2001, 2004), but not much is known about trends in vulnerability. How many people have fallen into poverty over the past 10 or 15 years? Has rising income vulnerability made life more precarious and risk-prone for poorer people? Are people in poor countries more likely to experience erosion in their wellbeing now compared to 10 or 15 years ago?[1]

Knowing the answers to these questions is critically important for policy design. If the risk of falling into poverty is relatively small, then policymakers can concentrate on moving the existing poor out of poverty. But if the danger of being plunged into poverty is large and growing, then policy resources should be concentrated, instead, on reducing these risks. It helps little to focus exclusively on raising people out of poverty where large and growing numbers are simultaneously falling in.

The appropriate choice of policies for combatting poverty depends critically upon knowing the extents of volatility and vulnerability. If the risk of impoverishment is low, governments can more easily go about their usual tasks of promoting economic growth, confident that increasing poverty will not erode the ground from under their feet. But where these risks are large and growing, economic growth will not serve as an effective antidote to poverty, as we will see below. Volatility and vulnerability will have to be tackled more directly, through addressing specific causes that give rise to these events. It is essential, therefore, to know how volatility and vulnerability are affecting each country's population.

It comes as shock, therefore, to find that information about vulnerability is simply not available for any developing country. Try asking any national statistics office how many people *fell* into poverty in your country over the last X years. You will learn that the available poverty data simply cannot answer any such question. National statistics offices – along with international agencies, such as the World Bank – routinely collect information about the stocks of poverty at particular moments in time. By calculating how much this stock has changed from time period t to time period t + 1, they can calculate the net change in poverty, and they can relate this change to particular changes in the economic situation. But they hardly have any means of knowing how this net change was actually obtained: how many people fell into poverty, and how many others escaped out of poverty? These questions – since they are not usually asked – cannot be answered with the prevailing systems of poverty measurement.

The collection of official statistics about poverty trends is preconfigured to answer only a narrow range of questions, such as the overall effects that economic growth has upon poverty in a country. More disaggregated (and more interesting and potentially useful) avenues of inquiry into poverty simply cannot be pursued.[2] Policy choices are restricted by the manner in which data collection has been organized.

Such evidence as is available has been put together for industrialized countries, and it points toward a worrying increase in volatility in recent years. A recent investigation in the United States concludes that 'over the past generation the economic instability of American families has actually risen faster' than income inequality, which has also been rising (Hacker 2006, p. 2). 'While the gaps between the rungs on the ladder of the American economy have increased, what has increased even more quickly is how far people slip *down* the ladder when they lose their financial footing [. . .] The chance that families will see their income plummet has risen; the chance that they will experience long-term movements up the income ladder has not' (Hacker 2006, pp. 12–13; emphasis in the original).

As unfettered market forces increasingly take over the economies of poorer countries and governments retreat, rolling back the safety nets that they used to provide, it is quite likely that similar trends are occurring as well within developing countries. Several critics of current-day neoliberal economic policies have suggested that volatility might be on the rise within developing countries (for example, Escobar 1995; Rapley 1996; Stiglitz 2002; Soros 2002). And evidence of increasing inequality, with the emergence of a dualistic structure of the economy – within which poor people are mostly confined beneath a low glass ceiling, while richer people embrace an ever-widening horizon of globally vast opportunities (see Krishna and Brihmadesam 2006) – also suggests that vulnerability and volatility might well be on the rise. But no hard evidence is as yet available that allows any firm judgment to be made about how volatility has been affected.[3] Consequently, policies get made without the knowledge that is essential for making these policies.

Hacker based his conclusions about the United States on data from the Panel Study of Income Dynamics (PSID), a nationally representative sample of nearly 8,000 US families that has been followed consistently since 1968.[4] The availability of this longitudinal data helps address questions related to income volatility in the US. The absence of anything similar in most developing countries makes it impossible to come to any equivalent judgment, based on studies of population samples representative of entire countries.[5]

We are left, therefore, with a worrying concern: that volatility and risk may have increased considerably, especially for middle-class and less well-off families in developing countries. But we have no way of checking – at least not with the help of official data – whether or not this concern may be valid and important. As a result, we might be rendered helpless to prevent a potentially great human tragedy in the making. Thousands of households might continue falling into poverty apace, and years from now we might end up saying – just as we do now for import-substituting industrialization, all the rage in the 1960s, and for structural adjustment, the flavour of the day in the 1980s and 1990s – that economic liberalization was wrong-headed and incomplete; it put at risk the livelihoods of too many poorer people. But lacking information, we do not act; we cannot attack something ill-defined and unproven.

New learning from recent disaggregated studies: trends in vulnerability

Some information, recently gathered, helps fill these important gaps in our knowledge about poverty. Decentralized studies, conducted over the past seven years, have generated important new information about household poverty dynamics in different locations. By providing data (that national statistics lack) about poverty dynamics – giving numbers of those who have risen out of poverty and numbers, simultaneously, of those who have *fallen into* poverty – these studies help us get a better grasp on vulnerability.

Table 3.1   Simultaneous escape and descent: some illustrations

(1) Country/ Region	(2) Study	(3) Period	(4) Sample (households)	(5) Percentage escaped poverty	(6) Percentage descended into poverty
Kenya (Western)	Krishna et al. (2004)	1978–2003	1,706	18	19
South Africa	Carter and May (2001)	1993–98	1,171	10	25
India (rural)	Bhide and Mehta (2004)	1970–82	3,139	23	13
Bangladesh	Sen (2003)	1987–2000	379	26	18
Egypt	Haddad and Ahmed (2003)	1997–9	347	6	14
India (Rajasthan)	Krishna (2004)	1976–2001	6,374	11	8
Uganda	Deininger and Okidi (2003)	1992–2000	1,300	29	12

Commonly, these studies show that descents – into poverty – have occurred alongside escapes from poverty. In every region studied, upward and downward movements have occurred in parallel. Even as some households have moved out of poverty, other households in the same regions and communities have fallen into poverty. Poverty has been created anew even as some existing poverty was overcome. Vulnerability is an ever-present feature, and it is a larger problem in some contexts compared to others. Reducing poverty requires not just raising poor people out of poverty – but also and more importantly, preventing the descent into poverty of households not currently poor. The second problem – arising because people are vulnerable to descents – is mostly ignored, a product of shortsighted methods of collecting national statistics on poverty.

Table 3.1 summarizes these results from a sample of recent disaggregated studies. The first row of this table shows that in 20 communities in Western Kenya, 18 per cent of households rose out of poverty over the past two decades, but another 19 per cent fell into poverty over the same period. Poverty increased by 1 per cent overall, even as nearly 20 per cent of households succeeded in escaping out of poverty (Krishna et al. 2004).

Other studies also show how descent occurs alongside escape in all parts of the world. Carter and May (2001) show how over a five-year period 10 per cent of households examined in Kwazulu-Natal, South

Africa, came out of poverty. These households formed part of the stock of poverty in 1993, but they were no longer poor in 1998. Movements in the reverse direction more than compensated for this positive achievement, however. More than twice as many households, 25 per cent, moved into poverty during the same five-year period. Similarly, another study shows that 14 per cent of a random sample of rural Indian households escaped from poverty between 1970 and 1982, but another 13 per cent of households fell into poverty over the same time period (Bhide and Mehta 2004).

Movements into poverty are large, and they occur alongside upward movements in all contexts. The figure for net reduction in poverty from time period t to time period t + 1 is merely a resultant of these parallel and opposite flows; it should not have any independent significance for policy. Too often, however, policy attention focuses exclusively on the figure for net change, paying no heed to the separate flows that make and unmake poverty.

In reality, the two flows need to be attended to separately; the factors responsible for each are independent of each other. While one set of factors is associated with escapes from poverty, a separate set of factors is associated with descents into it.

Different policies are required to deal with these separate sets of factors. Mounting the appropriate mix of policies requires knowing the respective rates of escape and descent. Simply knowing the net change from t to t + 1 will not help. While escapes from poverty are associated with income diversification and new jobs, descents into poverty are associated, most importantly, with health-care expenses, as we will see below. Because it is brought on by a different set of factors, controlling descents will require responses that are different from those required to accelerate escapes. The higher the rate of descents in a given context – that is, the greater the extent of vulnerability – the more policy resources must be directed toward deflecting the reasons for descent.

However, the existence of higher vulnerability needs to be detected before it can be ameliorated and rectified. Unfortunately, national statistical systems do not facilitate any such detection, and the existence of high vulnerability can continue, unidentified and unchecked, nullifying other efforts made to speed up escapes out of poverty. The few decentralized data sources in existence show that vulnerability is a large problem everywhere, but it is especially large within some specific contexts. Extending these forms of data collection into other areas is an essential aspect of understanding and then addressing vulnerability.

What about volatility, which is related to increasing vulnerability over time? Has vulnerability – considered here as the risk of descent into poverty – changed significantly over time, becoming more pronounced in more recent years? In order to learn about volatility, one must know how vulnerability has changed, that is, how the prospects for descent have changed from one time-period to the next. While 13 per cent of households fell into poverty in rural India in the 12 years ending in 1982 (Bhide and Mehta 2004), did more than this number suffer drops into poverty during the following 12-year period? Data about volatility is even scarcer; even the limited data about vulnerability seems large in comparison. In order to track how the rate of descent has changed, similar disaggregated data need to be available for at least two time periods. Very few studies are as yet available which provide such inter-temporal information, comparing trends.

I examine below results from five such studies with which I have been associated. Undertaken over the past five years in five separate countries and examining poverty dynamics for more than 25,000 households overall, these studies are by no means conclusive about volatility in a global context. They do not all draw upon nationally representative samples, and they do not employ a standardized measure of poverty, common across all countries, such as dollar-a-day. To the extent, however, that these separate studies nevertheless report a common conclusion – reporting *increasing* vulnerability and *growing* volatility within communities of all five countries studied – they are suggestive of a broader trend that would bear a closer look.

In disparate communities, studied in India, Kenya, Uganda, Peru, and the state of North Carolina in the US, common trends are evident. More important, similar reasons appear to be responsible for the common growth of vulnerability in all these contexts. Critical among these reasons are ill-health and high health-care costs. Examinations by other scholars working in a swathe of countries around the globe also show how a 'medical poverty trap' is beginning to have increasingly serious consequences.

I present below, first, the results related to vulnerability and volatility that were obtained in the different studies that I undertook. Next, I discuss the reasons identified for the worrisome observed increase in vulnerability. Finally, I introduce results from others' studies which show that – because of the operation of similar reasons – similar trends might also be operating elsewhere, resulting in an increase in vulnerability and rising volatility.

Indications of increased volatility

Between 2002 and 2006, I undertook nine separate studies, considering a total of 236 communities and tracking the pathways traversed by 25,866 households.[6] Not all of these studies have considered more than one time period, thus not all are relevant for studying volatility. The initial studies were focused upon a single time period. But becoming curious about volatility and gaining more confidence in the reliability of the new methodology used for these studies, I considered two separate time periods in the studies that I undertook at later dates. I base my conclusions in this paper on these later studies, including those of Uganda, Peru and North Carolina studies, and the second set of studies in Rajasthan, India and in Kenya.

A new methodology was developed for conducting these separate studies. The Stages-of-Progress methodology is an innovative, community-based approach for identifying and explaining households' movements *vis-à-vis* poverty. This methodology is rigorous but relatively simple to apply. It relies upon working with community groups to develop a ladder of successive steps consisting of capabilities and assets that people acquire sequentially as they move upward out of poverty. The Stages-of-Progress methodology serves as a useful device, benchmark or yardstick for assessing how high up the ladder of material prosperity a particular household has climbed within each of the two time periods considered. In the absence of official or any other data, it provides perhaps the only clue as to how vulnerability has changed in the past 10 compared to the previous 15 years. It also helps examine the reasons for any change in volatility. Triangulation of all data is an important feature of this methodology. Information about each household is obtained separately at both the community and the household level. The methodology has seven steps that were applied commonly in the studies reported below. Due to lack of space and because not all readers might be interested, I do not discuss (or further defend) this methodology here, but instead refer the interested reader to the website, www.pubpol.duke.edu/krishna, which provides a detailed description of these steps and a complete training manual.

These investigations showed, worryingly, that vulnerability is on the rise; people's livelihoods have become more volatile and precarious everywhere. Data collected in quite dissimilar contexts – 36 communities in two regions of Uganda; 40 communities in two regions of Peru; a countrywide representative sample of 71 urban and rural communities in Kenya; 13 communities in North Carolina; and 71 communities in Rajasthan, India – commonly point to the same worrying conclusion.

Uganda

A total of 36 villages were studied. Three dissimilar districts were selected in each of the Western and Central regions of Uganda. In each district, six villages were selected, two located near the district town centre, two located near a main road but not near the district town centre, and two located relatively far away from either a main road or the district town centre and therefore relatively remote and hard to access. The selected villages represent quite well the considerable diversity that exists within the two selected regions; they are not, however, 'representative' in the statistical sense of this term. A total of 2,631 households are resident in these villages, and following the participatory, community-based methodology described above, the poverty status of each household was ascertained for the present, for 10 years ago, and for 25 years ago. The trajectory of each household was compiled in this manner, and reasons associated with these trajectories were examined for a random sample of 1,068 households (Krishna et al. 2006a).

On average in these 36 villages, 45 per cent of all households lived in poverty 25 years ago, 37 per cent were poor 10 years ago, and 35 per cent are poor at the present time. Overall, poverty has fallen consistently over the 25-year period. But disaggregating these data shows that not everything has been going well.

Table 3.2 presents the data divided into two separate time periods, with the *first period* running from 1980 to 1995, and the *second period* from 1995 to 2005. An average of 13 per cent of households in both regions escaped from poverty during the first time period, with 15.6 per cent escaping poverty in villages of the Central Region and 10 per cent escaping poverty in villages of the Western Region. During the second time period, as well, an average of about 13 per cent of all households escaped from poverty in both regions. Thus, the pace of

Table 3.2   Escape and descent over two time periods in Uganda

	Communities of	Per cent of all households	
		Escaped poverty	Descended into poverty
1st time period (1980–95)	Central Region	15.6	6.4
	Western Region	10.0	4.6
2nd time period (1995–2005)	Central Region	17.2	13.4
	Western Region	10.4	11.6

escapes remained relatively unchanged on average from one time period to the next.

On the other hand, many more households *fell into* poverty during the second compared to the first time period. An average of 5.6 per cent of households fell into poverty during the first time period (6.4 per cent in villages of the Central Region and 4.6 percent in the Western Region). However, as many as 10.9 per cent of all households – nearly twice the earlier number – fell into poverty over the second time period. In both regions, a much faster rate of descent was obvious in the later period.

The pace of economic growth in Uganda was faster in the second time period compared to the first time period, and we had expected initially that poverty reduction would also have been faster in the second time period. But because descents have been almost twice as frequent in the second time period compared to the first time period, the pace of poverty reduction has slowed down in recent times.[7]

More volatility seems to have gone together with more liberalization and commercialization. Especially since the late 1990s, the pace of descents into poverty accelerated, with more than twice as many people falling into poverty during the 10 years between 1995 and 2005 as became poor during the preceding 15-year period. There are indications of similar trends in other regions of Uganda. Using data from the Uganda National Household Surveys, Kappel et al. (2005, pp. 28, 49) detected 'an increase in poverty between 1999/00 and 2002/3 ... from 7 million to 9 million in only three years'. Results of participatory poverty assessments also suggested that movements into poverty have become more frequent in recent years (McGee 2004).

Peru

The Stages-of-Progress methodology was applied in a group of 40 communities in two regions, Cajamarca and Puno (Krishna et al. 2006b). We selected these two regions because they are among the poorest in this country. Within each region we selected 20 communities, capturing diversity with respect to five criteria: altitude, economic activity, market access, size of community and, especially in the Puno region, ethnic group and language. The communities we selected are located from a low of 1,900 metres to a high of 4,500 metres above mean sea level. Economic activity varies as a result; for example, households in lower-lying communities are more dependent upon cattle-raising as a principal activity, while communities at higher altitudes are more dependent upon camelids, like llamas and alpacas. Market access also varies considerably. Ethnic group and language also vary. Spanish is the spoken language in the Cajamarca communities, while in Puno the 20 selected communities include 12 Quechua-speaking ones and eight that speak Aymara.

Even in these poorest regions of Peru, large numbers of households have made an escape from poverty. The dark side, however, is that large numbers have also fallen into poverty. Among all 3,817 households currently residing in these 40 communities, 38 per cent were poor ten years ago, and 28 per cent are poor at the present time. Overall, therefore, an improvement of 10 per cent has been experienced. Considering the longer 25-year period, poverty has fallen even further, from 47 per cent in 1979 to 28 per cent at the present time.

Quite disparate fates were met, however, by different households within the same communities. While 19 per cent of households escaped from poverty over the past 10 years, another 8 per cent of households simultaneously fell into poverty. This distinction between escape and descent was even sharper when one considers the longer period of 25 years. Twenty-nine per cent of households escaped poverty during the 25-year period (from 1979 to 2004), but another 10 per cent of households became impoverished at the same time.

The identities of the poor changed considerably because of these simultaneous up-and-down movements. Of the 28 per cent of households that are poor at the present time, 18 per cent have been poor over the entire 25-year period, and another 10 per cent have fallen into poverty anew during this period. *More than one-third* of currently poor households were not always poor; thus they joined the ranks of the poor during the last 25 years.

Table 3.3 presents results related to volatility, dividing the 25-year period considered into two separate sub-periods as before.

These data show that volatility rose substantially between the first and second time periods. While just about 4 per cent of households fell into poverty during the 15-year period, 1979–94, over 8 per cent of households fell into poverty during the next 10 years, 1994–2004. Escapes out of poverty were also more frequent in the second period. However, this achievement was nearly entirely offset by the rising pace of descents. Once again, as in the Ugandan case, volatility has risen sharply; the

Table 3.3   Poverty trends over two sub-periods in Peru (per cent of households)

	Escaped poverty	Became poor
1st time period (1979–94)	12.5	4.1
2nd time period (1994–2004)	18.6	8.1

danger of a downward slide – into poverty – has almost doubled in these communities of Peru.

North Carolina

Four counties in North Carolina – Beaufort, Burke, Gates and Vance – were selected for this study (Krishna et al. 2006c). Geographically and in terms of poverty incidence, these four counties represent a diverse selection. Within each county, four communities were targeted for this study.[8] For each selected community, a list of all resident households was compiled.[9] This list of resident households was randomized, and 30 households were selected for interviews in each community. This sample of households is ethnically diverse, corresponding to the diversity that exists within these communities.

While the pattern of poverty is somewhat different in these North American communities compared to the communities studied in Uganda, Peru, Kenya and India, the trend in income volatility is very much the same as in these other four countries. Table 3.4 reports these results. We considered two separate time periods, each five years long. Escapes out of poverty were more frequent in the first time period, while descents into poverty were more frequent during the second time period. Consequently, poverty reduction was faster in the first compared to the second time period.

A total of 35 per cent of households in the sample changed their situations over the entire 10-year period, either by falling into or coming out of poverty. While 23 per cent of households escaped poverty over these ten years, another 12 per cent of households fell into poverty over the same period.

However, while the pace of escape from poverty slowed down slightly during the second time period – 13 per cent of households escaped from poverty during the second period, compared to 16 per cent during the first period – the pace of descents accelerated. A total of 12 per cent

Table 3.4 Movements in two sub-periods in 13 North Carolina communities (per cent of households)

Trajectory	First sub-period 1995–2000	Second sub-period 2000–5
Escaped poverty	16	13
Became poor	6	12
Remained poor	44	27
Remained not poor	34	48

of households fell into poverty during the second period, compared to only 6 per cent during the first five-year period.

Similar trends appear to be operating more widely in the United States. Examining longitudinal samples from PSID and other data that in scope cover the entire continental USA, McKernan and Ratcliffe found that

> poverty entries and exits have changed over the past two decades, with the mid-1990s seeing an increase in both entries into poverty and exits from poverty [. . .] The number of people entering and exiting remained relatively constant from 1975 until the early 1990s, when both [trends] jumped dramatically (2002, p. viii).

In communities of the United States, as in those of Uganda and Peru, volatility has increased substantially in recent times. In all three locations, almost twice as many people fell into poverty during a more recent time period compared to the period before.

Cycling into and out of poverty was relatively infrequent in all three locations. Very few people moved into poverty in the first sub-period only to move back out in the next sub-period. The vast majority of households that moved out of poverty stayed out during the next sub-period, and the majority who fell into poverty remained poor subsequently.[10] This abiding nature of descents into poverty makes vulnerability an even more important concern. It seems so much better to prevent descents in the first place than to provide assistance only after someone has experienced poverty for a long time.

Kenya

While the studies undertaken in Uganda, Peru and North Carolina considered a specific set of communities selected purposively in a few selected regions or counties, the study in Kenya followed a selection technique that sampled communities randomly over all regions of this country. The Stages-of-Progress methodology was implemented in each of 71 sampling clusters (villages or urban neighborhoods), located across 18 districts in Kenya, selected through a process of stratified random sampling. Unlike the other studies, therefore, this Kenya study can lay claim to being nationally representative in a statistical sense.

The results from this study are not, however, qualitatively different from those found in the other studies: volatility has increased appreciably in more recent times. This study considered two separate time periods, with the first period running from 1991 to 1998, and

Table 3.5 Household-poverty dynamics in different livelihood zones of Kenya over two time periods

Livelihood zones	Per cent of households		
	Escaped poverty	Became poor	Net change
1st time period (1991–8)			
Livelihood zone 1	9	7	2
Livelihood zone 2	7	10	−2
Livelihood zone 3	7	12	−4
Livelihood zone 4	8	15	−8
Urban zone	10	7	3
2nd time period (1998–2006)			
Livelihood zone 1	10	11	−1
Livelihood zone 2	7	14	−7
Livelihood zone 3	11	13	−2
Livelihood zone 4	3	22	−19
Urban zone	14	15	−1

the second period from 1998 to 2006. Villages were clustered together into livelihood zones representing similar agro-ecological and livelihood options.

These results (presented in Table 3.5) show that across livelihood zones an average of 8 per cent of households escaped from poverty during the first time period while an average of 9 per cent escaped from poverty during the second period. Thus, overall, a slightly larger number of people escaped poverty over the second time period. However, *many* more households fell into poverty during the second period compared to the first time period. An average of only about 10 per cent of households became poor over the first time period while an average of 14 per cent became poor over the second time period.

In every one of the five separate livelihood zones considered, vulnerability increased over the second and more recent time period. This increase was most pronounced for people living in urban areas, with the chances of falling into poverty more than doubling, from 7 per cent in the first period to 15 per cent in the second period. The greater the exposure to commercial and market forces, it seems, the higher the exposure to risk resulting in poverty. 'The key point,' as Birdsall (2006, p. 8) emphasizes, 'is that open markets ... can be associated with greater volatility, and the resulting volatility is bad for the poor.'

Rajasthan

The results cited above present a common picture of increasing volatility and greater vulnerability to descents into poverty. Results from Rajasthan support a similar conclusion. Within 71 villages that I studied twice, once in 1997 and again in 2004, the pace of descents has accelerated. Many more people fell into poverty over the seven-year period 1997–2004 (8 per cent) than during the previous seven years (4 per cent).

In each of these quite dissimilar contexts, a similar story emerges: volatility has increased, and many more households are vulnerable to becoming impoverished. Compared to five, seven or ten years ago, the pace of descents into poverty has accelerated everywhere.

Curbing volatility: a focus on health

Governments should be doing much more to curb these growing risks of impoverishment; instead, they are preoccupied with accelerating economic growth. Growth can be good for poorer people as well as richer ones, but growth is hardly what it takes to slow down the pace of descents into poverty.

Very *different* causes are associated, respectively, with escaping poverty and falling into poverty. It is the latter set of causes toward which increasing attention needs to be paid; otherwise, more and more people will keep falling into poverty, cancelling out the positive effects of efforts intended to raise people out of it.

Tracking the poverty trajectories of more than 25,000 households in diverse communities in India, Kenya, Uganda, Peru and North Carolina, I found that ill-health and high health-care expenses played a principal role in all of them in propelling households into poverty. Let me narrate a few instances before providing these statistics.

A resident of the district of Cachachi, Peru, gave the following account of his descent into poverty: 'I was much better off than my neighbours when my wife of 25 years became ill with cancer of the uterus. I was obliged to sell my animals, my cows, oxen, and donkeys, and I also went into debt in order to care for her, and later, bury her. Today, old and sick, I have to find work as a day labourer.'

In Ntungamo District, Uganda, a woman recounted her experience of descent as follows:

Earlier my welfare was good. My husband was still alive, and we had plenty of land and animals. Then my husband was sick for 10 years before he died, and all the money that we had with us was spent on medical charges. We sold some animals and land to raise money for his treatment. My children dropped out of school because we could not pay school fees. Then my husband died. I was left with a tiny piece of land. My welfare became worse. Now I cannot even get enough food to eat. I work as a casual labourer on other people's farms.

Thousands of other households narrated similar accounts of their economic downfalls. Among households that fell into poverty in 20 villages of Western Kenya, 73 per cent cited ill-health and high health-care costs as the most important reason for descent (Krishna et al. 2004). Ill-health and health-related expenses were associated with nearly 60 per cent of all descents recorded in villages in Rajasthan (Krishna 2004), 74 per cent of all descents examined in Andhra Pradesh (Krishna 2006), and 71 per cent and 67 per cent of all descents investigated, respectively, in communities in Uganda and Peru (Krishna et al. 2006a, 2006b). In Gujarat, another Indian state, where annual economic growth rates in excess of 8 per cent have been achieved regularly for two decades, as many as 88 per cent of households that fell into poverty in the 36 communities studied blamed ill-health, hard-to-reach medical facilities, and high health-care costs (Krishna et al. 2005).

In every region of the world where these trends have been examined, ill-health and health-care expenses have been found to be a primary factor associated with descents into poverty. Evidence from many other countries, including Cambodia, Ethiopia, Haiti, Sierra Leone, Senegal and Vietnam, points unambiguously to the deleterious effects of health-care costs upon households' welfare (Asfaw and von Braun 2004; Barrett et al. 2001; Deolalikar 2002; Fabricant et al. 1999; Farmer 1999; Kenjiro 2005). Some – though not all – richer countries show similar trends. For example, more than half of all personal bankruptcies occurring in the United States were related to unbearably high medical expenses (Himmelstein et al. 2005).

Studies show that catastrophic payments for health care have increased in recent years across a vast swathe of countries (Xu et al. 2003). Large numbers of families are threatened by a 'medical poverty trap', becoming impoverished on account of medical conditions and health-care costs (Whitehead et al. 2001). Increasingly, families in China are becoming impoverished as health-care services are crumbling in rural areas. Experiencing one major health incident was calculated to result in a 13 per cent reduction in long-term family income in China, with successive health incidents ensuring faster descents into abiding poverty (Gan et al. 2005). A comparison in India of households' expenses over time shows that

Table 3.6   Principal reasons for descent into poverty (per cent of descending households)

Reasons	Rajasthan, India n = 364	Gujarat, India n = 189	Western Kenya n = 172	Andhra, India n = 335	Uganda: Central & Western n = 202	Peru: Puno & Cajamarca n = 252
Poor health and health-related expenses	60	88	74	74	71	67
Marriage/dowry/ new household-related expenses	31	68		69	18	29
Funeral-related expenses	34	49	64	28	15	11
High-interest private debt	72	52		60		
Drought/irrigation failure/crop disease	18			44	19	11
Unproductive land/land exhaustion			38		8	

average expenditure on all classes of medical treatment increased many times between 1986 and 1995. Average expenditure on outpatient care went up from Rs. 76 to Rs. 176, while average expenditure on inpatient care increased even further, from Rs. 597 to Rs. 3,202 (Sen et al. 2002). Signs of danger are becoming evident within these two icons of national economic growth.

Indebtedness is quite frequently associated with large medical expenses. A very large part of debt incurred by poor families in India arises on account of large health-care expenses (Dilip and Duggal 2002). In rural Vietnam, 60 per cent of poor households were found to be in debt, and more than one-third of these households cited medical expenses as the major reason for their indebtedness (Ensor and San 1996).

It should be noted that ill-health and health-care costs are not the *only* reasons for people falling into or remaining trapped in poverty. Some other factors are also important. Table 3.6 provides these statistics. It shows the percentage of households afflicted by different reasons for descent. Usually, descents have occurred on account of more than one reason.

Social and customary expenses – on funeral feasts, as in the example cited above, or on burial ceremonies, marriages or dowries – are an important factor in descents into poverty in some regions and countries. Persistent drought and land exhaustion have accelerated descents in some regions, while crop-price fluctuations have ruined families in some other places. However, the impact of these different factors varies considerably across countries and regions.

Health is commonly a key factor in descents everywhere. Millions of people are living one illness away from poverty. Not only does ill-health reduce the earning capacity of a household's members; in the absence of affordable and easy-to-access health-care facilities, it also adds considerably to the household's burden of expenditure, thereby striking a double blow, quite often resulting in tragedy.

Reducing volatility and vulnerability will require concentrating on improving health care. Countries in which health care is provided more reliably, affordably and effectively are those where people bear the lowest level of risk to their livelihoods. Consider the countries that have the lowest poverty ratios in the world. Sweden, Norway, Denmark, the Netherlands, Germany, France, Canada, South Korea, and Japan – all provide access to high-quality health care for all.

Conclusion: saving livelihoods by saving lives

Whether livelihoods have become more precarious in recent years is a question of critical concern to policymakers, but its study is marked by a curious lack of attention and evidence-gathering. Current-day data collection methods simply do not support the gathering of evidence that can help verify or reject claims about rising volatility. Much surmising, but very little hard information, results from the ensuing data gaps. Nationally representative data are simply not available that can help examine whether the livelihoods of the poor have become even more precarious.

Yet, the available sub-national studies point consistently toward this trend. Results from decentralized, community-based examinations show that the risk of impoverishment has increased in recent years. In Uganda, Peru, Kenya, India and the United States, wherever such disaggregated inquiries have been carried out, the same results were obtained: vulnerability is consistently on the rise.

The story in these developing-country communities is very much like that which Hacker (2006) found for communities and families in the United States. The single biggest factor, he finds, causing increased risk of descent into poverty in America is related to health care. 'Every thirty seconds, someone files a bankruptcy claim that is due in part to medical costs and crises.' Major unexpected expenses, 'particularly health expenses', have driven increasing numbers of American families down the road to poverty (pp. 138, 167).

Health is also, within developing-country contexts, the largest factor affecting descents into poverty. The examples of over 25,000 households that I examined in diverse communities show that the risk of impoverishment has increased substantially. Over the past 10 years many more households have fallen into poverty compared to the previous 10 or even 15 years. And the reason for this accelerated descent into poverty is also the same: ill-health and rising health-care costs account for the vast majority of descents.

It is not clear why the importance of health-related factors has increased so much in recent times, although a number of factors appear to play a role. The spread of new illnesses, most notably HIV/AIDS, has almost certainly been important. However, the poverty-inducing effects of health-care costs have also increased because people, including poorer ones, are increasingly feeling pressured to avail themselves of more expensive interventions and remedies. More frequent visits to doctors and hospitals and the availability of ever-more sophisticated and expensive interventions have gone together with rising expectations that the best remedies should be sought when one's near and dear are sick.

An elderly villager in Rajasthan explained this trend to me as follows:

> In the old days, the aged people would fall sick and they would die. Their survivors would grieve and be unhappy, but they would pick up their lives eventually and carry on much as before. Now, the old people fall sick, and their children run up huge debts caring for them. The old people die, nevertheless, and they leave behind ruined families.

People live longer than they used to, but their livelihoods are more insecure. Sharply rising expenditures on health care are prominent among the factors responsible for this trend. The increased commercialization of medical treatment coupled with weak or absent regulation has resulted in a proliferation of fly-by-night operations, over-prescription, overcharging by private providers, and spurious or counterfeit drugs. Whitehead et al. note how

> in developing countries, pharmaceutical drugs now account for 30 to 50 per cent of total health-care expenditures, compared with less than 15 per cent in established market economies. Private drug

vendors, especially in Asia and parts of Africa, tend to cater for poor people who cannot afford to use professional services. These vendors, who are often unqualified, frequently do not follow prescribing regulations. In parts of India and China, [such unqualified] drug vendors can be found on nearly every street corner. Limited access to professional health services and aggressive marketing of drugs on an unregulated market have not only generated an unhealthy and irrational use of medicine, but also wasted scarce financial resources, especially among poor people [...] Cultural access is a special problem that encompasses lack of responsiveness [involving humiliation and] disrespect shown towards disadvantaged groups of people and widespread use of informal, so-called under-the-table, payments (2001, pp. 833–5).

Further, there is the problem of widespread absenteeism in public health-care systems. 'The commodification of medicine invariably punishes the vulnerable,' comments Farmer (2003, p. 152). As health systems are privatized with little or no regulatory discipline and no concurrent investments in risk-pooling institutions, ever-larger numbers of people have become vulnerable to the risk of falling into poverty.

I found while speaking to hundreds of households that they do the best they can to have their ailing members provided with medical attention – even if it means selling off productive assets and accumulating debt at very high interest rates. When locally available remedies are no longer effective, they take their patients to a hospital in a bigger city, quite often a considerable distance away. They wait a long time to be treated, suffer humiliation frequently at the hands of medical staff, and they pay quite large amounts in fees, an expense which often turns out to be ruinous over the longer term. But it does no good to let one's father or mother die without trying to give them the most modern medical care within one's reach.

The crushing burden of health-care costs needs to be brought under control. Countries that have succeeded in making affordable and effective health care accessible to their citizens are also the ones where vulnerability to poverty has been best kept in check.

A comparative examination of health data from 11 low- and middle-income Asian countries shows that countries where people pay a higher proportion of health expenses from their own pockets – where public-health and health-insurance schemes are not widespread or effective – are also the ones in which a higher proportion of people are at risk of falling into poverty. More than 78 million people in the 11 low/middle-income countries included in this study – nearly 3 per cent of the total population of these countries – get pushed *every year* below the very low threshold of $1 per day due to ill-health and high health-care costs. These proportions range from a low of 0.05 percent of the population in Malaysia (where out-of-pocket expenses add up to just about 40 per cent of all health-care costs) to a high of 3.7 percent of the entire population in India (where out-of-pocket expenses constitute more than 80 per cent of all health-care expenses). Across countries, a monotonously increasing relationship can be observed between the risk of falling into poverty and the share of health-care expenses borne directly by households (EQUITAP 2005). Countries such as Thailand, Indonesia and Sri Lanka, which have implemented health-insurance or health-card systems, are those where vulnerability has been best brought under control. Catastrophic payments for health care – amounting to 10 per cent or more of a households' annual expenditure – are most prevalent in Bangladesh, Vietnam, China and India, suggesting that the vast populations of these countries are disproportionately at risk. It seems shocking how commentators applauding the rapid economic strides of India and especially of China can so easily turn a blind eye to these large-scale tragedies occurring in parallel.

Examinations in OECD countries have returned a similar verdict connecting affordable health care with reduced volatility: 'More generous benefits for sickness and pensions are associated with large reductions in absolute poverty in advanced industrial countries' (Scruggs and Allan 2006, p. 901). They find that economic growth rates matter less than public benefits, especially benefits related to public health care. Vulnerability and volatility are consequently much lower in Norway, the Netherlands, Germany, Sweden, Austria, Canada and Denmark and much higher in Australia, Ireland and the United States.

Economic growth is neither a guaranteed route to health improvements nor is low growth necessarily a barrier to progress. 'The problem of catastrophic health payments will not simply go away with rising incomes; rather, the complex process of developing social institutions to effectively pool financial risk must be placed on the agenda' (Xu et al. 2003, p. 116). Richer countries have not always provided adequate and affordable health care for all citizens. The United States is a contemporary example. Other countries, poorer in comparison, have done comparatively better; Costa Rica, Cuba and Sri Lanka (during the 1970s) are three examples.

Greater wealth can certainly be helpful, but social institutions are essential. The emergence of commercialized health care in the absence of both insurance and regulation is largely responsible, I believe, for the large negative impacts of ill-health, with millions of households living only one illness away from poverty. Pooling risks through suitable insurance mechanisms is important. In addition, it is also important to have more effective regulation. Capitalism, the hidden hand of private incentives, works best when regulations are enforced that can help keep individual greed in check, directed toward the collective fulfilment of socially desirable objectives. Along with health insurance, about which a great deal of concern is rightly expressed, more attention needs to be paid to health-care regulation.

The blind rush to faster economic growth has shut our eyes to the impoverishment that has been occurring in parallel to it. Very large numbers of people are falling into poverty with a regularity that needs to be much better recognized and controlled. Instead of falling, these numbers (for descent into poverty) have tended to become greater in more recent times. The prevalent data-collection methods are not designed to measure vulnerability and – since in today's policy world 'what can be measured and manipulated statistically is not only seen as real; it comes to be seen as the only or whole reality' (Chambers 1997, p. 42) – little or no policy attention is being paid to the worrying increase in vulnerability.

Both the micro-level data examined here as well as examinations by other analysts show that, largely on account of unavailable or unaffordable health care, large and increasing numbers of people are falling into poverty. Vulnerability is on the rise. Efforts made to accelerate economic growth are of little consequence, at least for poorer people, unless vulnerability can be reduced and livelihoods rendered less volatile.

Notes

1. Vulnerability is understood here as the risk at a given point of time of a household or individual becoming impoverished. Volatility is understood as an increase in this risk over time.
2. As a result, we can make calculations, as one much-cited article does, about whether growth in the aggregate economy is good for the poor overall (Dollar and Kraay 2002). But whether growth is good enough to reduce poverty in some country – or whether something else might be better – cannot be readily examined. The data simply do not exist that can support disaggregated inquiries intended to examine the reasons why some people escape from poverty and others fall into poverty.
3. Relatively few studies examine volatility trends in developing countries, and they do so in broad, macro contexts, looking at possible effects on entire countries, but without providing any estimates of how many people fell into poverty in any given country, and without saying much about how falling into poverty might have become more or less prominent. See, for

example, Breen and Garcia-Penalosa (2005); Jansen (2004); and Whalley and Yue (2006).

4. http://psidonline.isr.umich.edu/

5. Some recently initiated studies will help bridge to some extent these important existing gaps in poverty knowledge. Initial results from these studies include, for example, Barrett et al. (2006); Baulch and Davis (2007); Davis (2007); and Quisumbing (2007).

6. In chronological order, these studies were undertaken in Rajasthan, India (Krishna 2004); Western Kenya (Krishna et al. 2004); Gujarat, India (Krishna et al. 2005); Andhra Pradesh, India (Krishna 2006); Central and Western Uganda (Krishna et al. 2006a); two regions of Peru (Krishna et al. 2006b); 13 communities of rural North Carolina, USA (Krishna et al. 2006c); once again in Rajasthan, India in 2006; and finally, a countrywide study was undertaken in Kenya in 2006–07.

7. Cycling into and out of poverty was relatively rare. Of all households that fell into poverty during the first period (5.6 per cent) only about one-third (1.9 per cent) were able to overcome poverty during the second time period. The majority of these households, two-thirds in all, remained poor at the end of the second time period, indicating that falling into poverty is not merely a temporary inconvenience. Similarly, of 13.3 per cent of households that escaped from poverty during the first time period, less than one-tenth (1.1 per cent) fell back into poverty during the second time period. Falling into or escaping from poverty was not a transient phenomenon; in most cases, those who fell into poverty stayed poor.

8. While we aimed to study four communities within each county, time and money constraints necessitated that we could only study two communities in Vance County and three communities in Gates County, making for a total of 13 communities in all.

9. A household was defined as a group of individuals – usually related, but not always so – who live under the same roof. In the other countries studied, a similar definition was employed. More stringently, however, we considered as one household all those that commonly ate together and lived in the same compound.

10. One reason for why relatively few in-and-out movements were recorded in these studies has to do with the reliance of the Stages-of-Progress methodology on asset-based indicators of poverty. Studies that use consumption-based (or income-based) measures of poverty usually record larger short-term fluctuations and more frequent oscillations around the poverty cutoff that they employ. Assets, however, are more durable than consumption, fluctuating less in relation to shorter-term variations in fortunes.

Part II
Emerging Societies

4
Globalization and Development: Learning from Debates in China[1]

James H. Mittelman

How can a developing country capture the advantages of globalization? In grappling with this question, China has played to its strengths and picked itself up by the bootstraps, though not without mounting signs of apprehension. Indeed, many observers are looking to China to find clues to what spurs development in the context of globalization. Largely overlooked in this search is the range of China's internal debates. This creative dialogue, an interrogation of globalization, could have an exhilarating impact on development studies.

China is surely a special case, but which case is not distinctive? Or free from structural conditions in the global environment? Besides, how could one understand leapfrogging in globalization and development if the largest and foremost national experience with maintaining high-speed economic growth is not taken into account?

Specifically, it is worth turning to China for three reasons: the possibility of resuming its historic pattern as world leader circa AD500–1000; the immense impact of its political economy on other regions as well as globalization itself; and the broad implications of the internal debates even for small and less powerful actors.

A developing country that astutely navigates the currents of globalization, China has sustained an annual growth rate above 9 per cent in gross domestic product (GDP) for the last two decades, the highest in the world, and has achieved improved living standards for the majority of its people. In embracing globalization, China, of course, commands unique assets, including 26 per cent of the world's population (more than the combined total of Latin America and sub-Saharan Africa) and thus a massive domestic market, a sizable domestic savings rate, large-scale foreign investment, a hard-working and inexpensive labour force, and substantial cultural resources. Whereas nearly all studies project that the

Chinese economy will surpass that of the United States as the biggest in the world in about 2020, as calculated in purchasing power parity, Chinese government sources indicate that the country's real per capita GDP is less than $1,000 (as cited in Ye Jiang 2002, p. 64). According to *The Financial Times* (London), the real income per head is 15 per cent of the US level (Wolf 2005, p. 13).[2] Yet, as will be shown in the ensuing pages, severe weaknesses and uncertainties about how to adjust to a changing world order abound.

What then are China's internal debates over globalization? Buried in this question are more specific issues:

1. Are the globalization debates in China, with its strong economic engine and authoritarian regime, entirely focused on economic globalization, as many outside observers believe?
2. Do the country's policymakers, academic intellectuals and nascent civil-society groups share outsiders' worry about China's emergence, or 'peaceful rise'?
3. Insofar as politics in China is dominated by the discursive power of the state, are globalization debates there confined to official transcripts?[3]
4. Thus, are China's internal debates about globalization really distinctive?

In addressing these questions, it is important to note that with Beijing's official portrayal of globalization as a win/win situation for building a 'harmonious society', China has its own brand of political correctness. Yet authoritarian politics is not fixed and unvarying. Although there is increasing freedom of expression in China – apparent, for example, in criticism voiced by academic intellectuals at universities – it is accompanied by stringent restrictions on written dissent. The sharp debates among China's power holders and the populace are often masked, partly by design and partly neglect or perhaps due to blinders on the outside.

Hence, the main objective in this article is to bring forth voices in the debates prompted by the embedding of globalization in China. Insofar as voicelessness hinders comprehending globalization and jump-starting development, attention should be given to unofficial transcripts that extend beyond state narratives.

This approach is designed to help decentre globalization research, most often produced in the West and then disseminated in the form of travelling paradigms, a major aspect of the reproduction of established ways of thinking. To ferret out the subtleties in evolving processes, emphasis is placed on the interplay between the manifest and latent content of the transcripts, and China's globalizing text and its subtext, as well as between the political elite, dominated by authoritarian conservatives, and a burgeoning political culture.

Another goal here is to stimulate critical responses from other analysts engaged in these debates, thus advancing inquiry into the variability and intricacies of globalization. My aim is to encourage specialists to articulate the specific debates on globalization formulated in multiple contexts. Researchers could then compare how diverse nodes and their prevailing discourses are similar to and differ from those in China.

Toward these ends, I will draw on my five visits to China (1986, 1988, 2000, 2002 and 2005), one as a guest of the government of the People's Republic invited to observe and discuss market reforms; the others involving teaching at three universities (Nankai, Fudan and China Foreign Affairs), lecturing in various venues, and carrying out research. I will summarize – for obvious reasons, without attribution – interviews and discussions (either with assistance by interpreters or in English) with hundreds of people in China: government officials, representatives of international organizations, students and colleagues at universities and research institutes, managers and workers in industry, and internal migrants. I will offer my own understanding of these discourses, and clearly do not have license to represent others'.

It will be shown how debates are framed in light of specific processes within the ambit of what I call the 'globalization syndrome' – that is, in regard to the syndrome's constitutive elements and rarely the whole structure, which, after all, is a large, abstract force.[4] The debates may thus be directly or indirectly tethered to globalization: for example, although not the ostensible purpose, reshuffling local–national relations definitely is a strategy for reaping globalization's benefits. Furthermore, aspects of China's globalization debates overlap with one another but are not identical. They are dynamic and their fluidity marks an indigenous discourse. Yet endogenous features are interlaced with exogenous ones – there can be no stark separation between the internal and external components.

The advent of these framing arrangements in China takes place against a backdrop of antidevelopment: the multipronged attack on the basis of the whole developmentalist paradigm. In this context, the debates may be divided into three domains: material power, institutions and ideology. In the first, the frame concerns the interactions between inclusiveness and exclusiveness; the second, the nexus of status and identity; and the third, globalism and nationalisms. After taking into account calls for a retreat from developmentalism, let us examine a turn toward another way of conceptualizing the issues, in this case grounded in China. Finally,

I want to reflect on the extent to which the framing discourses are interrelated and on the openings that the Chinese narrative may provide.

Antidevelopment

Development theory has fallen on hard times. This field arose at a particular historical moment, the onset of the Cold War, and soon became a growth industry. A motivating force was to know the terrain of the presumed enemy, including in newly decolonized countries. Amply funded, the outpourings of development studies from think-tanks, universities, and governmental and intergovernmental agencies have been massive. To fast-forward the story, the end of the Cold War meant that development theory lost its original *raison d'être*. The halcyon times came to a halt by 1989. Historically constituted, development theory reached a dead end.

Many policymakers and policy intellectuals have found successive theories – modernization, dependency, Marxism, and so on – too abstract and too formulaic to be useful. This mood coincides with the postmodern deconstruction of grand theory, pilloried for preaching about universalisms, including narratives about the structured process of development. So, too, postcolonial sensibilities draw attention to differences and bolster reservations about building models of development.

Numerous intellectuals specializing in development have become atheoretical, preferring to just get on with it. They either migrate to other fields of study or seek to disaggregate development, focusing on single problems such as privatization, or simply 'projects' like housing or water in a particular locale. This move entails prescribing piecemeal solutions and conceptualizing the structural challenges of development as matters of pure management.

Closely related is a tendency toward the kind of institutionalist analysis that seeks to fix problems while paying scant attention to the foundations that underpin them. In some cases, the problematic is shifting toward security and the concrete institutions that would underwrite it, because development requires peace and a measure of stability (Duffield 2001).

Feeding into this current is disillusionment with stagnation and corruption in the Third World, much of it tied to interests in the West and its perspectives on development. Mindful of this tendency, some cultural theorists regard development as an ideology of domination and call for more critical reflection on the production of knowledge (Escobar 1995, p. 216 and passim; Eagleton 2004). And as the late Claude Ake, one of

Africa's leading political economists, put it: '[Development] ... was the ideology by which the political elite hoped to survive and reproduce its domination' (Ake 1996, p. 7). He traced this ideology to 'the former colonial masters', who also promoted development and invented concepts such as partners in development (p. 8).

In addition, development theory has been faulted, if not jettisoned, because it sidelined patriarchy. Subsequent efforts have sought to unveil the gendered division of labour, including its global dimensions: a key stratification system that places women in subordinate positions. Moreover, there is a focus on the changing role of the national vector in relation to globalizing processes. In one conceptualization, it is argued that the 'globalization project' is superseding national development and that individual states are helping to install a global enterprise in their locale (McMichael 2004). From this standpoint, notwithstanding the enormous contextual differences in the magnitude of state power, the role of the state in the developing world is becoming the administrative coordination of flows as they penetrate national nodes in the global economy. The state is said to exercise reduced control, leading to a growing sense of powerlessness. As in Europe with the European Union, slices of sovereignty are being stripped away or surrendered: surrendered perhaps as a defensive measure to preserve the state.

However, developmentalism – the ideology of development – survives this structural shift. It was part of the Washington Consensus, a global template of neoliberal ideas and a policy framework centred on deregulation, liberalization and privatization, that organizing institutions such as the World Bank and the International Monetary Fund (IMF) sought to universalize. Their one-size-fits-all modus operandi ran aground on the shoals of 'shock therapy' – market reforms in the former Soviet Union and parts of Eastern Europe, spectacularly in the 1997–8 Asian economic crisis and the 2001 Argentine debacle.

After the discrediting of the Washington Consensus, there followed several efforts to forge a new consensus, including, intriguingly, the Beijing Consensus. Delineated by Joshua Cooper Ramo, a former journalist and now a lecturer at Tsinghua University, this consensus is thought to consist of: an emphasis on 'bleeding-edge' innovation (such as fibre optics) to start change more quickly than the emergence of problems caused by change; avoidance of large-scale contradictions by stressing contemporary quality-of-life concerns and chaos management; and new security priorities to avert the ill-effects of hegemonic power (Ramo 2004, pp. 11–12).

Careful observers may disagree about what constitutes a Beijing model and the degree to which groups outside China are adopting it. Implicit in Ramo's construction is a national framework for development. In seeking to conceptualize it, Ramo fails to offer insight into the processes and mechanisms of consensus-building. He does not delve into the fragmentation of discourses nor note competing policy agendas in China and the extent of infighting. Moreover, in an authoritarian political context, the level of consent may not be as high as Ramo posits. In the Gramscian understanding, consensus itself can reduce political space, for it is the major component of hegemony, with coercion always being part of the mix. From this perspective, consensus-making could be a means of exclusion. In this sense, the goals of development may be better served by rejecting a *pensée unique*, a singular way of thinking that its champions trumpet as a consensus; by going beyond the work of commissions on 'North–South' development and decommissioning development, and by invoking a series of debates internal to local encounters with the global. If antidevelopment leads in this direction, it becomes developmentally interesting. The Chinese case is a venue for exploring this proposition.

Inclusiveness and exclusiveness

Since the onset of market reforms in China in 1978, there have been many debates about how to enhance material power and the route to it – What is a 'socialist market economy'? How far to extend the market and reduce the role of the state in the economy? And how fast to hasten this process? The importance of 'patience', especially after a long period of feudalism and then a planned economy, is stressed. Compared to the 'shock therapy' in Russia and elsewhere, the opening to the market in China has been a gradual one. This strategy is related to the conundrum of how to engage with global competition. And with the advantages mentioned above – a labour-intensive economy, cheap wages and an enormous home market – what are the best ways to gain a competitive edge?

In China, there is self-confidence in the ability to direct global flows as they meet local conditions. This assurance is linked to ample investment in infrastructure, provision of basic education for all citizens, and extensive industrialization. Just as countries in Europe and Canada have sought to restrict the amount of foreign content in television and films, so Chinese authorities have regulated the quantity of imported television programmes, which convey global flows. Similarly, the state protects indigenous culture by subsidizing the Beijing opera, crafts and artefacts for festivals.

In state–market relations, democratization is presented as a goal. Whereas the Chinese Communist Party (CCP) seeks to build legitimacy through its notion of 'socialist democracy', the Beijing leadership does not define democracy in terms of constitutional protections for liberty, competitive elections with a formal opposition or other institutional arrangements such as a separation of powers. Rather, democracy in China today is regarded as a way to resolve problems and to make adjustments in politics. Not easily amenable to an abstract theoretical model, the content of democracy in China is a negotiation that remains ongoing while the regime strives for legitimacy and other actors seek political space (Sun 2005, pp. 63–4). As many of my interviewees attest, now there is slightly more freedom in daily life than a decade ago or, as Robert A. Scalapino puts it, a move from the 'hard authoritarianism characteristic of the Mao era to what might be described as authoritarian pluralism' (2005, p. 50; for a competing interpretation, see Pei 2006). Within limits, criticism is expressed. Political disagreements surface, though, without the right to organize alternative power structures.

In foreign policy, democracy serves as a contentious issue, especially in regard to Taiwan and thus with the United States. Many Chinese strategic thinkers contend that globalization can be used to democratize US hegemony by restraining its unilateralist policies and making Washington more reliant on sources of legitimate authority. Thus, if the interests of more countries, including a strong China, are more tightly interlocked, globalization may serve as an affirmative force in democratizing the US-dominated world order. Pursuing this logic, Chinese think-tanks and other policy analysts argue that globalization heightens competition in a positive-sum game: different actors may win, though not equally, through multipolarization (Deng and Moore 2004).

A key factor is migration from the United States, traditionally a receiving country, which sends mobile Chinese who bring investment, technology, corporate culture and business acumen that differ from the skills of local tycoons, as they are known in China. There are other streams of migrants, such as North Koreans, who are less welcome; in some cases, they have been expelled or not granted entry. Moreover, internal migration is a marked pattern. China has a vast floating population numbering 130 million people, and the state is considering moving 400 million more, roughly equivalent to the size of Europe's population.

In comparison to the EU, whose Schengen zone provides for the free movement of people and security cooperation among its members, the construction of a regional order in Asia remains more problematic. Regionalism presents risks, as in the 1997–8 Asian financial crisis, as well as opportunities. For China, the questions are – Which Asia? The Association of Southeast Asian Nations (ASEAN) plus China, Japan and Korea? Or East Asia? Or Pacific Asia? Would the latter extend Cold War measures, with a heavy US military presence? Surely the Cold War lingers in East Asia, and the Realist lens of a state-centred world is used to view international relations, albeit represented as 'Realism with Chinese characteristics'.

From this perspective, China seeks to improve coordination in Asia and become even more of an epicentre of globalization. Its competitive landscape, booming markets and world-class scientists follow the prosperity achieved by Japan, Hong Kong, South Korea and Taiwan after the Second World War. While China's transformation, with its vast scale, is undoubtedly shaping globalization, the dynamics of intra-Asian relations are also striking. For example, in developing Asia, India, the world's largest democracy, maintains an advantage in tradable services. Moreover, the complexity of manufacturing supply chains upsets wobbly formulations in policy circles in the West about trade and currency imbalances with China.

Whereas Beijing maintains a $200 billion trade surplus with the United States, it has a $137 billion trade deficit with the rest of Asia. Yet, although up-to-date, reliable data on the movement of goods and money to and from China are lacking, it is reported that most profit from manufacturing supply chains in China goes to American and other overseas firms (Barboza 2006).

While Asia's macroregionalism and impact on globalization are manifest, many underlying issues about coordination within the region persist – To what degree should the activities of the Shanghai Cooperation Organization countries in Central Asia be enhanced? What is the concrete form that subregionalism, in dialogue with ASEAN 10, should take? A primarily economic, military-strategic or sociocultural constellation? In addition, microregionalism occurs within China and is expanding, as in plans to partner Beijing and the industrial city of Tianjin in order to increase their competitiveness. Meanwhile, cities such as Shanghai, a financial power and trading centre, are linking into the global economy and becoming major players in their own right.

To discuss the region's future, China's Boao Forum for Asia (BFA) is an alternative to the annual World Economic Forum usually held in Davos, Switzerland. Adopted in 2001, the Declaration of the BFA provides for a yearly conference, a platform for an exchange of views among more than 1,000 senior government officials, business leaders and researchers.

But with the enormous diversity and many conflicts in East Asia, how can strategic trust be established? Notwithstanding the rhetoric about Asian values, what norms are held in common? And are civil-society organizations, increasingly emergent in China, included in regionalism? This is part of the identity question that in China is tied to its status in the world.

Status and identity

China's attempt to attain world status befitting a major power involves a strategy of multilateralism and building military might. Yet these issues ignite trying debates in China. Following the Mao period, China inserted itself in the global arena by joining the United Nations as a permanent member of the Security Council. Along with China's accession to the World Trade Organization (WTO) in 2001, and its membership of the IMF and World Bank, Beijing has increasingly participated in UN peace-keeping activities, its role raising questions about the People's Republic's own dedication to maintaining peace in its neighbourhood.[5] International crises, especially the 1999 US bombing of the Chinese Embassy in Belgrade and a 2001 crash involving an American spy plane and Chinese aircraft near Hainan Island, have complicated this issue (Pang 2005). But, on balance, the Chinese authorities find international organizations to be useful instruments for enhancing status and employing the symbolic power of serving as a leader in the developing world.

Emblematic of improving its image in the global arena, the watchword in China is 'responsible country'. The principle of responsibility means not only meeting obligations but also safeguarding sovereignty. The options include choosing among numerous security forums and multiple meanings: national security, regional security, human security, comprehensive security and global security, some of which take into account nontraditional threats such as environmental damage. Beginning in 1996, the Chinese authorities and state-controlled media have favoured what they call the 'new security concept': a positive attitude extending beyond the historical weight of being victimized by outside powers towards 'pragmatism' in international affairs (Xia 2004; Jin 2005).

In practice, pragmatism signifies an increase in military expenditure and also a means of establishing space for endogenous development. Military spending is deemed necessary in that some influential Western liberals and Realists, such as John J. Mearsheimer (2005), contend that China's rise requires pursuing national interests that will inevitably collide with those of the United States and thus constitute a threat.[6] From their perspective, Chinese policymakers and scholars believe that it is imperative to achieve a rising status suitable for a global power, but that it need not threaten others (Yu 2004).

The trope 'peaceful rise', widely employed by China's leaders until early 2004, is no longer in vogue. An undercurrent in China is that, without wanting to appear hostile, surely political authorities are not willing to relinquish a sovereign state's prerogative to use force, as in hotspots like Taiwan or in territorial disputes with neighbours. Whereas the debates in China do not altogether discard the word 'peaceful', the other component of the phrase 'peaceful rise', fails to resonate in Mandarin, for 'rise' translates as 'surge', which would be an abrupt phenomenon. In a nation that values stability and order, the implication of a rupture is to be avoided. Discursively, 'peaceful development' is a better fit, and riding the wave of globalization is deemed the way to achieve it.

Just as development may take myriad forms, so it spawns multiple shades of identity, among others, Sinocentric and pan-Asian images. This part of the self/other distinction operates in the global arena and reflects a long perspective. The historical memory of 'the Century of National Humiliation' prior to the accession to power of Mao Zedong in 1949 still persists. This experience is seen as a period of wars, exploitation by foreign powers and decadence. Thus, trust in external actors within East Asia is generally low. Even when focused on the here-and-now of globalization, this discourse about China's history is unavoidable.

Another shade of identity relates to domestic pluralism. In China, the question of diversity partially relates to national minority populations, including large Muslim communities. Many of these ethnic groups live mostly in remote regions, border areas that lag far behind the country's average standards, as measured in income, education, health care, water supply and transport. Whereas concrete policies are being adopted to develop the frontier areas, the official discourse continues to stress 'harmonious relations' within the compass of one society.

A third shade concerns the definition of Chineseness. In depicting China's transnational relations with its diasporic community, Beijing officials no longer favour the phrase 'Greater China', because it may be perceived as intimidating (for example, to Southeast Asians). No idiom has replaced it in the political lexicon. Rather, there are mixed intersubjective meanings, variously invoking Confucianism and the accumulation of wealth. For dealing beyond China's territorial boundaries, a narrative of flexibility lubricates the negotiation of practices.

In other words, there are diverse ways to be Chinese (Goodman and Segal 1994; Ong 1999; Ong and Nonini 1997; Callahan 2002; Ames 2004).

How then does a 'harmonious society' attempt to harmonize the quest for status and varied identities? In the blend, realizing 'prosperity' is accorded priority, if not primarily in word, then in deed. Yet this move requires stability, which, in turn, entails balancing the state. The decentralization of political authority is a key policy initiative, one that shifts dimensions of power from national to local government (Wang 2004, pp. 534–5). Nonetheless, periodic swings from balancing to rebalancing can be safely anticipated. This restructuring of the state also involves reform in the ministries (pp. 536–7). Matters of commerce, tax and the legal code, among others, are subject to slow-paced institutional adjustments in the mode of regulation.

Many problems appear in, or are even heightened by, reforms partly aimed at winning gains from globalization. Foremost perhaps are rapidly increasing inequalities in income, among regions, and between the countryside and the city. In 2005, a Chinese government press agency reported that the top fifth of the population received 50 per cent of national income while the bottom fifth earned less than 5 per cent (cited in *Le Monde* 2005). Although figures differ slightly, most up-to-date sources calculate the ratio of average urban income to average rural income in China as more than three to one.

The country's growing number of millionaires and billionaires, especially in Guangdong province, an economic powerhouse in southern China, coexist with impoverished workers and a multitude of unemployed citizens; the ranks of the latter are swollen by layoffs in state-owned and collective enterprises, mainly in large industries, many of them in the northeastern rust belt and poor inland areas. More frequently, these public enterprises are declared financially defunct. Some of the bankruptcies are attributed to unsound banking practices, including massive bad debts and new sources of vast corruption. The pursuit of prosperity is accompanied by shortages in housing, sewage and transportation. The challenges of meeting escalating energy needs (up 65 per cent between 2002 and 2004, making China the second biggest oil market in the world) and coping with rampant pollution, hazardous waste and other forms of environmental degradation strain state capacity. Safety nets are being established, but are big projects in the west and other poor areas of the country the answer to the needs at the grassroots?

These and other questions are debated by China's 'New Left', as it is called. The 'New Left' is a heterogeneous group of disgruntled intellectuals and other, often young, citizens. Edited by Wang Hui, a professor of literature, the journal *Du Shu* offers a forum for criticism of the calibre of governance and the impact of policies that favour an export-oriented economy at the expense of the wellbeing of several sectors of the population, especially subaltern groups in the countryside. Certain articles in *Du Shu* focus on topics such as freedom of expression and damage to the environment (Pocha 2005). Some of the dissent from the 'New Left' endorses select elements of Maoism, aspects of its criticism resonate with the concerns of the global social justice movement, while other restive sentiments about quality-of-life issues are in fact supported by members of President Hu Jintao's government.

Since becoming president in 2003, Hu, and the premier, Wen Jiabao, have sought to calm critics by introducing the policy of 'five balances': the need to reach equilibrium between 'domestic and international, the inland and the coast, the rural and urban, society and the economy, and nature and man' (*Financial Times* 2005). For each balance, Chinese officials at all levels are supposed to give priority to the first rather than the second factor. This discourse is crystallized in the motto 'green GNP', shorthand for the desiderata delineated by China's leaders.

At the same time, the state seeks to restrain online dissent by relying on filters, firewalls and other security tools. Some of them are sold to China by US companies such as Cisco Systems, Microsoft, Yahoo and Google, which have signed pledges to respect local censorship laws. Nevertheless, considerable discontent appears on the Internet. Understanding globalization as a double-edged sword, sundry voices decry the excesses of market expansion. They also debate the impact of the WTO, focusing attention on its deleterious effects. Frequent talk about workers' rights is part of this trend. Furthermore, artists are pushing social mores. Some internal migrants, too, are dissatisfied, refusing to take the worst jobs in factories. Among peasants and villagers, riots and protests each year, involving tens of thousands of people, are vivid expressions of frustration with the Chinese 'miracle'.

Another social force building political space is the Falun Gong, introduced to the public in 1992. This spiritual practice purports to improve mind and body, but causes the political authorities a great deal of worry. Subject to crackdowns by the government since 1999, many of its adherents have their roots in rural areas and are poor. Some are women who have lost jobs in state agencies and are vulnerable to the effects of globalization. For the power holders in Beijing, the Falun Gong represents and is perceived as a political challenge. In a country with a historical tradition of redressing grievances, a government increasingly prone to prizing order and stability is sensitive to the activities of a movement constituted outside the realm of state politics.

To a certain degree, a discourse resistant to market-led and state-induced globalization is emerging in the expanding space carved out by China's nongovernmental organizations (NGOs). These may be best understood as both a response to and a component of the power of globalizing forces, refracted and shaped by the state. This contradiction manifests itself in the efforts of NGOs to mitigate the jagged impact of the deepening of the market – say, by tackling widespread environmental damage – and in their compliance with the state or even extension of state policies.

China's NGOs have called for changes in the regulation of their activities. The current rules stipulate that under the dual-management system they must register with the civil rights department and a relevant industry watchdog. In other words, these organizations must be officially endorsed in order to receive tax exemption, sponsorship from domestic enterprises, and preferential treatment in governmental purchasing policy. Another requirement, one that may be relaxed, but which is particularly stringent for regional NGOs, is meeting a threshold of activity funds, currently 30,000 yuan, or $3,614, before organizations are permitted to register (Zong 2005, p. 4).

Empirical research, for example at the Tsinghua University NGO Research Centre, documents the expanding role of NGOs in China. The Ministry of Civil Affairs puts the number of officially registered NGOs at 283,000, but scholars such as Wang Ming, director of the Tsinghua NGO centre, report approximately three million. There are also township or community-based unregistered NGOs, which are required to submit documents (Zong 2005, p. 4). Another category is foreign NGOs, numbering perhaps 3,000 to 6,000, according to Wang Ming, who says: 'The number of foreign NGOs is small, but they are financially powerful and have impressive activity capacity and thus wield huge influence in society' (quoted in Zong 2005, p. 4). Although NGOs such as Greenpeace are not officially registered, the state clearly acquiesces in their presence. However, while they are supposed to be subject to the legal requirements of the dual-management system, the legislation – an aspect of how the state accommodates globalizing activities – is in flux.

Globalism and nationalisms

If globalism, the dominant ideology of globalization, provides the normative architecture for the expansion of the market (Steger 2002), in China it also embraces cosmopolitan norms that are built on the foundations of a more than 5,000-year-old civilization. Indeed, the cosmopolitan dimensions of globalism easily come into play in daily life. Examples are legion: an outpouring of contributions for tsunami relief signifies a display of empathy with humankind beyond China's territorial borders. Also, the growing number of Chinese tourists travelling overseas bring back images of alternative ways of life, including varied intersubjective frameworks. Many Chinese students enrol in universities abroad, and an increasing number of foreign students and teachers come to China. Political leaders and business people in China send their children for schooling in other countries. And, nowadays, marriages to non-Chinese are common and without the stigma they used to have. With greater frequency, diasporic Chinese are returning to the mainland to take advantage of the economic opportunities there and injecting new norms into the local mindset. No doubt, borders are blurred; Great-Walling, latticed.

Yet there is a contradictory phenomenon. Accompanying the mounting globalism is the ascendance of nationalisms. This tension is manifest in Shanghai, China's most globalized city. There, more than anywhere else in the country, the 2005 demonstrations against Japan took a violent form. Triggering the explosion of nationalism in Shanghai was the downplaying by Japanese newspapers of the acts committed by Class A war criminals found guilty at the postwar Tokyo trials; Prime Minister Junichiro Koizumi's annual visits to Yasukuni Shrine, where these soldiers are buried; and the failure of Japanese textbooks to deal in a forthright manner with the history of militarism in Asia. Consequently, in the display of anti-Japanese hostility, Chinese nationalism and globalism encountered one another.

What kinds of nationalism? What is its content? One form is linked to pride in the country's real recent achievements: more prosperity, better housing and advances in technology. It was apparent in the fervour of sports teams fuelled by preparation for the 2008 Olympics in Beijing.[7] This type of nationalism can be animated by incidents with Taiwan and other hotspots offshore (Zhao 2005). Disputes with the United States over trade and protectionism, and revaluing currency add to the nationalist zeal. State sovereignty and self-determination are components of the official discourse. Mostly top-down before the mid-1990s, this nationalism is dominated by the CCP and feeds off patriotism (Chen 2005).

More bottom-up beginning in the early 1990s, popular nationalism has a different character (Chen 2005). According to Chen, popular nationalism consists of different strands: traditional or culturalist notions emphasizing Confucian philosophy; neoauthoritarianism repackaged as neoconservatism with an emphasis on rejuvenating the strong state and patriarchal power; and the call for political will strong enough to say no to the United States and Japan in the country's foreign relations, reflected in survey data and bestselling literature in China that expresses criticism of the state (Ong 1999, pp. 196–201; Chen 2005). More than ten years on in this debate, is another form or forms of nationalism evolving? A robust construction of the global nation?[8]

Conclusion

The constructs examined above convey multiple, dynamic and chaotic meanings. But given the complex dynamics of globalization, the arduous transition on which China has embarked, and the sheer scale of this shift, it would be foolhardy to expect coherence. In delineating patterns, however inchoate, the four specific questions posed at the outset of this article may serve as guideposts. Let us now revisit these themes and consider the implications.

1. The globalization debates in China are no longer single-mindedly concentrated on economic issues, and have shifted since the 1978 advent of market reforms. Now, they take on a decidedly political hue. Encapsulating politics, society and culture, the framing discourses incorporate realpolitik; to be sure, some of them are centred on the state, which can play a key role in garnering the benefits of globalization. As indicated, they coexist with other discourses. Above all, the leaders, many of whom were trained in engineering and other technical fields, regard themselves as pragmatists.

2. The redefinition of political life in China is shot through with technological innovations and more mobile spaces, such as the Internet. Subject to contestation, new state–market–society relations are evolving and run side by side with China's involvement in the globalization syndrome. The linkages between the domestic complex and the global political economy have precipitated perplexing questions. In China, the discourse about the country's 'peaceful rise' is mainly framed in terms of development paradigms, ensconced as they are in an amalgam of internal and external relations.

3. Globalization debates in China are definitely not confined to official transcripts. In the face of mounting prosperity, matters pertaining to the

ethical framework of development are surfacing. Interventions critical of policies such as bans on begging in public places in certain cities are prompting further debates on provisions for the losers in globalization. Undoubtedly, resistance to the incursion of neoliberal globalization, pushed, for example, by the WTO and private corporations, has become apparent. Chinese police records document a seven-fold increase in incidents of unrest, including mob violence, in the last ten years (reported in Bardhan 2005). Helping China's growing rights movement is an informal network of journalists, scholars and lawyers; they gather information, write articles, file court cases and provide expertise. Yet, given semi-authoritarian politics, some of the resistance must be read as subtext. Much of it is covert, though overt displays take such forms as workers' unrest over conditions in factories and peasants' discontent with inadequate social policy and with failings in meeting the needs of the most vulnerable citizens in an increasingly prosperous society.

4. In China, the bundling of globalization debates includes some elements that derive from without, while others spring from a local knowledge system. An 'indigenous' epistemology concerns how problems are formulated, the methods for resolving them, and the ways to reconcile differences. Over the long term, a knowledge structure absorbs and develops part of its 'common sense' from outside national borders through inter-civilizational contact, including conquest, long-distance trade and migratory flows. For China today, as elsewhere, pushing this thinking forward relates to control over globalization processes, in particular to a professed self-confidence in the ability to steer them. Of course, it remains to be seen whose priorities will prevail. For instance, although China has not experienced structural adjustment under the guiding hand of the Bretton Woods institutions, Beijing is the World Bank's biggest client in terms of outstanding loans; and in the post-2000 period, all of them have been at commercial, not concessionary, rates. Notwithstanding China's sizable foreign exchange reserves, the World Bank estimates that the country is home to about 18 per cent of the world's poor. Today, the World Bank's large-scale involvement in China's educational projects, presented as a poster child of the Washington-based agency, provides a means for not only basic skills but also the dissemination of universalizing ideas. Meanwhile, the Bank offers largesse to Chinese consultants; and some of these *nouveaux riches* are moving into gated, upscale communities. Even among the winners, however, concern lurks about the uneven rewards of globalization.

More often, however, the explanations of the causes of vulnerability are directed at outside forces. In this vein, the 1997–8 Asian financial crisis dramatically demonstrated the risks of globalization, even if China was not one of the most severely affected countries in the region. So, too, standardization policies, required in international accountancy procedures and for joint ventures in China's high-tech centres, show that the benefits of globalization require a high level of integration into the world order.

In China's official transcripts, the antidote is represented as a stable Confucian order. Despite this move to essentialize culture, a flexible value system is in fact emerging. Folklore, aesthetics and material power are combined. Shared meanings must be negotiated. Like Beijing opera and traditional medicine, China's encounter with globalization has its own speed and rhythm, markedly different from the crescendo and swiftness characteristic of Western forms. In China, the discourses offer searching reflections on a way to balance globalizing processes, one that calls for a gradual, sequenced and directed strategy. Today, participants involved in this debate pose the political question of who should be entrusted, or empowered, to look after the public good. When politics increasingly crosses the line between the public and personal, as well as the national and global, realms, the telling question becomes – How is this trust being reimagined?

In sum, it is useful to tell the story of China precisely because we cannot afford to keep repeating the old tales of globalization and development. The debates underway there can contribute importantly to remaking these narratives.

China, I want to say emphatically, is not a model to be copied. But it is a compelling case of a home-grown strategy for transformation. It is a case in which hope and self-confidence have been expressed in the developing world. Without structural adjustment, it presents a case of a large measure of self-determination within the globalization syndrome. It is a case in which indigenous cultural resources have been mobilized while values worth localizing have been derived from other systems.

Outside China, these issues are ripe for debate and may give rise to different answers. The point is that there is no reason for other countries and regions to remain engrossed in bleak discourses about their unremitting 'crisis'.

The operative challenges become: how to reframe issues; how to imagine alter-globalization in the encounter with development and achieve a measure of autonomy; how to tap a cultural endowment, generating not merely resources and inventions but fostering resourcefulness and inventiveness. In other words, how to write a fresh script for the future while in the grip of neoliberal globalization. The issues to wrestle with are how far these debates can be taken, and how different communities can find their own alternatives. One lesson is clear: not to learn from the debates over globalization, the foray into antidevelopment and a newly informed quest for the self-realization of collective potential would be a great error.

Notes

1. This article is a revised version of the Annual Globalization Lecture sponsored by the Economic and Social Research Foundation, Dar es Salaam, Tanzania, 11 October 2005. Special thanks to Josapahat Kweka for organizing this event. For stellar research assistance, I am indebted to Patrick Besha and Carl Anders Härdig; for helpful suggestions, Jeremy Paltiel; and for comments on earlier drafts of this paper, Chen Zhimin, Fantu Cheru, Barry Gills, Linda Yarr, Wang Yong, Wang Zhengyi, Samuel Wangwe and Zhao Quansheng, though they are not implicated in the final product, for which I alone am responsible.

2. Computed in purchasing power parity, the US GDP per capita of $37,800 in 2004 was second worldwide to Luxembourg's, whereas China's at $5,000 ranked 122nd. See Central Intelligence Agency (2004), available at: http://worldfactsandfigures.com/gdp_country_asc.php (accessed 2 June 2005).

3. I am adapting the distinction between 'public' and 'hidden transcripts' introduced by James C. Scott (1990). Public transcripts refer to verbal and nonverbal acts by the dominant party or, 'to put it crudely, the *self*-portrait of dominant elites as they would have themselves seen' (Scott 1990, p. 18; emphasis in the original). For Scott, they are the public record of superior–subordinate relations, whereas hidden transcripts are what subordinate parties say and do beyond the realm of the superordinate group.

4. Elsewhere (Mittelman 2000, 2004), I have argued that globalization is not a single, unified activity, but a *syndrome* of processes and activities: a historical transformation in the interactions among market forces, political authority and the lifeways embodied in society and culture.

5. The domestic debates over the WTO in China are explored by Wang Yong (2000).

6. Military developments in China and its security policy are perceived as a major threat in Washington, as is evident in US Defense Secretary Donald H. Rumsfeld's sharp criticism of Beijing: 'China's defense expenditures are much higher than Chinese officials have publicly admitted. It is estimated that China's is the third-largest military budget in the world, and now the largest in Asia' (as quoted in Shanker 2005, pp. 1 and 7). Recent data compiled by the Stockholm International Peace Research Institute (SIPRI, 2004, appendix 10A) show that in 2003, US military spending, calculated at market exchange rates, came to roughly as much as the total for the rest of the world, while China's expenditure was about 4 per cent of world expenditure. The United States spends

approximately $1,500 per citizen; China, less than $100 (SIPRI 2004, appendix 10A). China's increases in its defence budget since 2003 could also be compared to the spike in the US's, or relative to the growth of its GDP and then measured as a percentage against India's and those of other burgeoning economies. Whereas the Pentagon warns that China's defence spending is now mounting rapidly and may exceed Beijing's official figure, it is not clear why China would engage in an arms race with the United States and deflect funds from development rather than attack the US economy by withdrawing its massive holdings in the bond market, thought by many American economists to be propping up the dollar. Similarly, Washington would seem to have little incentive for a shooting war with Beijing. The United States is not only militarily engaged elsewhere but also amassing huge budget and trade deficits, thus making China's goodwill an increasingly important factor.

7. With construction of exercise centres and other facilities as well as the demand for equipment, production in China's sports industry is already growing by 50 billion yuan, or $6.04 billion per year, and the annual spending on average by Beijing residents for physical exercise is now 888 yuan ($107) (*China Daily* 2005, p. 4).

8. Fusing these components, Thomas G. Moore (2000, pp. 123–6) posits the emergence of 'global nationalism' in China.

5
Internal Migration in Mainland China: Regional and World-Systemic Aspects

Ganesh K. Trichur

Introduction

I argue in this paper that the phenomenal internal migration in the People's Republic of China (PRC) is closely related to the equally phenomenal emergence of China as a leading agency in the economic expansion and regional integration of East Asia. From 1978, when China launched its economic reforms and opened up to the outside world (*gaige kaifang*), to the onset of the Asian financial crisis in 1997, its socialist market economy sustained average growth rates of over 9 per cent per annum (Ping and Pieke 2003, p. 2). The region's financial crises had relatively few harmful effects on China which maintained a GDP growth rate of 8 per cent in 2000 and an estimated 7 per cent growth rate in 2001 (So 2003, p. 4): 'the sharp setbacks experienced by the other economies in the region and the relatively limited impact of the crisis on China provided the country with an unexpected opportunity to exert leadership in Asia' (Naughton 1999, p. 209).

The economic reforms of 1978 also contributed to 'the world's largest ever peacetime flow of migration' (Tunon 2006, p. 5) after almost three decades of stringent restrictions that prevented farmers from leaving the land. If the unrelenting 'separation of people from the land is etched into the making of the modern world,' as McMichael (2008, p. 205) observes, the restless tide of rural Chinese migrants leaving the farmlands is endlessly reshaping Chinese modernity. The floating population[1] that migrated from the countryside grew from two million in the mid-1980s to 70 million in the mid-1990s to 120 million in 2002 (Ping and Pieke 2003, p. 6–7), to as many as 150 million in 2006 (Tunon 2006, p. 5). According to the latest Chinese census in 2000, some 20 million Chinese farmers leave the land annually. Although it is not clear 'exactly how many Chinese have exchanged their land for one of China's 670 cities', the migrants 'arrive by the thousands at the train stations in the big cities to find their way as construction workers, factory workers, cooks, waiters and waitresses, hairdressers, au pairs, or prostitutes in the countless construction sites, factories, restaurants, beauty parlors, city families, and brothels' (van Luyn 2008, pp. xiv, 2). These tidal waves of migrant farmers (*mingong chao*) correlate with the rapidly rising rate of urbanization: from 17.6 per cent in 1977 to 40.5 per cent in 2003 (Ping and Shaohua 2005, p. 68). If the absolute size of *internal* migration in the PRC compares only with the magnitude of *international* migration of 191 million in 2005,[2] the speed and density of migration in particular parts of the PRC appears more challenging in the context of China's emergence as a world power. With fast widening rural-urban income gaps since the mid-1980s, extensive interprovincial income disparities fostered by coastal development strategies and over 150 million surplus rural labourers in agriculture, the current pace of rural-urban migration may be expected to continue at least for the next two decades (Ping and Shaohua 2005, p. 68). The floating population of migrant workers is 'the flip side of the shiny façade that China so often presents'. Driven by a deep desire to escape rural poverty and the huge demand for cheap labour in the cities, more and more farmers leave the countryside. Although relatively larger proportions of rural migrants are male migrants, female migrants constituted 44 per cent of all migrants from 1985 to 1990 and 55 per cent between 1995 and 2000 (Fan 2004, p. 243). Thanks to this huge floating population, 'China's skyscrapers are becoming taller, its highways wider, its airports greater in number, its computers more modern; and its market increases constantly. But the strength of this renewal derives from the peasants who, on the land, in the factories, in construction . . . respond to China's need for modernization. Without the peasants there would be no modernization' (van Luyn 2008, pp. xiii–xiv); or no Olympics for that matter – more than a million migrants built the Olympic village in Beijing. In April 2006, migrant workers constituted 58 per cent of China's industrial labour force and 52 per cent of the tertiary sector labour force (Ngok 2008, p. 56). They make up 70 to 80 per cent of the total workforce in the garment, textile and construction industries (Lee 2007, p. 6). At the same time, migrant farmers also share their new prosperity with rural China. In 2004, according to the Ministry of Agriculture, migrants' remittances were estimated at $45 billion (Tunon 2006, p. 16). According to Chan (2003, p. 127), the value of migrant farmers' remittances to rural areas is 15 per cent of China's agricultural GDP. To this we should add Ping and Pieke's (2003, p. 15) observation that between 1995 and 2003 rural-urban migration contributed 16 per cent of total GDP growth in China. If the emergence of the 'China Circle' during and after the mid-1980s promises 'a broader and more integrated East Asia' (Naughton 1997, p. 289), it also underlines the crucial role played by migrant workers in the political integration and economic expansion of the region.

Arrighi et al. (2003, pp. 301–17) deploy the term 'East Asian resurgence' to denote the succession of spectacular economic 'miracles' that unfolded in the region since the late 20th century. The ascent of the region in the global hierarchy of wealth, its rapidly increasing share of the world market, the late 1960s crisis of US world hegemony and the rise of Japan, Hong Kong, Taiwan and the PRC as the world's leading creditor nations since the financial expansion (Arrighi 1994) of the 1980s, are related dimensions of the East Asian miracle. They argue that each of the overlapping stages in the regional miracle has been spearheaded by a series of different agencies – each agency creating the conditions for the emergence of the next agency – leading the expansion and integration of the East Asian region. In the first stage (1950s–80s), a 'political exchange' between the US and Japan during the Cold War – in which the US specialized in the provision of protection and the pursuit of political power and Japan specialized in trade and the pursuit of profit – launched the 'most spectacular' (Arrighi et al. 2003, p. 301) of the regional miracles. A US-centred East Asian regime not only set the 'outer limits' (Cumings 1984, p. 6) to participation by its dependencies in the region's dynamics, it also effectively excluded communist China from commerce, trade and diplomatic relations with the rest of the region after the Korean War (1950–3). The Sino-Soviet split in the late 1950s further isolated Mainland China. It was US defeat in the Vietnam War in the early 1970s that created the conditions for the PRC's re-entry into diplomatic and commercial relations with the region following US President Nixon's 1972 visit to China. In the second stage (1970s–80s), Japanese multilayered subcontracting business networks that encompassed the entire East Asian region were the leading agency of expansion and integration. In the process Japanese business relied heavily on vital networks of ethnic Overseas Chinese who occupied commanding positions in local businesses in most of the region. In this stage, restructured, vertically disintegrated US business enterprises began to compete with and undermine Japanese business leadership in East Asia in the 1990s. If the 1990s marked the onset of prolonged Japanese economic stagnation, the ascent of China – through an alliance between the political leadership in the Mainland and the Overseas Chinese business networks all over the region – in East Asian and world markets (1980s and 1990s) marks the current stage of the sustained regional miracle.

As Arrighi and his collaborators point out, common to the second and third stages of the regional miracle was the role played by the Overseas Chinese business diaspora. Common, however, to *all* the three stages of the regional miracle has been the 'concatenated, labor-seeking rounds of investment that promoted and sustained a region-wide economic expansion'. Labour-seeking flows of investment from higher-income jurisdictions to lower-income jurisdictions are matched by counter-flows of labour-intensive exports from lower-income jurisdictions such as China:

> In this regional space-of-flows, labor-seeking investments mobilize the cheaper or more abundant labor supplies of lower-income locales to contain costs of production and consumption in higher-income locales, while labor-intensive exports tap the wealthier or larger markets of higher-income locales to boost the prices fetched by the productive combination of lower-income locales (Arrighi et al. 2003, pp. 301–2).

I make three related arguments in this paper. First, I argue that Arrighi et al. (2003) do not specify *how* lower-income locales like the PRC are able to mobilize the labour power needed to sustain the labour-intensive exports that feed into the dynamic 'space-of-flows' in the region. There appears to be no engagement in their narrative with the question of migrant workers as agents in China's ascent in East Asia – despite the revolutionary role peasants played in propelling the Communists to power in 1949. Although Communist land reforms eliminated feudal agrarian relations and created more egalitarian social relations, farmers struggled against myriad restrictions on their mobility and against ascriptive status differences between rural and urban workers. Powerful grassroots peasant initiatives formalized the post-1978 household production responsibility system (*baochan daohu*) although the mid-1980s marked a reversal in rural fortunes, and intensified rural-urban income disparities as well as inter-regional disparities. This strengthened rural migratory flows, especially those towards the richer coastal areas. Second, I claim that large-scale internal migration (spontaneous as well as state-channelled) in the PRC after the mid-1980s is closely related to the PRC's export-oriented development strategy of national integration for upward mobility in the world-system. This strategy unfolded in the context of the 1985 Plaza Accord which spurred economic integration with Hong Kong and Taiwan by attracting Overseas Chinese foreign direct investment (FDI) in the coastal regions of China. Super-exploited rural migrants' labour power, however, built what is known as the 'China Circle'. Finally,

I argue that the livelihood struggles of rural migrant workers against exploitative work conditions in the special economic zones (SEZs) and the struggles of the urban unemployed and laid-off workers have created considerable social unrest in the country. Perhaps this escalating social unrest can redefine the PRC's market-based development such that it substantially uplifts those at the very bottom of the world-system. Can the Communist Party rise to this challenge?

Migrants as agents in the socioeconomic transformation of China

Restrictions on population mobility as well as restrictions on rural marketing were relatively rare before 1949 (Solinger 1999, pp. 28–32; Davin 1999, p. 40; Skinner 1985, p. 394). By contrast, the PRC's rulers (1949–78) followed the Soviet *propiska* (exclusive permit for living in cities) system (Solinger 1999, p. 33; Davin 1999, p. 5) to facilitate food transfers for industrial workers by segregating city from countryside and prohibiting rural-urban movement. A special household registration system, the *hukou* (State Council Directive 1955), was invented to fix people permanently to particular places based on their birthplace or their husband's residence. The essential characteristics of the *hukou* emerged clearly only during the 1960s. As Hein Mallee (2002, p. 424) explains, 'a number of initially separate strands which were not part of a pre-existing blueprint . . . came together in a rather haphazard, path-dependent way'. After 1954, when the State Food Monopoly was established, rural trade was diverted to cooperatives and state trading companies. All marketing activity was curtailed and the number of rural markets was sharply reduced (Skinner 1985, p. 405). The great 1959 famine (that followed the Great Leap Forward) played a key role in linking household registration to a grain-supply and rationing system (Davin 1999, p. 7). China's industrialization took place through this grain-rationing system that provided subsidized grain for urban factory workers organized in socialist work-units (*Danwei*). The socialist contract between the state and its workers worked through the urban *hukou*, possession of which gave urbanites access to the 'urban public goods regime' (Solinger 1999). To feed urban dwellers, farmers organized in rural agricultural cooperatives and communes produced cheap grain at below-market prices for the State Procurement System which distributed subsidized grain in the cities. Farmers' movement to urban areas was not only controlled, it was almost impossible because without an urban *hukou* they could not purchase state-distributed grain. The *hukou*, along with the fetishistic control over food grain, consolidated the strict boundaries between rural and urban areas even as it reinforced a new spatial hierarchy in China (Davin 1999, pp. 5–6). Except in emergencies when rural labour power was needed in the cities, farmers were effectively prohibited from migrating to cities (Solinger 1999, pp. 40–4). In order to limit the numbers of the urban population, the state made children inherit their mother's *hukou* status: children born to rural *hukou*-holding mothers inherited this lower rural status regardless of their fathers' registration status (Davin 1999, pp. 5–6, 18). An ascribed, inherited residential status thus determined an individual's entire livelihood and welfare, based simply on where the registration was located.

As Hsiao-Tung (1989, pp. 221–40) explains, these practices were directly opposed to Chinese agricultural traditions in which agriculture and rural industry had long been complementary activities. Apart from cultivating food, a variety of side occupations such as family handicraft industry had supplemented annual farm household income. Although the 'first big leap of the productive forces' associated with the land reforms of the early 1950s eliminated feudal exploitation, returned land to the tiller and stimulated agricultural cooperation and producers' cooperatives, at the same time it restricted commodity production, prohibited side occupations and adversely affected family handicraft industry and rural society. It was only with the introduction of the household production responsibility system in 1982 that a 'second big leap' in productivity transformed the structure of the rural economy.

However, the origins of the second big leap in the form of the household production responsibility system (*baochan daohu*, the practice of turning production over to the household) can be traced back to a long line of farmers' resistance to forced collectivization that began in 1956–7 with the *la niu tui she* (formally withdrawing from the cooperative, taking back one's family ox or buffalo) farmers' movement. Kate Zhou (1996) explains that this movement began in Zhejiang province and spread widely to other provinces. Although it was repressed and the People's Commune (the new form of the collective system) set the stage for the 1958 Great Leap Forward, the famines that followed renewed farmers' cross-provincial practices of *baochan daohu*. In response to farmers' pleas during the famine in Anhui province, provincial and local leaders in 1961 introduced the *zerentian* system (responsibility land system) which was supported then by Deng Xiaoping, but rejected by dominant Party factions who launched first the Socialist Education Movement (1963–5) and then the Cultural Revolution (1966–76) which forced farmers back to collective farming. It was only after 1977 that the 'spontaneous, unorganized, leaderless, nonideological, apolitical movement' (SULNAM) of farmers succeeded in convincing the Communist Party of the effectiveness of household family farming. Even though the Third Plenum of the Party Congress in 1978 declared *baochan daohu* illegal, the agricultural reforms that followed raised farm-product prices and gave farmers access to rural markets. These incentives from above were followed by spectacular farm-supply responses from below in the form of bumper grain harvests in 1980 and 1981, which in turn affected the Party's policy decisions. In October 1982 Party leaders finally lent their support to the farmers' movement for decollectivization (Zhou 1996, pp. 46–75); and a 1984 directive allowed peasants to move as 'temporary migrants' ('non-*hukou* migrants') to cities and towns (Fan 2004, p. 249). Farmers followed their success in *baochan daohu* by making use of state-subsidized fertilizers and seeds to increase land productivity and create larger farm surpluses, which stimulated the creation of new rural markets. Since the pre-reform collectives concealed massive farm labour surpluses, the 1978 reforms set the stage for rural-urban migration. With the basic production quota fixed by the State Procurement System, farmers were allowed to keep or to sell the rest of the harvest: 'farmers' incentives soared, leading to the greatest increase in productivity... in Chinese history' (Zhou 1996, p. 77).

By 1985 however, bumper food crops and poor State warehousing facilities made the State Procurement System increasingly unwieldy, while the practice of urban subsidies drove the state into a fiscal crisis. One outcome of the 1985 fiscal crisis and the state's inability to maintain grain purchase prices as well as to store grain surpluses was that farmers began to commercialize agricultural production and to expand networks of rural markets (Zhou 1996, pp. 79–84). In short, traditional dynamics began playing themselves out in the reconstitution and extension of marketing systems: in 1979 there were 36,767 rural markets; in 1980 there were 37,890; by 1983 there were 43,500 rural markets. 'It is almost as if China's pragmatic leaders were letting commercial capitalism run its course in the countryside' (Skinner 1985, pp. 408–12). Rural markets synergized with spectacular rural industrial development. Revival of rural trades complemented the dynamic township and village enterprises (TVEs) that tapped rural surplus labour.

The success of *baochan daohu* and the impact of the farmers' movement (SULNAM) on agricultural productivity exercised strong demonstration effects on state policy not only towards rural China but also towards workers in State Owned Enterprises (SOEs). In 1980 a new labour-policy framework (*sanjiehe* or 'three in one') reflected the Party's decision 'to allow the urban population to create job opportunities themselves'; it 'allowed urban people to engage in self-employed businesses, i.e., private business (*getihu*)'. By 1984, faced with massive unemployment and economic stagnation, the CCP Central Committee believed that the old *Danwei* (socialist urban work units) system – of guaranteed lifelong employment, egalitarian wages and a welfare package that offered subsidized housing, healthcare, schooling and pensions – had 'depleted the autonomy of SOEs'. Strong competition from TVEs exposed the rigidity of the wage and employment system in SOEs and forced their restructuring through labour and employment reforms introduced in the 1986 Labour Contract System that effectively abandoned the socialist labour contract with urban workers. In this way farmers also undermined the *Danwei* (urban work unit) system, which was dismantled in 1991 (Ngok 2008, pp. 46–7). At the same time small-scale rural merchants and peddlers restored the longstanding interdependence between countryside and the city through longer-distance trading (legalized in 1983). Trading not only ensured upward rural social mobility, it also weakened the effectiveness of regulations relating to migration that had been enforced by urban food coupons. Rural migrants bypassed the grain-rationing system by providing and exchanging services and commercial goods to urban people (Zhou 1996, p. 143). Farmers and migrant entrepreneurs reduced transaction costs by drawing upon networks their neighbours had forged with migrants who shared with them place-based kinship and associations. For instance, Zhang Li (2001, p. 47) explains how, in the early formation of the Wenzhou migrant community in Beijing, traditional social networks like kinship ties and native-place networks 'were not opposed to the development of a modern market economy'; in fact they 'provided the organizational framework for Chinese rural migrants' social life and private businesses'. Uprooted from rural communities, migrants rely on ascriptive bonds and on intermediaries as a strategy for survival in harsh environments (Solinger 1999, p. 176).

The above depiction of farmer-migrants' agency in China's great social transformation needs some qualifications, however. First, migrant workers have not yet overcome the rural-urban *houkou*-based social status divide (Li 2001, p. 23; Tunon 2006, pp. 22–3). Chinese migrant workers are still second-class citizens deprived of citizenship rights enjoyed by those who hold the urban *hukou*. In addition, poverty, low skills and lack of education or inadequate social connections are formidable barriers blocking migrants' upward social mobility. Solinger (1999, p. 5) goes on to claim that the Chinese migrants' lot in the city 'was much more akin to that of black people in South Africa before the 1990s or of blacks and Asians in the United States throughout the first half of the twentieth century', in that 'they all bore the brunt of a form of institutionalized discrimination so stringent that it barred them from becoming full citizens in their own home countries'. Zhou (1996, p. 33) even suggests that urban-rural segregation based on the *hukou* system created a caste-like society in China (see also Davin 1999, p. 8). According to Davin (1999, p. 39), 'the complete abolition of the household registration system does not seem to be on the horizon' because it supports the functioning of the entire socioeconomic system and works as an effective means of social control. Be that as it may, the social effects of the *hukou* are not qualitatively the same as the relatively deeper and more durable social inequalities produced by the Indian caste system. Unlike the majority of Indians who belong to the underprivileged and exploited lower social castes, in China the majority (including most migrants) belong to the dominant ethnic Han majority. The State's desire to regulate migrants' movements derives in part from perceived threats to urban privileges from the 'swarm' of rural migrants. And in part it derives from the corruption of the 'sticky' bureaucratic structures: confronted by the myriad challenges of a rising market economy, state bureaucrats seek to resist the erosion of their former power and privileges. Sustaining the rural-urban status difference in the course of China's market-based development is the thorough commodification of the *hukou*, so much so that counties in different provinces began selling, in the late 1980s, local urban household registration papers, known as blue cards (*lanka*) or blue seals (*lanyin*). By 1991 the sale of blue cards had spread 'to all levels of urban places throughout the country' (Woon 1999, p. 479). The *hukou* remains much more expensive in the coastal areas to where most migrants desire to migrate. It continues to be a social and economic status-marker, and it is part of a more widespread system of policing of rural migrants in China (Shukai 2000, p. 102). In short, the effects of the urban *hukou* continue to make rural migrants a socially inferior group. On the other hand, as Solinger (2003b, pp. 76–7) notes, a growing similarity of economic predicament confronting laid-off urban workers – between 1995 and 2002 some 150 million workers (including their dependents) were effectively laid off out of an urban workforce of 200 million and a total urban population of 450 million – and super-exploited rural migrants makes for a common (if uneven) devaluation or forfeiture of rights of citizenship.

Secondly, migrant subjectivity needs to be situated within the context of gender differences in migration patterns. If 'Chinese women's level of labor-force participation is among the highest in the world', it is in part because the Maoist period promoted women's engagement in production as fully as men (Fan 2004, p. 246). The post-1978 economic reforms that reduced restrictions on mobility also enabled Chinese women to migrate on their own rather than as 'tied movers'. Some women use marriage as a strategy for migration while others move to become *dagongmei* (rural 'working girls' in urban areas) in coastal south China (pp. 246–8). By and large more women tend to remain in the countryside given their reproductive roles in rural households, while men increasingly become wage labourers in rural TVEs or in urban industries. Sustained inequalities in women's and men's educational levels and hence also in access to opportunities in the labour market outside the countryside appear to have led to a growing 'feminization of agriculture' (Fan 2004, pp. 262–3; Cartier 2004, p. 286). On average, according to L. MacLeod, women now perform over 70 per cent of farm labour; and, according to T. C. Carino, women constitute 80 to 90 per cent of the agricultural labour force in the provinces of Jiangsu and Shandong (cited in Cartier 2004, p. 280; see also Ping 2006, p. 240).

Third, ethnographic studies of the changing relationship between the state and migrant communities in different urban areas suggest that the state develops different strategies to regulate migrants (Li 2001, p. 2). In general, the process that transforms farmers into a 'floating population' – apart from migrant subjectivity – works through a combination of state policies (the macro-structural determinant) and the specific ecosystem formed by the geography of migrants' native places.

Three state policies in the period 1949–78 – a pro-natalist stance, prohibition of departure from the village, and a commune-provisioning regime that offered no incentive for planning family size – worsened the gap between available arable land (which dropped from 107 million hectares in 1957 to 99 million hectares in 1977) and population growth. By the mid-1990s, between 100 million and 200 million farm labourers became redundant on the farmland (with close to 75 per cent in central and western provinces) and TVEs were able to absorb only 50 per cent of the redundant farm labourers. At the same time the rural-urban per capita income (PCY) gap that had been significantly shrinking between 1978 and 1985 significantly widened after the 1985 bumper food harvest. New grain-procurement policies, reduced prices for farm products (especially above-quota grain), and increased official prices of agricultural inputs raised the costs of farm production. State investments in agriculture were also slashed (from 11 to 5 per cent) in the course of the 1980s (Solinger 1999, p. 159). After the mid-1980s, poverty-alleviation measures stalled and the proportion of poor actually increased through 1991 as inflation turned the terms of trade against agriculture (though during the 1993–6 period there was dramatic progress). From its minimum level in the mid-1980s, the urban-rural household income gap widened over the next two decades (Naughton 2007, p. 211). If rural PCY as a percentage of urban PCY rose from 50 per cent in 1982 to 54 per cent in 1983 and 1984, starting in 1985 rural PCY dropped to 53 per cent of urban PCY; in 1990 it was 41 per cent of urban PCY. By 1994, the urban-rural PCY gap had widened to 2.6:1 (Solinger 1999, p. 161);[3] in 2005 the ratio was 3.22:1, and in 2006 the gap became 3.27:1 (China Labor Bulletin 2008). This widening urban-rural gap remains an endless stimulus for internal migration.

From the mid-1980s differences between rural ecosystems of labour-exporting and labour-importing provinces also determined processes of inter-provincial migration. The Inland Provinces (Anhui, Guangxi, Guizhou, Gansu, Henan, Hubei, Hunan, Sichuan and Jiangxi) were the major labour-exporters from the mid-1980s to the mid-1990s; six of them (four with relatively lower arable land per capita), with 35 per cent of the PRC's population, accounted for nearly 50 per cent of the total migration. If we include Chongqing, over 80 per cent of migrant workers flowed out of these Inland Provinces (China Labor Bulletin 2008). By and large, TVEs have stayed away from western and central China. In the poorest parts of northwest and southwest China ecological conditions make for low productive forces; low educational assets and lack of information prevent poor people from migrating. TVEs have tended to concentrate in six eastern coastal provinces favoured by littoral location, topography and climate (Jiangsu, Guangdong, Hainan, Zhejiang, Fujian and Shandong) that accounted for 65 per cent of all TVE output, while central and western provinces accounted for only 30 per cent and 4 per cent of TVE output respectively (Solinger 1999, pp. 163–71). As Naughton (1996, p. 274) points out, the exceptionality of Chinese growth is really the exceptional story of the five coastal provinces of Fujian, Guangdong, Zhejiang, Jiangsu and Shandong. Between 1983 and 1994, the eastern coastal provinces (excluding Hainan), with a total population in 1994 of 217 million, grew more rapidly than the national average GDP growth rate, by at least one percentage point per year. These disparities in regional endowments, coupled with TVE concentration in favourably endowed provinces, contributed to deepening inter-provincial and inter-regional income disparities. Internal migration patterns reflect these general eco-systemic and state-induced parameters. And they reflect gender differences (Fan 2004, p. 248; Cartier 2004, p. 286). In the following section I situate these parameters and patterns within the context of the relationship between the floating population's coastward surge – dominated by female interprovincial migrants (Fan 2004, p. 256) – and the unfolding of larger regional and world-systemic forces at work since the mid-1980s.

Internal migration and the greater 'China Circle' in the global conjuncture

Bruce Cumings (1984, pp. 38–9) has argued that if history is any guide to the future of relational power hierarchies in the region and if it is clear that the world-system does not provide access to upward mobility for all states (Wallerstein 1979), we should expect Taiwan and South Korea to move into a middle position between the US and Japan on the one hand and the PRC on the other. However, it appears that a somewhat different configuration of wealth and power is emerging in East Asia in regard to 'the Chinese triangle of Mainland-Taiwan-Hong Kong'. During the period of US hegemony (1945–67/73) these three states pursued different developmental projects. The PRC prioritized self-reliant growth through industrialization; Overseas Chinese capitalists and cheap refugee labour from the PRC fuelled British colonial Hong Kong's pursuit of export-led industrialization. Taiwan pursued import-substitution industrialization in the 1950s and export-led industrialization and industrial deepening in the 1960s and 1970s. The frontline position of Taiwan (and South Korea) in the Cold War made it a recipient of massive US aid and gave it access to US markets (Hsiao and So 1993, pp. 133–4). Nevertheless by the late 1970s all three encountered developmental limits. Taiwan and Hong Kong encountered rising labour shortages, escalating land prices and growing environmental protests (Hsiao and So 1993, p. 134; Lee 1998, p. 45), while the PRC faced high urban unemployment and economic stagnation in part because of 17 million returnees from the countryside after the Cultural Revolution and in part because of the adverse impact of the *dingti* system of occupational inheritance in urban state-sector jobs (Ngok 2008, p. 46). And yet, as Ching Kwan Lee (1998, p. 1) remarks, '[s]ince the mid-1980s, China has become the world's new "global factory", with the southern province of Guangdong (including Hong Kong) as its powerhouse'; and since 1988 Taiwan itself began to trade and invest in the PRC on a large scale (Hsiao and So 1993, p. 142) especially in the coastal Mainland provinces of Guangdong and Fujian. Even more remarkable is that '*despite* political and military conflict and long-standing, deep-seated suspicion and mistrust' between three sharply different political entities 'that until recently had seemed to be permanently sundered by political divisions', a 'natural' economic and trading region cutting across territorial jurisdictions has unfolded in 'a series of concentric economic circles, centered on Hong Kong' (Naughton 1997, pp. 3–5, emphasis added; see also Ong 2006, p. 114). The smallest circle encompasses the metropolitan core of Hong Kong, although between 1985 and 1995 almost all of Hong Kong's manufacturing relocated to the PRC's coastal province of Guangdong in the Pearl River hinterland.[4] As Lee (1998, p. 90) observes, 'Hong Kong's deindustrialization since the 1980s occurred in tandem with Guangdong's industrialization'. In a similar manner, Taiwan's manufacturing industries relocated between 1987 and 1995 to both Guangdong and Fujian, thereby constituting with Hong Kong the next largest circle. Lying beyond this circle is the greater East Asian region defined by two flows of capital spreading northward and southward along the entire coast of Mainland China – one from Hong Kong and Taiwan (spreading out from Guangdong and Fujian) and the other from Japan and South Korea (spreading out from Shandong and Liaoning) – and meeting and overlapping in the lower Yangzi provinces of Shanghai, Jiangsu and Zhejiang (Naughton 1997, pp. 5–6; Selden 1997, pp. 329–30). If, prior to the mid-1980s, foreign trade in East Asia was dominated by *trans-Pacific trade*, between 1986 and 1992 *intra-regional trade* assumed greater importance: it surged from 32 per cent to 44 per cent while the region's trade with the US dropped steeply from 37 per cent to 24 per cent (Selden 1997, p. 321). Although this trend increase in intra-regional trade was 'abruptly reversed' by the Asian financial crisis, it has since resumed (Naughton and Macintyre 2005, p. 88). At the same time, the share of the combined exports of the China Circle in world exports between 1985 and 1995 increased from some 3 per cent to 7 per cent (Naughton 1997, p. 7). Since the 1980s Guangdong's share of the PRC's foreign trade grew from 7 per cent to 23 per cent (1979–91); and Fujian's share over the same period grew from less than 1 per cent to 3 per cent (Selden 1997, p. 331). Between 1987 and 1996 the US began to run a large trade deficit with the China Circle that rose from $26 billion to $47 billion, with virtually the entire recent deficit recorded against the PRC (Naughton 1997, p. 17). Finally, foreign direct investment (FDI) in the PRC grew from almost nothing to $5 billion in 1991 to $28 billion in 1993 and to over $40 billion in 1996, with most of it concentrated in Guangdong and Fujian. This China Circle has emerged not only as a global workshop manufacturing labour-intensive toys and garments; especially after the mid-1980s, it has become the world's third leading producer and exporter of electronics with the massive relocation of assembly lines from Hong Kong to the Mainland (Naughton 1997, p. 7; Lee 1998, p. 51).

What conjunctural and world-systemic circumstances account for the emergence of the China Circle in the mid-1980s and for the growing concentration of intra-regional trading within this Circle? In the first place the turn toward business strategies of flexible accumulation (and away from the large multi-unit, vertically integrated business form that had dominated the organization of the most successful businesses in the Cold War period) as a means to overcome the overaccumulation crisis of the US Fordist regime in the late 1960s and 1970s (Harvey 1989), fitted well with the predominantly small-firm environment not only in Hong Kong and Taiwan, but also within the PRC. Naughton (1997, p. 20) notes how small and medium-size firms have played the predominant role in the emergence of the China Circle and that 'the size distribution of China's firms has changed in the direction of that of Hong Kong and Taiwan'. However, as Hamilton and Chang (2003, p. 203–5) demonstrate, subcontracting through networks of small family household firms and buyer-driven commodity chains had long been an established business practice in late-imperial China: it was this late-imperial 'pre-modern' legacy that allowed coastal China to fit in seamlessly with late 20th-century 'postmodern' processes of globalization. Further, if the contemporary and successful revival of this business form in the East Asian region is in part due to the sharp reduction in transaction costs among the participants in the China Circle as Naughton (1997, p. 10) correctly notes, the role played by the Overseas Chinese business diaspora in reducing these transaction costs in the ethnic-Chinese-dominated environment of the China Circle is no less important, as is the role played by the PRC in successfully attracting Overseas Chinese capital (in Hong Kong and Taiwan) to invest in coastal China's Special Economic Zones (SEZs).

Second, I want to argue that the currency realignments of the mid-1980s strongly favoured the emergence of the Greater China Circle. The 1985 Plaza Accord – 'an attempt to bring under control Japan's enormous trade surpluses with the United States and other nations' (Selden 1997, p. 323) – led to sharp appreciation of the yen and the Taiwan dollar between 1985 and 1988. From the viewpoint of Hong Kong and Taiwanese capital, rising land costs and labour shortages made it imperative to restructure their export production networks; in this context the 'opening of China to foreign investment at this time created a dramatic opportunity to transfer labor-intensive export production to the People's Republic' (Naughton 1997, p. 9). The PRC responded to the mid-1980s conjuncture in two ways. In the first place it introduced in 1986 'the most significant break with the old employment system' through the Labour Contract System which discontinued the earlier practice of lifelong employment, and made all new recruits sign labour contracts with their respective SOEs (Ngok 2008, p. 47). At the same time the PRC sought to further the expansion of SEZs by facilitating the coastward movement of migrant labourers towards south China and by offering preferential treatment for Overseas Chinese investments in that region alone, reasoning that 'the potential for rapid wealth generation was greatest along the coast' (Solinger 1999, p. 46). Moreover, Guangdong's remoteness from Beijing reduced risks that political and social unrest among migrants from the experimental changes in the SEZs would spread to the interior (Lee 1998, p. 40). There was also, however, an important political motivation behind the strategy of coastal development. As Ong (2006, p. 98) argues, the economic integration of the 'disarticulated political entities' of Hong Kong, Macao and Taiwan may also be seen as a strategic 'detour to eventual political integration'. If the PRC's opening in 1979 of four SEZs to attract high-tech capital investment from US and Japanese TNCs was unsuccessful (Hsiao and So 1993, p. 135), its coastal development strategy (the opening of 14 coastal cities and Hainan in 1984 and the extension of the open door in three Delta areas in 1985) was enormously successful in luring Overseas Chinese FDI into coastal China.[5] Economic and administrative autonomy in these SEZs attracted Overseas Chinese investments in almost wholly export-oriented production where market conditions alone determined wages and work conditions for the migrant millions. As 'spaces of economic exception' to the centrally planned socialist economy, the political order within SEZs promoted 'freewheeling entrepreneurial activities and labor exploitation to a degree not allowed in the rest of China' (Ong 2006, pp. 106–9). The economic success of the SEZs in turn enabled the PRC in the mid-1990s to formulate its 'one nation, two systems' policy for politically reintegrating the breakaway territories of Hong Kong, Macao and Taiwan by reconstituting them as Special Administrative Regions (SARs). SARs constitute a 'political exception' to the general socialist politics of the Mainland in the sense that they represent unique orders of political autonomy, a formal and flexible accommodation of different political entities within the PRC's 'one nation, two systems' policy. However, the synergy between the 'economic exception' (SEZs) and the 'political exception' (SARs) 'is creating a kind of regionalization that makes political unification of China and its breakaway parts inevitable' (Ong 2006, pp. 109–11).

While it is certainly a myth that the rise of China is attributable to its adherence to the neoliberal creed (Arrighi 2007, pp. 353–61), may we not see in the creation of SEZs 'spaces of exception' to the centrally planned socialist economy that are 'informed by neoliberal reason to combat neoliberal forces in the world at large' as Ong (2006, p. 99) argues? If the PRC has pursued market reforms with 'Chinese characteristics', are these reducible to the 'positive kinds of exception' promoted in the SEZs – the 'kinds of exception that create market opportunities, usually for a minority, who enjoy political accommodations and conditions not granted to the rest of the population' so that these privileged groups can face the challenges of neoliberal globalization (pp. 101–2)? In the last instance did not the success of China's coastal development strategy evolve out of the state policy of making floaters out of migrant farmers, and by influencing the direction of the flow of low-waged rural labourers? In the late 1980s, 90 per cent of internal migration involved workers leaving central and western China for the east: 'this coastward surge derived directly from state policies that expressly privileged that region' (Solinger 1999, p. 46). In 2000 one out of every three migrant industrial workers in China lived in south China's Guangdong province; 37 per cent of China's migrant industrial workers were drawn to Guangdong, which accounted for 42 per cent of China's exports, 90 per cent of which came from the eight cities in the Pearl River Delta area (Lee 2007, p. 161). According to the State Statistical Bureau's 1987 survey, women comprised 58.3 per cent of migrant workers from within Guangdong and 63.2 per cent from outside Guangdong. Shenzhen is the most important 'floating' city in the Delta, 'the rite of passage for China's peasant generation coming of age in the 1990s' (Lee 1998, p. 81). Three-fourths of Shenzhen's six million labouring migrants in 2005 (out of a population of close to eight million) were employed in export-processing and foreign-invested industries, making Shenzhen 'China's major link to the global marketplace' (Lee 2007, pp. 161–2). The industrial takeoff in the coastal SEZs in short depended upon unrelenting tides of migrant workers floating into the coastal provinces. Since the mid-1980s, young and single rural women have made up the larger portion of the migrant labour deluge (*mingong chao*) in Guangdong (Lee 1998, p. 68).

And yet, it appears as though after 20 years of spectacular growth, southern China is increasingly haunted by the spectre of labour shortage. A government report in 2005 noted a shortfall of two million workers and 'particularly of women aged between 18 and 30 who are badly needed in factories and companies' in both the Pearl River Delta and in east China's Yangzi River Delta (Croll 2006, p. 300). In August 2004 'an industrial panic' spread throughout the Pearl River Delta's export-driven industrial belt: 'the seemingly bottomless pool of migrant labor is reaching a limit, at least a limit of tolerance for low pay and miserable working conditions'. Migrant wages in 2006 ranged between 300 yuan and 800 yuan per month compared to urban workers' wages which averaged 1,842 yuan per month (Ong 2006, pp. 137–8; see also Ngok 2008, pp. 57–8). Voting with their feet is one expression of migrant workers' lower tolerance for exploitation and unequal exchange between city and countryside. Croll (2006, p. 127) notes that since 2003 at least some migrants are finding work nearer their home villages. A more striking expression of this intolerance is the surge of insurgencies against the shameless exploitation of their labour power.

Labour unrest in the global factory

According to the UN's Country Assessment (2004, p. ix), with the Gini coefficient of national inequality now exceeding 0.4, the PRC has crossed 'the threshold considered by many to indicate potential social unrest'. In general, Ching Kwan Lee (2007, pp. 164–70) identifies three types of grievances among migrant workers: unpaid wages, illegal wage deductions or substandard wage rates arising out of non-contractual employment status; disciplinary excesses and assaults on workers' dignity in the workplace; and innumerable workplace injuries and fatalities. I make two arguments in this section.

First, China's 1994 Labour Law, the first of its kind in the history of the nation, emerged as the dialectical outcome of countrywide labour unrest since the mid-1980s on the one hand, and a spate of legislation on labour policy passed by the central government on the other. The resumption of nationwide waves of labour unrest despite the new Labour Law produced the recent Labour Contract Law which came into effect on 1 January 2008. Since the mid-1980s the state had reduced its administrative intervention in labour relations and relied on legislation to regulate labour relations and to maintain its legitimacy through the rule of law (Ngok 2008, p. 46). Since market reforms decentralized production decisions to the local level, they made local governments responsible not only for developing a business-friendly market economy, but also for implementing the central government's labour policies that sought to resolve labour conflicts in the workplace. The tension between the interests of 'local accumulation' and the centre's pursuit of legitimacy by the rule of law has led to endemic violations of labour rights and entitlements, with the local state as the target of workers' struggles (Lee 2007, pp. 10–11). Myriad instances of 'organized agitation' by migrant workers in the form of unauthorized unions and illicit strikes began to appear by the mid-1980s. There were more than 100 strikes per year in 1992 and 1993 (Solinger

1999, pp. 284–5). The escalating labour unrest in the nation involved unemployed, laid-off and retired urban workers as well, after the 1986 Labour Contract System restructured the SOEs (Ngok 2008, pp. 47–8). In 1993, some 8,700 'mass incidents' involving protests and demonstrations by urban workers were recorded by the Ministry of Public Security. In mid-1994, incidents of industrial unrest appeared to be occurring once or twice a week in the provinces of Hubei, Hunan, Heilongjiang and Liaoning (Lee 2007, pp. 5–6; Ngok 2008, p. 50). The common predicament underlying both types of labour unrest – urban rustbelt workers' 'protests of desperation' and rural sunbelt workers' 'protests against discrimination' – is 'the illiberal nature of China's legal system' (Lee 2007, p. 202). Although the state issued more than 160 labour regulations and rules between 1979 and 1994 (Ngok 2008, p. 49), they did not have much impact at the lower levels of local government where the imperative to enhance economic growth and investments conflicted with protecting the rights of workers. Faced with growing social instability, the PRC finally passed the 1994 Labour Law. Its three pillars – the individual labour (written) contract system, collective negotiation between trade union and employer, and labour dispute mediation, arbitration and litigation processes – defined the new labour policy regime but remained largely unenforceable at the local level. In particular they failed to provide any legal protection for migrant workers, who continued to occupy a twilight status between peasants and workers (Ngok 2008, pp. 49–56). At the same time, SOE reforms and bankruptcies continued to unmake Mao's urban working classes. As a result the period after 1994 was marked by an upward shift in labour unrest. The number of mass incidents by unemployed and laid-off rustbelt workers spiked from 11,000 in 1995, to 15,000 in 1997, to 32,000 in 1999, to 58,000 in 2003, to 74,000 in 2004 and 87,000 in 2005 (Lee 2007, p. 5). Migrant workers' unrest also surged: by 1996 migrant workers' strikes had involved the participation of over 200,000 workers (Solinger 1999, p. 286). Shenzhen witnessed 600 protests and strikes by migrant workers each year in the period 1998–2001 alongside an explosion of officially mediated and arbitrated labour disputes, most of which related to wage arrears and illegal wage rates (Lee 2007, pp. 6–7). The State's response to the deepening social strains was the decision to 'strike a balance among economic growth, social development, and environmental protection'. This led to the release by the State Council of the first comprehensive policy document on migrant workers in which migrants were formally recognized as working classes. It was followed by the 2007 Labour Contract Law. Effective from 1 January 2008, the new labour law appears to be more specific and operation-oriented compared to the 1994 Labour Law: it mandates stringent punishment for employers who violate the law; and it stresses building a harmonious society and putting people first. Nevertheless the new laws still fail to clearly define the legal status of migrant workers (Ngok 2008, pp. 57–60).

Second, despite widespread social unrest, no horizontal combinations between urban unemployed and laid-off workers (*xiagang*) *or* between migrant workers (*nongmingong*) *or* for that matter between urban workers and migrant workers have yet emerged. This is all the more surprising considering that *all* workers have experienced varying degrees of downgrading of their citizenship status (Solinger 2003b, p. 12), and considering that they all also see themselves as *ruoshi qunti* or subaltern social groups in weak and disadvantaged social positions (Lee 2007, p. 64). Why have the combined weaknesses of the different subaltern groups not translated into stronger workers' combinations?

In part this is because the Communist Party-dominated All China Federation of Trade Unions (ACFTU) remains the only legal workers' union in the nation despite its widespread crisis of membership, credibility and legitimacy. In general there is no workers' right to strike in China; the pro-production mediating role played by unions only heightens workers' cynicism towards unions. At the same time, the state's numerous instances of labour legislation have catalyzed 'cellular' labour activism without union support, against local cadres who are denounced as acting 'against the law' (Lee 2007, pp. 57–61, 21). Why have the forms of labour protest generally been confined to local enterprise levels and to particular localities?

In the case of state-sector workers, government policies have fragmented the interests of retired pensioners, laid-off workers and the unemployed by stipulating different terms of employment and retirement for each group. Retirees with moral economy claims on SOEs see their livelihood crises as different from those of unemployed and laid-off workers. In general these groups do not combine forces except in times of enterprise bankruptcy, 'because the Bankruptcy Law bundles their rights together, and because bankruptcy always implies cadre corruption and illicit sales of enterprise assets perceived by workers as their collective property'. State repression, however, is swift and decisive whenever these groups join forces in large numbers or when their protests invite inter-factory or community participation. Lateral mobilization and solidarity are thus rarely sustainable (Lee 2007, pp. 72–91, 112–15). Migrant workers are also divided by shop floor, local origin, rank and skill level. Their strongest moment of solidarity is at the moment of plant closure or relocation – at the moment of their exit from the factory – but since they have no organization to sustain connections they also rapidly disperse (pp. 175–6, 197, 206). Localized, workplace-based cellular activism thus remains the form of labour activism common to state-sector and non-state sector workers. Finally, state-sector workers and migrant workers have never been inclined to form political alliances (p. 202), in large part because of the *hukou* system that privileges the former and devalues the social status of the latter.

Wallerstein (1999, pp. 45–6) observes that, unlike other parts of the world, anti-statism has not found any purchase in East Asia. This is because East Asia is 'the only area that has not yet lived through a serious decline in economic prospects during the period 1970–95, and therefore the only area where disillusionment with incrementalist reformism has not taken place'. In China, of course, economic growth has been stronger than anywhere else in the world economy. Rawski and Perkins (2008, p. 857) anticipate that China's future real GDP will continue to grow at average rates of 6 to 8 per cent per year between 2005 and 2025. Apparently those at the bottom of China's wealth pyramid 'still believe that the whole nation is getting wealthier so that the rich are simply those who got there first and that others will follow in their footsteps via hard work and further education'. And the Party leaders appear to have succeeded in conveying the hope to those at the bottom that 'China's growth is moving fast enough to lift the majority of the population into the middle classes' (Croll 2006, pp. 321, 329). At least in terms of its capacity to ensure reasonably rapid economic growth, the future legitimacy of the Chinese state appears secure. In general, subaltern groups in China have a 'bifurcated view of the State'. Both state-sector workers and migrant workers see the Party-State as representing the general interest and 'their faith in the moral and political integrity of the central state has remained largely unwavering'. At the same time they perceive that the general interest is sabotaged by corrupt and predatory local cadres; and they see themselves 'as supplicants to the state, which in turn has the responsibility to protect and lead' while the masses have 'the moral responsibility to rebel against immoral leaders' (Lee 2007, pp. 117–19, 201). But their rebellions have not become national in scale and character.

There are two other factors that help us understand why social unrest in China has not yet produced political instability in the PRC. There is firstly the housing entitlement for state-sector workers that has survived the post-*Danwei* (socialist work unit) society. Although urban joblessness is everywhere there is nevertheless 'no sign of homelessness even in the worst hit areas in the rustbelt. Near universal provision of housing is perhaps one of the most significant keys to the regime's capacity to maintain overall social stability'. And although workers are unhappy about inequities in housing allocation and about the fuzziness of housing property rights, the reality is that 'workers are provided with basic housing. No matter how destitute, they have a home to go back to at the end of the day' (Lee 2007, pp. 125–6). To this we should of course add that the land-rights system in rural China after the dismantling of the communes has not led to 'accumulation through dispossession' from the land. 'Migration is usually accompanied by a very considerable remigration [...] a reflux toward the village' (Polanyi 2001, p. 96). In particular when migrants find working conditions intolerable in south China they exercise the option to exit to the countryside. Like their unemployed urban counterparts they have a safety net to fall back into: no matter how destitute, they have a piece of land to return to when they experience overexploitation in coastal China. For 'the distinctiveness of the Chinese agricultural reform is that it returns farmland to the village collective, which then allocates land use rights to individual peasant households'. These land-use rights act as a buffer for rural migrants; it allows for subsistence in times of unemployment and non-payment of wages, even though 'working for the bosses' (*dagong*) in the city is increasingly necessary to reproduce livelihoods (Lee 2007, pp. 229–30, 204–5).

Conclusion

What kind of implications may we draw from the arguments in the preceding sections? I have argued that the efforts and contributions of migrant workers to the resurgence of East Asia is central to understanding the growth, integration and expansion of the region since the late 20th century, insofar as it provides us with a 'bottom-up' perspective on the region's ascendance in the global hierarchy of wealth and power. Doing so balances the emphasis Arrighi et al. (2003) place on the 'political exchange' and symbiosis between the Chinese Party-State and the Overseas Chinese diaspora. While this symbiosis is undoubtedly real and productive (even as it is productive of a discourse on 'the rise of East Asia'), it raises other questions that are relatively unaddressed in Arrighi's path-breaking works on the East Asian region. For Arrighi argues that unlike the Western developmental path where capitalism was *internalized* by Western territorial and national states, in the East Asian developmental path represented by Mainland China, capitalism was largely *externalized* to its outer rims (the coastal areas) and never allowed to become the 'general interest' of the state whether in the Ming and Qing imperial states or in the contemporary PRC. The PRC-Party-State, it is argued, is in control of its relationship with the capitalist overseas diaspora, in the sense that the PRC-State is *not* a committee for managing the affairs of the Overseas Chinese bourgeoisie (in the sense in which Marx speaks of the capitalist state as nothing but a committee for managing the affairs of the ruling bourgeoisie or in the sense in which Fernand Braudel speaks of capitalism triumphing only when it becomes identified with the state). In this argument, China's post-1978 development is largely the development *not* of a capitalist state: it is represented as a market-based development (in the sense of Adam Smith and Braudel) in which (in Polanyi's terms) the economy is still embedded within society, within larger social and political relations that regulate it effectively.

And yet, in the interpersonal relationships (based on 'cultural affinity') between Overseas Chinese and decentralized local coastal governments, large land sales have become one of the major sources of revenue for local governments – in the Shenzhen and Zhuhai SEZs revenue from land sales to overseas investors is often as high as 50 per cent of the total revenue of these cities (Hsing 1997, p. 147) – even as farmers confront a growing crisis of landlessness. As capitalists driven by 'promiscuous opportunism' (Ong 1997, p. 175) in the pursuit of profit, what incentives do overseas Chinese have to invest in the social and material advancement of Chinese workers? As decentralized local governments (with substantial autonomy from the centre) strive to compete among themselves for Overseas Chinese investments, what incentives do they have to make the livelihood concerns of migrant workers a pressing priority? In fact, the subaltern groups who bear the main burden of China's great transformation are almost never mentioned in the ruling discourses of the putatively 'Asian way' of rising up in social and material life. 'Though indispensable to capitalist success in the region, they are rendered invisible and speechless, an effect of the symbolic violence . . . of triumphalist Chinese modernity' (Ong 1997, p. 192; see also Dirlik 1998). The Party-State's interest in promoting 'harmonious development' is thus in sharp contradiction to the local-level dealings (*guanxi*) with Overseas Chinese. If this contradiction continues, so will migrant unrest; and insofar as the circumstances that produced this contradiction (whose effects include both rising social unrest and increasing income inequalities) continue to be essential for China as a regional (and global) growth engine, what is the virtue of speaking in terms of the 'externalization' of capitalism in contemporary China? Perhaps a more important question is to ask how these contradictions and limits may be overcome in the future in such a way that market-based development in the PRC remains embedded in social relations. To prioritize harmonious societal relations over the market relations entails keeping a sharp eye on material and social inequalities. In short, we need to raise challenging questions that concern the rise of particular social classes and the exclusion of other social groups from the benefits of Chinese (and regional) growth. If it is the *conjoint* motions of commodities, capital *and* labour that create and re-create the Pacific and East Asia as regional spaces, then an exclusive focus on the flows of commodities and capital does little justice to the great flux and reflux of exploited labour (in particular migrant labour) that intersects in complementary *and conflicting* ways with the path of flows of commodities and capital.

As Arrighi (2007) argues, drawing upon McNeill (1982), the Euro-centred inter-state system successfully expanded and globalized only through its superiority in the art of war: in developing and accumulating means of violence (militarism), inter-state European military competition synergized with the development of capital- and resource-intensive industrialization. This synergy between militarism and capitalism produced what McNeill (1982) calls the industrialization of war, which in turn drove Western capitalism on its globe-girdling imperialist path which resulted not only in the 19th-century subordinate incorporation of the East Asian regional system into the European developmental path, but also in the most inegalitarian world-system in human history, whose contemporary form is reflected in the persistent global North (rich nations)–global South (poor nations) divide.

As the leading agency in contemporary East Asia's market-based development, the rise of China presents a unique occasion to undermine the material inequalities that have formed the basis of this global North-South divide. As the holder of the biggest foreign exchange reserves in the world, amounting to $1,810 billion as of June 2008 (Dyer 2008, p. 1), the PRC has an unprecedented opportunity to carry forward a different kind of world-embracing material expansion that imparts a distinctive socialist foundation to the world-system. But the challenge begins on the domestic front. How may the Communist Party forge a different developmental path that makes redistribution of the benefits of growth in the interests of its lowest social strata the foremost priority? In 1983 with a Gini coefficient of inequality of 0.28, China was one of the most equal countries in the world; since the mid-1980s the Gini spiked sharply and consistently rose upward, from 0.35 in 1990 to 0.45 in 2001 to 0.46 in 2002, making China significantly more unequal than most

Asian nations, more unequal than the average semi-peripheral nation, and as unequal as the average nation in the periphery. As Naughton (2007, pp. 217–8) observes, 'there may be no other case where a society's income distribution has deteriorated so much, so fast'. One social effect of growing inequalities within China is growing social unrest. Another important effect of growing inequalities of income is the restraint it places on the growth of the domestic market. Insofar as the future of East Asian integration depends significantly on the growth of intra-regional markets so as to fully overcome the region's dependence on Northern markets – rendered even more important in the light of the stagnation of the Euro-zone and the staggering indebtedness of the US economy – growing inequalities within China (and between nations in the region) limit the potential of Chinese markets to support and reinforce regional growth and expansion.

The elimination of the *hukou* system would work towards removing entrenched *social* inequalities within the country. As such the *hukou* system, with its built-in urban bias, devalues the inestimable contribution of migrant labourers to the Chinese growth miracle and provokes social unrest in the face of widespread discrimination against ruralites. Eliminating the *hukou* may help fulfil the dream of erasing the pernicious divide between city and countryside. It may also exert a powerful demonstration effect on social inequality in India where the enduring legacy of the caste system remains the biggest obstacle to South Asian development.

Investing a larger share of its foreign exchange reserves in rural development projects that privilege and protect rural land rights and rectify what appears to be a growing urban bias may become a challenging priority for the Communist Party. As Solinger (1999, p. 187) observes, the exclusion of farmers from the right to urban citizenship makes their rural land-use rights more than a supplier of sustenance in times of economic hardship. It is also 'a means of psychic security'. It is therefore disconcerting to note that a 'looming crisis of landlessness' appears to be unfolding as local cadres coercively requisition farmland in the countryside (Lee 2007, pp. 206, 241). Huang Ping (2006, p. 27) argues that the social security provided under the land-rights system 'ensures that there will be no urban slums such as those in other developing societies'. And yet by the mid-1990s 'with the reform era, China's cities came to appear more and more similar to those elsewhere in the third world, as slum-like spaces reappeared for the first time in post-1949 China' (Solinger 1999, p. 250). Against this we should note that conscious urban planning by the CCP has promoted a more balanced urban hierarchy through the growth of small-to-medium-sized cities and towns that have absorbed the majority of rural surplus labour. Nevertheless, 37 per cent of the urban population in China (as in Indonesia) lives in slum-like habitations (Davis 2006, pp. 7, 23–4). More than half of the migrant workers in Shenzhen, Beijing and Shanghai live in high-density 'urban villages' (*chengzhongcun*) with poor-quality housing, limited infrastructure, and poor safety and hygiene (China Labor Bulletin 2008).

As Polanyi (2001, p. 165) recognized in the ruins of the world created by Western liberal civilization, 'life in a cultural void is no life at all'. The disintegration of the cultural environment – that is to say, the disintegration of the relationship between the land and its people through environmental degradation of land and water as well as the alienation from the land through extensive land sales that provide much of the revenues of local governments – can only intensify the disenchantment with farmland-based livelihoods. How may the Communist Party rejuvenate life in the countryside through initiatives that restore the integrity of habitation in farmlands and women's labour in farm households so as to 'nourish the people' – and in turn be nourished by the immense social and cultural productivity of the people – and thereby sustain a long-run *project* of what Arrighi (2007) calls 'accumulation *without* dispossession'? Over the past 30 years the Communist Party and the people of China have constructively offered their resourcefulness and ingenuity to overcome different kinds of obstacles to the PRC's participation in the international community of nations. The courage, resilience and determination of Chinese people was everywhere in evidence in the aftermath of the 2008 earthquake in Sichuan province. The same determination drove the nation to host one of the most successful (and expensive) Olympics in August of the same year. As Naughton (2007, p. 11) observes, 'the Chinese political system has a striking ability to target a few critical issues and mobilize talent and resources to address these issues when it is absolutely necessary to do so. This provides the system with a degree of resilience that is one of its key strengths'.

I have claimed that the few critical issues or challenges facing the nation include the widening social and economic inequalities that have occurred in spite of sustained economic growth and enormous accumulations of foreign exchange reserves. Above all, there is the critical issue of popular social unrest of subaltern groups excluded from the benefits of growing economic prosperity. If Perry and Selden (2004, p. 19) are correct, then the long history of popular social unrest in China suggests that 'it could ... be managed by adept state leaders in such a way as to under*pin*, rather than under*mine*, their rule'. It remains to be seen how the Communist Party will rise to meet these challenges in the new millennium.

Notes

1. The Chinese term *liudong renkou* (floating population) is often used to differentiate it from *qianyi* (migration). The former applies to the population (*renkou*) that has *not* been granted permanent, official household registration (*hukou*) in the place where they are currently residing, while the latter applies only to those whose *hukou* has changed. 'Permanent migrants' who have altered their *hukou* are sometimes distinguished from 'temporary migrants' who have not. The 1990 Census tabulated only 'long-term temporary migrants', that is, those who have remained more than a year within their current place of residence, but not 'short-term temporary migrants' (present in a given city for less than a year). See van Luyn (2008, p. 1) and Solinger (1999, p. 15; p. 295n). At the same time the floating population is also a socially constructed category (Li 2001, p. 23).
2. See Global Commission on International Migration (2005, p. 84). Overseas Chinese currently number 35 million worldwide.
3. Solinger (1999, p. 161) notes some 200 scattered rural uprisings from 1992 to 1993.
4. Deindustrialization took place in Hong Kong between 1985 and 1995 (the industrial labour force declined from 0.93 million to 0.386 million); in Taiwan it took place between 1987 and 1995 (the manufacturing labour force declined to 2.4 million in 1995 after reaching a peak at 2.8 million in 1987). See Naughton (1997, pp. 12–13). To explain the massive relocation of Hong Kong's manufacturing operations into Guangdong, Lee (1998, p. 47) points to a combination of labour shortages, the size structure of the manufacturing sector, the non-interventionism of the colonial state and the underdevelopment of trade unionism in Hong Kong. Wage differentials between Hong Kong and Shenzhen are revealing: in 1989, wages in Shenzhen were one-seventh those of Hong Kong and the price of land was one-eighth that of Hong Kong (Selden 1997, pp. 328–9). In 1993, the basic wage for an assembly worker in Shenzhen was 6.3 yuan per day (Lee 1998, p. 55).
5. In the early 1990s, close to 75 per cent of realized FDI in Guangdong came from Hong Kong because of the PRC's preferential policies (Solinger 1999, p. 305n); and in 1985 the Pearl River Delta's designation as an open economic zone initiated 'a new round of interdependent development' between Hong Kong and Guangdong (Lee 1998, p. 4).

6
Paradigm Shift in India: Analysing the Impact of Liberalization and Globalization[1]

Anand Kumar

India is regarded as an emerging economic power and is one of the fastest growing countries in the world. Only China has growth faster than India in the last 20 years [...] It is important to bear in mind that despite some positive movements like more openness in trade or investment in the 1990s, India is today one of the most insulated among the large economies of the world. It is nowhere near integrating with the world, or being 'absorbed' by foreign powers [...] India's share of world trade is only one per cent whereas that of China is six times as large. Similarly, annual foreign investment in China by overseas companies is one hundred times larger than their investment in India.

Bimal Jalan in The Future of India (2005), pp. 200–1

India is a nation on the move. I am confident that our time has come.

Dr Manmohan Singh, Prime Minister of India (2007a)

The macro overview and other analysis show that the [Indian] economy is witnessing rapid growth for the fourth year in succession, but the fast growing sector perhaps touches the lives of only a small part of the work force and most of the population is left out of this growth process. The stock market is also aggravating the disparities.

Alternative Economic Survey (2007), p. xvi

The question however is the sustainability and the wider reach of economic growth from the point of view of the desired level of social development. To what extent is the high economic development compatible with unsatisfactory social development?

Social Watch India (2007), p. 15

It is true that globalization has multiple causes and is contributing to significant changes in the modern world-system. Many processes of globalization are interrelated and have been found to be producing contradictory effects in the context of countries of the South. For example, it is well known that globalization has created a comfortable situation in the field of foreign direct investment as well as the inflow of foreign capital in India, creating financial flexibility and control over fiscal crises. But at the same time finance capital uses globalization to escape the controls organized around the imperatives of nation-building. In the field of governance globalization is creating the opportunity for a regional network of nation states which reduces the problem of national security-related conflicts in a given region. But there are doubts about the impact of globalization upon the sovereignty of individual nation states as the modern world system is found to be drifting towards a 'unilateralism' of the dominant countries such as the US and China. It is clear that nation states are going to be challenged by new social actors like transnational corporations in their quest for consolidation of power in territorial and population terms. There is new opportunity for assertion by sub-national groups against existing nation states with help from the network of transnational diaspora and global social movements organized around issues of human rights. The pressure for opening borders for facilitating global flows is another common concern among major nation states in the context of politics of globalization.[2]

If globalization can be understood as the process of shrinking of time and space beyond the nation state, then liberalization can be recognized as the process of pushing forward the market forces and rolling back the state from its role in the economic management of a given country (Gray 1998). According to political observers, globalization poses serious challenges to the sovereignty of nation states, which have been evolving as the dominant system in the modern world since the Treaty of Westphalia in 1648 (Krasner 1995). Globalization has been interpreted as the shrinking of the planet in such a way that there has been a continuous decline in the significance of nation states in Europe in favour of regionalization, in the shape of the European Union. This process of regionalization has also taken root beyond Europe, but it has promoted anxiety among the postcolonial nation states of Asia and Africa.

India provides a significant example of such a response to the process of the declining significance of nation states as a consequence of globalization. At the same time, liberalization has provoked a positive response from policymakers in India. To quote Prime Minister Dr Manmohan Singh:

> The economic reforms we initiated in the 1980s and took up with greater vigour in the 1990s helped push this growth rate to an average close to 6 per cent over the last two decades of the last century. It is important to appreciate that this acceleration of growth is not a flash in the pan. There has been an increase in our gross investment and savings rate, particularly in the last three years. I believe that India's growth process is based not only on the expansion of the home market, but also largely on the rise of domestic enterprise. The economic reforms of 1991 unleashed a new era of entrepreneurial growth in India (Singh 2007a).

Even the critics of liberalization find no difficulty in agreeing that in India there was an average 8.6 per cent rate of growth in gross domestic product (GDP) between 2004 and 2007, which made India the second-fastest-growing economy in the world. It was accompanied by a remarkable improvement in the indices relating to the country's external sector. For example, in the year 2006–7 foreign direct investment (FDI) was $16.4 billion, inflows from foreign institutional investors stood at $9.18 billion, while external commercial borrowing by 812 companies totalled $20.24 billion and foreign exchange reserves were over $225 billion. With imports constituting about one-fifth of Indian GDP, clearly the expansion of GDP in India translates into a major market for multinational corporations (MNCs). It is obvious that India has won the confidence of international investment communities.

The problem with all these successful liberalizing reforms is that they constitute a narrow corporate-sector-based expansion of the economy, while marginalizing agriculture and the informal sector (Palat, Chapter 2 in this volume). It is argued that the inverse relationship between the movement in shares of different sectors in output on the one hand and the workforce on the other has given rise to structural regression. This is a major indicator of a structural and socioeconomic imbalance with critical adverse regional implications (Alternative Economic Survey 2007, p. 4). It is obvious that the present wave of liberalization and globalization has made a deep impact on India since 1990–1. India has moved away from economic strategies based on self-reliance-oriented planning to the liberalization, privatization and globalization (LPG) syndrome, which has created a thrust towards market-mediated economic direction. On the one hand, the Indian engagement with (and the Chinese participation in) globalization has created stability and positive results in the context of poverty levels and social inequalities. On the other hand, there has been a consistent improvement in India's global rank and India has avoided any major economic crisis. Thus, there is a significant relationship between India and liberalization and globalization (World Bank 2006).

This paper aims to underline the paradoxes of this paradigm shift. It argues that the processes of liberalization and globalization have to be understood with reference to two sets of questions, which are presented from two opposite directions. Optimists talk about the problem of perpetuation of structural bottlenecks – energy, employment, education and environment. New tariff rules are creating a decline in the financial capacity of the state to continue its social commitments to the underprivileged sections of the society. It has been argued that the declining role of the state has resulted in discontent in spite of a rise in foreign currency reserves and export performance. A number of serious questions have been asked about the orientation of the better-off sections of society, particularly the business community, towards wider social responsibilities. It has been pointed out that unless affluent sections eschew conspicuous consumption and care for the less privileged through charity there may be a deepening of distress and the polity may become anarchic. Critics have raised the issues of growing maldevelopment causing a pampering of corporates and a marginalization of agriculturalists and the unorganized sector and the deepening of social disparities and divides due to the uneven impact of growth. They assert that a very large number of Indian people are found to be 'working poor'; at least 836 million Indians live on less than Rs. 20 or a half dollar a day each, according to the report of an Indian government committee enquiring into conditions of work and livelihoods in the unorganized sector. This group points to the problem of lack of investment in infrastructural development. Another official expert group has reported that there are 125 districts spread over 12 states of the Indian union which are affected by naxalism (Maoist political agitation) rooted in discontent among the poor and the landless; these regions are also known as the 'red corridor' which has been growing since the adoption of LPG policies in 1991–2. The experts point out that India's strong growth has done little to improve conditions among the landless and poor in these areas.

The complaints of the optimists

The Indian experience of globalization has gone through three phases in the last two decades: a crisis in foreign currency reserves (1990–6); the enchantment of liberalization (1996–2003); and a quest for liberalization 'with a human face' (2004 onwards). The present phase is marked by cautious optimism due to a number of paradoxical conditions. For example, the process of liberalization has created consistent growth rates of around 7 per cent over the past several years. But it is mostly 'jobless growth'. Similarly, while there has been enlargement of the service sector accompanied by the expansion of information and communication technology (the 'ICT revolution'), there has also been a growing crisis in the agricultural sector due to negative growth rates: the latter has caused a wave of suicides among farmers as well as widespread rural unrest. The twin challenges of poverty and regional disparity are becoming more and more complex for the proponents of the LPG approach. It is true that India has been successful in avoiding the recurrence of financial crisis. It is widely recognized as a country that has all the basics correct and strong, as well as an increasing flow of foreign investment and a consequent rise in the number of 'gainers'. But the 'rolling back of the state', commercialization of education and health, rising prices of the basic necessities and lack of growth in employment have created a much larger number of 'losers'. Thus, there is an 'anti-poor' image of globalization in India, which has made it an issue of nationwide debate between 40 million gainers and 400 million losers.

Energy is a major cause of concern for the promoters of the LPG paradigm. From a nuclear deal with the US to gas-pipeline cooperation with Iran and Pakistan, a number of major initiatives are in the making to create some hope for energy security. The energy scenario in India is marked by urban-centric energy policies where 80 per cent of the commercial energy is used by the 30 per cent of the population which is urban. The 70 per cent of the population living in rural areas and dependent upon agriculture, animal husbandry, handicrafts and the like is largely dependent on non-commercial sources of energy. Electricity generation has grown from 4.2 billion kWh in 1947 to 600 billion kWh in 2003–4 through a combination of thermal (71 per cent), hydro (25 per cent) and nuclear (2.7 per cent) systems. But there is still a shortage in capacity of at least 10,000 MW causing an energy deficit of 40,000 million units. The problem of energy deficit is further compounded by the dependence on oil resources, as 70 per cent of the needs are met by imports. This number is expected to grow up to 85 per cent by 2012. The oil import bill for India in 2003–4 was $20.4 billion. At the same time, investments of $8 trillion are planned to generate an additional capacity of 100,000 MW by 2012. In terms of energy potential in the country, it is estimated that there is a potential of 1700 MW from urban and industrial waste, 4500 MW from wind power, 15,000 MW from small hydro units and 10,500 MW from biomass. The employment situation is becoming more and more disappointing. It has created a demand for urgent steps to make the liberalization–globalization process inclusive and sustainable in social terms. It has been noted that globalization has created jobless growth because the acceleration in GDP growth in the 'reform' period has not been accompanied by a commensurate expansion in employment, particularly in the organized sector. The share of organized-sector employment in the total employment of the country is very small (only 7 per cent), so even if the growth in GDP increases further, there is little possibility of a significant increase in the share of the formal sector as far as employment is concerned. The bulk of economic activity (93 per cent) takes place in the unorganized sector. In fact, the agricultural sector has almost zero employment elasticity because there was no growth of employment in this sector during this period. There has been some increase in the share of employment in construction, trade and transport. But it is small. The growth in unemployment during recent years was almost three times (3 per cent per annum) the growth of total employment (1.03 per cent during the same period). The emerging labour market offers scope for employment and income to those with skills, often with more than one skill. Unfortunately, the educational and skill levels of a large proportion of the Indian labour force are quite low. According to a national survey of 1993–4, only 20 per cent of the Indian population has any marketable skills, even among the urban labour force. So, there is a need for strengthening the unorganized sector – both absolutely and relatively – if the people in general and youth in particular are to be provided with adequate and secure means of livelihood (Ramchandran and Arora 2004, pp. 39–49).

After the defeat of the National Democratic Alliance government in the national elections of 2004, the political implications of growing unemployment were recognized by the political elite. The new coalition government has gone ahead with a national minimum employment guarantee programme for the rural workforce, as there had been a dangerous drift towards a 'radicalization of poor youth' due to the labour-market crisis. The issue of employment is now being addressed by a proactive state, as there was little hope remaining in the market mechanism for a solution. The launching of the rural employment guarantee scheme in 2006 in 200 of the most needy districts was the first step in this direction. It promises 100 days of work per annum on minimum wages for one person from each household. It has now been enlarged to cover all rural areas of India. The failure of the LPG model in the context of mass employment generation in agriculture and allied activities has worried even the prophets of liberalization.

The educational bottleneck in today's India is related to the large backlog in the provision of basic education for the children of the economically weaker sectors, including women, the scheduled castes, the scheduled tribes and Muslims. India had a literacy level of just 18.3 per cent in 1951; this percentage had increased to 65.2 per cent in 2001, according to the census of that year. But there is a large inter-state variation in literacy rates; over 90 per cent in Kerala are literate but less than 50 per cent are in Bihar, Orissa, Jharkhand and Chattisgarh. In recent years, this issue has been addressed through a nationwide drive for 'education for all', raising the gross enrolment ratio in classes 1–5 to 94.9 per cent in 1999–2000. Similarly, higher education has been expanding rapidly, with more than 300 universities and 15,000 colleges in existence by the end of the last century. But in global terms, only 7.2 per cent of youth in the 17–24 age group have the opportunity for higher education in India, compared to 80 per cent in the US and Canada, and 52 per cent in the UK (Pathak 2005). Moreover, Japan has 684 universities for a population of 127 million, the US has 2,364 universities for a population of 270 million, Germany has 330 universities for 80 million and the UK 335 degree-awarding institutions for 60 million inhabitants. According to the Knowledge Commission of India, the country needs at least 1,500 good universities and 50,000 well-equipped colleges to be able to meet the challenge of becoming a global player in the modern world-system. This expansion of opportunities may be achieved by promoting public–private participation. At the moment, the education system in India is facing a resource crunch in the public sector and lack of quality in most of the private institutions.

The environmental crisis of India has reached dangerous levels in several towns and districts. Unplanned urbanization, concentrated industrialization, deforestation, chaotic transportation, population pressure and lack of infrastructure are identified as the major factors which together have led to a serious environmental crisis. What are the indicators of this crisis? India is the sixth-largest and fastest-growing producer of greenhouse gases. Three of the largest Indian cities are among the 10 most polluted cities of the world. There is a loss of 10 per cent of national income due to environmental degradation. There has been a decline of two-thirds in the availability of fresh water in recent decades. Fifty one per cent of country's cultivable soil (80 million hectares) is facing soil degradation. There is only 21 per cent forest coverage, half of which is low-density or degraded forest. In rural areas, due to over-exploitation of underground water, there has been a rapid decline in the ground-water level. There has been a six-fold increase in sewage generation from urban centres in the past 50 years and a seven-fold increase in municipal solid waste without a proper system of collection, transport and disposal.

This situation has led to the growth of a vibrant environment movement in India in the past few decades, which is supported by the judiciary, the media and scientific communities in various ways. A series of pro-environment laws have come into existence, and there has been a growth in the 'environmental market' of 10 to 12 per cent annually. The new policies have been consistently supported by a group of eminent economists since 1991–2 under the leadership of Dr Manmohan Singh. Dr Singh optimistically piloted the process of 'structural adjustment' in this period, first as the finance minister (1992–7) and now as Prime Minister (since 2004). But the realities on the ground have forced even him to alert the better-off sections, particularly 'corporate India', to become more aware of their social responsibilities. A social charter for the business community has underlined 10 conditions to be followed by the business class to fulfil its obligations towards the new partnership for inclusive growth and for a more humane and just society:

1. Care for workers' welfare
2. Community-needs fulfilment
3. Co-active role for employment of the less privileged, particularly SC/ST/OBCs/Minorities and Women
4. Preventing excessive salaries to senior executives and discouraging conspicuous consumption
5. Investment in people and their skills
6. Avoiding non-competitive behaviour
7. Environment-friendly technology
8. Promoting innovation and enterprise within each firm and outside
9. Fighting corruption at all levels
10. Promoting socially responsible media and advertising.

The presentation of the social charter to the gainers from globalization in India was concluded with a call to the better-off to come forward to be 'role models of poverty, moderation and charity'. It also expects that corporate India will fulfil its obligations towards 'the new partnership'. Therefore there seems to be hope for the less privileged and for 'the making of a more humane and just society' in the near future via a liberalization-privatization-globalization approach (Singh 2007b).

This call to the gainers from globalization has been further underlined by another economist-cum-policymaker, Professor Joseph Stiglitz. By his assessment, globalization has played an important role in strengthening the Indian economy since 1991–2. The impact of the reforms can be seen in the progress of the IT industry, the information technology revolution and a growing interest of the rest of the world in Indian markets and commodities. But India must be warned about the need to strengthen spending on its people's common needs, including education, health and poverty relief. India has to be careful about the increasing threat to the environment caused by resource-intensive growth. In the case of water, India is living on borrowed time as the water table is falling in large parts of the country. In short India has to avoid economic melt-down, political and social instability, and environmental crisis. India has a strong asset in democracy but the failure to invest adequately in education and health poses risks for the future.[3]

The objections of the critics

Most of the objections coming from the critics of the LPG paradigm point to the problems of the narrow social base and the weakening relationship between democracy, development and governance. It is argued that without sufficient deepening of the roots of the Indian parliamentary system and strengthening of economic stakeholding among the masses, India will become merely a partner in the corporate strategies of market-led globalization. This may cause a crisis of legitimacy for the state and may give rise to protests and violent social unrest. The mismatch between the political environment on the one hand and the socioeconomic on the other has proved to be the main challenge to making Indian democracy meaningful and participatory (Social Watch 2007, pp. 61–95). Corruption in high places and criminal behaviour in politics have created a crisis of confidence in democratic politics (Das 2006).

On the other hand, the policy orientation since early 1990s has increased the vulnerability of the poor, the weaker social sectors and the more backward regions. The country is facing the challenge of 'failed development' among large pockets of the population. Growth performance in the 1990s has been impressive in aggregate terms, but has also created a paradoxical impact due to the unevenness of growth, creating new disparities and deepening old imbalances. The case of agricultural decline has been one of the most depressing aspects of the total picture.

Similarly, commercialization of education and health services have contributed towards the making of a 'new poor' and more chronic poverty in the past decade. India's performance in the field of health services is marked by intra-state differences and income-based variations. The disparities are also due to caste and gender inequalities.

The critics point out that 'the market has failed' in promoting the welfare of the masses but has succeeded in rapidly increasing the wealth of corporates. According to the latest NSSO figures, 19.9 per cent of the rural population of India was found to spend less than Rs. 950 per month. In urban India, 83.6 per cent of the population spent less than Rs. 1,500 per month. In other words, around 700 million Indians are subject to low, inadequate and uncertain incomes and little access to basic public goods and services. On the other hand, the share of the corporate sector in the national income rose by 290 per cent between 2001–2 and 2006–7.

According to the Report of the National Commission for Enterprises in the Unorganized Sector (2006) an overwhelming 836 million people in India (77 per cent of the population) live on a per capita consumption of less than Rs. 20 a day; 88 per cent of the Scheduled Tribes and the Scheduled Castes, 80 per cent of the Other Backward Classes and 85 per cent of Muslims belonged to the category of 'poor and vulnerable' who earnt less than Rs. 20 a day in 2004–5. Landless households of small and marginal farmers account for 84 per cent of this proportion and also struggle under substantial and crippling debt. A total of 90 per cent of agricultural labourer households are landless or hold less than one hectare of land. The conditions in the non-agricultural sector suggest that 21 to 46 per cent of men and 57 to 83 per cent of women are employed as casual workers, who get less than minimum wages. Between 1993–4 and 2004–5 the middle class and the rich have grown in number from 162 million to 253 million, with the new rich class numbering 91 million. According to the report the LPG approach has benefited around 43 million among the extreme poor as their per capita consumption has gone up from Rs. 9 to Rs. 12 per day. In India a person is classified as absolutely poor if their per capita consumption is less than Rs. 9 per day. However, if per capita consumption is Rs. 13 a day, then the individual is above the poverty line (People's Democracy 2006).

These paradoxical consequences found reflection in a growth in discontent, unrest and extremism in different parts of India after the late 1990s. The Planning Commission of India published a report in 2008 about 'development challenges' to the country. It attempted the identification of processes and causes contributing to continued tensions and alienation in the areas of unrest and discontent, such as widespread displacement, foreign issues, unsecured tenancy and other forms of exploitation such as usury and land alienation. It is obvious that the widespread discontent plaguing the Indian polity has not exclusively been caused by the LPG paradigm. Most of the unrest is associated with issues of non-performance of the state machinery in the context of effective implementation of existing constitutional provisions, protection of civil rights and the prevention of atrocities against the weaker sections, particularly the Scheduled Castes and the Scheduled Tribes. At the same time there has been deepening of the hold of extremist movements in recent years.

It is to be noted that three new Acts have been created in response to the popular discontent among the underprivileged sections of the society in the LPG era, associated with the problems of grassroots democracy, rural employment and forest rights among the Scheduled Tribes. Similarly, there has been recognition of the problem of large-scale displacement caused by the promotion of LPG-based industrialization, and a solution has been offered through a national rehabilitation and resettlement policy (2007).

The expert committee found fault with the official approach towards the challenge from extremists in that it focused narrowly on the law-and-order aspects of naxalite activities. It recommended the deepening of democracy through the wider participation of people in developing strategies of development and in their implementation. It specifically asked for creative policies that bridge gaps between the state's interests and those of tribal communities. It concluded that there is widespread pessimism about the possibility of ensuring respect and dignity for the dalits, adivasis, women and the poor in general, because current laws are proving to be inadequate. The market forces that have been encouraged in recent years have left much to be desired in bringing about improvement the lives of these groups. To quote from the report:

> There is no denying that what goes in the name of 'naxalism' is to a large extent a product of collective failure to assure to different segments of society their basic entitlements under the Constitution and other protective legislation. There is also no denying that the nation is now caught in a vicious circle of violence and counter-violence [. . .] There is an urgent need to generate a will to ensure that every man, woman and child gets his/her legal rights and entitlements in order to make each one feel that he or she is an integral part of the Indian nation (Planning Commission 2008, p. 83).

Conclusion

The Indian experience of globalization has two levels of challenges – sociopolitical and structural. Sociopolitically, it has to democratically diffuse the polarization between the 'gainers' (40 million) and the 'losers' (400 million) in the population. Structurally, it has to become sustainable through solutions to the problems of energy deficit, unemployment, education and environmental degradation. Only after success is achieved at these two levels is there any chance of India becoming an autonomous global player in the modern world-system through pursuing its sustained paradigm shift to follow policies of liberalization, privatization and globalization.

Notes

1. I am grateful to Jan Nederveen Pieterse and Boike Rehbein for their useful suggestions on the first draft of this paper. I wish to thank my research scholar Mr. Ashish Kumar Das for his invaluable help in giving final shape to this paper.
2. Theorists of globalization have been led in this discussion by the writings of Anthony Giddens, David Harvey, Arjun Appadurai, Stuart Hall and Jan Scholte. A critique of the globalization processes has been brought together by the co-editors of the *Socialist Register* in Panitch et al. (2005).
3. India warning on globalization. http://news.bbc.co.uk/2/hi/south_asia/6195617.stm.

7

Hierarchical Integration: The Dollar Economy and the Rupee Economy[1]

Anirudh Krishna and Jan Nederveen Pieterse

Introduction

An early notion in development studies, raised by the Dutch economist J. H. Boeke, is the 'dual economy' thesis of a split between a traditional and modern sector. This idea was one of the starting points of modernization theory and was taken up by Arthur Lewis and other scholars.[2] The general implication was that development policy should focus on strengthening and expanding the modern part of the economy and the traditional sector would follow eventually. This was criticized in subsequent work. Dependency studies argued that rather than the economy being split, the modern sector was parasitical on the traditional sector and received subsidies in the form of cheap labour and agricultural goods from the traditional sector, so the two economies were interdependent. Moreover, since the 'traditional' sector served as a reserve army of labour, wage rates were kept low. In the 1970s modes-of-production debate economic anthropologists noted that multiple modes of production (such as subsistence agriculture, farming and colonial or neocolonial economies) often coexist in societies. This led to the question of the articulation of modes of production, in which the dominant mode of production sets the terms of exchange for the others (Foster-Carter 1978). Workers in the modern economy – such as urban migrants and seasonal labour – relied for part of their reproduction on agriculture in their villages, to fall back on in lean times, and on agricultural produce that was brought to the towns, while their families subsisted in the rural economy. Thus a major reason why the modern sector functioned as it did was that it received hidden subsidies from the traditional sector. The proletariat in the modern sector was a semi-proletariat with one foot in the rural economy.

These questions – we could call them questions of social cohesion and development – keep coming back in different guises and for different reasons, such as the relationship between the formal and the informal sector, and gender and the valuation of women's work.[3] Another recurrent theme is cultural diversity. World Bank studies (1998) argue that ethnically divided societies show lower rates of growth. According to Amy Chua (2003) globalization benefits 'market-dominant minorities' such as the Chinese in Southeast Asia, which increases ethnic divisions and spawns hatred and violence between ethnic groups. Both perspectives are static and, at best, partial. They generalize ethnic frictions, homogenize ethnic groups, uncritically recycle stereotypes and overlook *inter-ethnic* economies (Nederveen Pieterse 2004, 2007). Contemporary globalization is, of course, grafted onto and constantly reworks existing cleavages. As Western companies move production offshore to low-wage countries, they benefit from the subsidies that the formal sector receives from the informal sector. In India the rupee economy supports the dollar economy in many ways. The back-office services that move from the United States to India and other emerging economies are supported by low-wage services of the urban poor. China as the 'workshop of the world' relies on cheap labour from the countryside. As more land is devoted to manufacturing and special economic zones and to the work and recreation of the new middle classes, China and other Asian countries increasingly rely on imports of agricultural products and commodities from other developing countries. A case in point is Brazil's massive and growing exports of soybeans to China.

In all these instances, low-paid or unpaid labour from the informal sector and the countryside supports the flourishing of operations in the formal sector. 'Urban parasitism' has been a long-standing criticism of national development policies (Lipton 1977). A further implication is that cheap manufactured goods in western stores receive a double subsidy: from cheap labour in manufacturing (often in sweatshop conditions) and from the countryside in the exporting countries. Agriculture in these countries – while under increasing pressure of competition, input demands, and weak prices – supports workers in the formal economy and their families.

This chapter argues that this is an under-researched part of the emerging 21st-century international division of labour. The first section examines the dollar economy and the rupee economy in India, pointing out their inherent inequality. The second section goes on to discuss analytics that seek to come to grips with these relationships and suggests three possible perspectives: asymmetric inclusion, enlargement-and-containment, and hierarchical integration.

The dollar economy and the rupee economy

Large and growing distinctions in spending patterns become obvious when one travels from the capital city of New Delhi to Shishvi, a village in India with about 2,000 people, located 40km from the city of Udaipur in Rajasthan. A meal for four in a better restaurant in New Delhi will cost about the same as it would in New York or Amsterdam; expenditures of $70–80 per head are hardly unusual these days. In Shishvi, you would be hard put to spend sums of 70 *rupees* per head (approximately $1.44 at current exchange rates). Anywhere within 30km of this village, a sumptuous meal in a restaurant will cost much less than this amount. In the rupee economy of Shishvi, Rs. 70 provides for a feast. In the dollar economy functioning in (the up-market parts of) Delhi and Mumbai and Bangalore, Rs. 70 will not get you past the inevitable mustachioed gatekeeper.

Economic and social processes accompanying globalization have cleaved India into two separate yet interrelated economic spheres. In the sphere that is more directly connected to global economic flows, the appropriateness of incomes and (most) prices have begun to be assessed in dollar terms. In the second sphere, images of dollar-based lifestyles are still physically unavailable, except as blurry and intermittent black-and-white television signals. In the farms and the villages and little towns that are inhabited by more than 80 per cent of all Indians, the rupee economy prevails. A one-rupee coin still commands purchasing power in the rupee economy; its worth in the dollar economy is just a little more than two cents.[4]

A schoolteacher is one of the richest men in Shishvi. Making a monthly salary of about Rs. 5,000, and earning another Rs. 2,000 by giving private remedial tutorials, the schoolteacher has a relatively high disposable income. The small farmers and agricultural labourers who make up the bulk of village population have much less to spend, except immediately after harvest, but that is also when repayments of old debts come due. A steady monthly income of Rs. 7,000 (about $144) is enough to place the schoolteacher among the highest-spending people in Shishvi. He can use this amount to live comfortably for an entire month in the village – or he can blow it all on treating his wife to one fine meal in New Delhi.

Very few villagers make sightseeing trips into big towns. When they go into towns, villagers mostly do so as day labourers. All over Delhi and

Mumbai and Bangalore and other large towns of the dollar economy you can see the rude shacks of the poor, most of whom have come into the city from villages near and far. It is here – in the slums and tenements and on the streets of these big cities – that the dollar and the rupee economies meet, with the latter providing some critical support to the former.

Home to a reserve army of surplus labour, the rupee economy is rarely the canvas upon which pictures of economic growth get drawn. Few influential people worry much about sponsoring growth in the rupee economy. Growth is all about expanding further the rising dollar economy of India. The health of the stock market – in which less than 3 per cent of Indians have invested (George 2004) – gets equated in the Finance Minister's mind with the overall health of the national economy.[5] In popular media, too, accounts of economic growth are studded with stories about foreign investment in new airlines and hotels and advertisements from manufacturers of fashion garments and exotic watches. Very little is ever mentioned about goods and services purchased by rupee-economy people, and less still is said about the services most often sold by them, for it is in occupations of servitude that most rupee-economy people interact with the dollar economy.

Subservient and neglected, the rupee economy nevertheless provides a crucial basis upon which growth in the dollar economy is built. It is because the rupee economy continues to exist that the dollar economy of India remains internationally competitive. If the denizens of the rupee economy – the cooks, maids and gardeners, the construction labourers, messenger boys, lorry loaders, and so on – were to become suddenly unavailable to the dollar economy, or if they could only be hired on dollar-denominated terms, then the game, now taken for granted, would substantially be over. If software engineers in India had to pay their cooks and nannies, not 2,000 *rupees* but 2,000 (or even 500) *dollars*, then what they demand from their employers would tend to rise commensurately. As upward pressure gets put upon salaries in the dollar economy, it will no longer be possible to hire a qualified software engineer in India for one-quarter or one-half of the amounts paid to a similar worker in the West. And to the extent that these salary differentials matter – and by all accounts they matter a great deal – keeping them from becoming narrower is essential for preserving the health of the dollar economy in India.

The continued vigour of this dollar economy is premised upon two sets of earnings differentials. First, it requires that highly qualified technical manpower in India be hired for a fraction of what is paid in Western Europe, the US or Japan. Second, it requires that despite lower dollar earnings managers and engineers in India can still enjoy better lifestyles, as cheap human services are available from within the rupee economy. If either earning differential were to become smaller – if technically qualified manpower were to become more cheaply available abroad or if earning expectations in the rupee-economy were to be adjusted upward – the competitiveness of India's dollar economy would come under serious threat. The second of these threats can be held in abeyance as long as the rupee economy continues to serve as a source of cheap services.

In the present scenario the rupee economy sustains and keeps alive the dollar economy. Without the cheap labour and the cheap produce from villages, lifestyles in the dollar economy would become severely eroded. Restoring these lifestyles would require cutting into the international wage differentials that hold up an important basis of the dollar economy in India. For the continued health of the dollar economy it is imperative that things remain this way: the rupee economy must function in rupees while the dollar economy functions in dollars. Expectations in the rupee economy must not be allowed to creep upward, for if nannies, laundrymen and delivery boys start seeing visions of dollar lifestyles for themselves, then it will not be long before competitiveness gets eroded in the dollar economy.

In other words, for globalization to continue being of advantage to India's elites, it is important that its benefits be kept away from non-elites. Separation is required. Rather like gated communities, the outposts of the dollar economy fence themselves in. Dollar-economy people come and go easily through the gates. But rupee-economy people are mostly kept out; their entries are regulated on conditions that keep most subservient to dollar-economy people – or altogether out of dollar-economy domains.

By preventing all but a few rupee-economy inhabitants from making their way in the dollar economy, separation helps hold expectations low in the rupee economy. Few rupee-economy people have achieved high positions in the dollar economy, and young people today do not aspire to much more. In terms of a 'capacity to aspire', people in rural areas generally face a 'lack of opportunities... less easy archiving of alternative futures, and have a more brittle horizon of aspirations' (Appadurai 2004, p. 69).

Over the past 10 years, not one individual from Shishvi has travelled past the fence and risen high. Hardly any young adult here aspires to a high-paying position in the dollar economy. The highest position anyone from Shishvi has achieved to date is that of village schoolteacher.

Table 7.1 Highest positions achieved in 20 Rajasthan villages (1996–2006)

Accountant	2	Lineman	2
Clerk typist	4	*Panchayat* secretary	2
Doctor	1	Police constable	4
Driver	2	Messenger	2
Civil engineer	1	Schoolteacher	22
Land records assistant	3	Soldier (*Jawan*)	9
Lawyer	1	Software engineer	1

Source: Original data collected in 2006.

Young adults in Shishvi shape their career ambitions based upon the role models they know. Very limited achievement in the past has given birth to equally limited aspirations for the future. Shishvi is hardly unique in this respect. Table 7.1 provides data from a survey that Krishna and his colleagues conducted in 2006 in 20 villages selected at random from two districts, Ajmer and Udaipur, in Rajasthan, a state in the north of India. Focus groups in each village were asked to name the three highest positions – in any walk of life – that anyone from their village had achieved within the past 10 years. These highest positions are reproduced in Table 7.1. Over the ten years, hardly any of the more than 60,000 residents of these villages obtained a better-paying job. About 300 individuals in these villages graduated from high school during this ten-year period, yet only one was able to become a software professional, one other became a civil engineer, one became a medical doctor, and one is practising as a lawyer in the district courts. Others who were able to get jobs mostly joined government departments at very low levels, becoming clerk typists or linemen or messengers or land-records assistants, while many – most – who graduated from high school (and some who completed college) were unable to find any acceptable position. The highest-ranked occupations actually achieved by villagers in any significant numbers were those of schoolteacher and soldier in the army, firmly embedded within the rupee economy.

Globalization and new opportunities seem to have largely passed by educated youth in these villages. Hardly anyone has managed to cross the fence into high-paying dollar-economy positions. Table 7.2 provides similar information collected in the second half of 2006 in 20 villages of two districts, Dharwar and Mysore, in Karnataka, a state in the south of India, whose capital city, Bangalore, is an icon of globalization-led economic growth. While a slightly larger number of individuals have

Table 7.2   Highest positions achieved in 20 Karnataka villages (1996–2006)

Accountant	3	*Panchayat* secretary	2
Clerk typist	6	Police constable	11
Doctor	1	Messenger	2
Driver	2	Nursing assistant	1
Engineer	3	Schoolteacher	20
Land records assistant	3	Soldier (*Jawan*)	8
Lawyer	4	Veterinary assistant	2
Lineman	2		

Source: Original data collected in 2006.

obtained jobs in these villages compared to those of Rajasthan, the character of these jobs is similar across villages of both states. One doctor, three engineers, and four lawyers from among some 60,000 people – these are the highest achievements in the past 10 years from these 20 Karnataka villages. Collectively, they do not amount to any significant inroads into the dollar economy, particularly when one considers that most of these doctors, engineers and lawyers practise in large villages and nearby small towns, and few among them have any direct connection or regular transactions with the dollar economy.

The career aspirations that young people in these villages currently hold are similarly confined to positions within the rupee economy. Many do not know what dollar-economy positions exist, and those who do have no idea about how such positions are attained in practice. As one villager told us about his son, Dhruva, 'He is good at mathematics, and he wants to be an engineer, but no one in this village knows how an engineer gets made'. How – through passing what examinations, attending which classes, filling out what forms – does someone gain eligibility to get hired as a dollar-economy engineer? Hardly anyone in any Indian village could tell you with much certainty about the processes involved. Consequently, for lack of examples and lack of knowledge, aspirations remain low within the rupee economy. The fence (or, to change the metaphor slightly, the dyke) helps keep the tide low in the rupee economy.

We asked each of more than 1,000 young village respondents what they hoped to become, what careers they wished to follow and what positions they aspired to achieve after finishing their studies. We divided these reported career aspirations into two broad types: first, all those that could be – sometimes by stretching one's imagination – classified

Table 7.3 Percentage reporting different career aspirations

	Rajasthan	Karnataka
Dollar-economy positions		
Accountant	>1%	>1%
Business manager	>1%	>1%
Doctor	2%	2%
Engineer	3%	4%
Lawyer	2%	1%
Senior government official	3%	1%
Other well-paid positions	1%	2%
Rupee-economy positions		
Schoolteacher	43%	39%
Army recruit	13%	5%
Policeman	11%	12%
Other low-level government positions	15%	22%
Other low-paid private occupations	5%	11%

Note: 1,456 respondents aged between 14 and 22 years.

as dollar-economy positions; and second, all those that were firmly entrenched within the rupee economy. We took a rather generous view of the first type of positions including within it, for example, everyone aspiring to become an accountant, doctor, engineer, lawyer or business manager, regardless of what type of lawyer they hoped to become and regardless of what type of business they intended to manage, be it a small village grocery store or a Toyota franchise in a big city. Table 7.3 reports these results, which show that young villagers' career aspirations are limited in the extreme. A large majority believes that, despite studying hard, the most that he or she can become is a schoolteacher or a low-paid government employee. Very few villagers see any better prospects in store for themselves. The modal career aspiration is schoolteacher, with around 40 per cent of young adults in these villages aspiring to this career. Another large chunk of young people – 15 per cent in Rajasthan and 22 per cent in Karnataka – aspire to become low-level government employees, such as bus conductors, typists, messenger boys and so on. A third large chunk wishes to enlist as soldiers in the army or the police. Most of them know of nothing else that they could possibly become. Schoolteachers, low-level government employees, and soldiers are what they see in their everyday lives – few other occupations make their presence felt in villages – with the result that a total of 87 per cent of young villagers in Rajasthan and as many as 91 per cent in Karnataka aspire to these low-paying occupations. Their parents, interviewed separately, had a largely similar pattern of aspirations for their sons and daughters. Results from official national surveys in India suggest that these trends are not specific to these particular two states. The 61st Round of the National Sample Survey Organization's (NSSO) large-sample survey studies showed that employment growth in the organized sector, public and private combined, *decelerated and may actually have declined* during the 1990s, even as the economy was growing fast (indiabudget.nic.in/es2006-07/chapt2007/chap104.pdf). Commenting on these results, Chandrasekhar and Ghosh (2006) note that 'for urban male workers, total wage employment is now the lowest that it has been in at least two decades, driven by declines in both regular and casual paid work'. Aspirations in rural areas, already low, have hardly been raised higher as a result of these trends.

Experiences from the past, mostly consisting of low achievements confined within the rupee economy, along with expectations for the future, also similarly contained, combine to keep non-elites in proper order *vis-à-vis* the dollar economy. Very few among rupee-economy inhabitants have vaulted themselves into high-paying dollar-economy positions, and very few aspire – and fewer still plan and actively work to – make any such move for themselves in the future.

Studying the problem from the opposite end, by looking at new entrants into the dollar economy, a similar conclusion related to low permeability was supported. Krishna and Brihmadesam (2006) examined the social and educational backgrounds of a random sample of newly minted software engineers employed in Bangalore. They found that city residents brought up within dollar-economy households were 20 times more likely to find dollar-economy jobs compared to others of their age groups brought up in rupee-economy households.

The fence separating the dollar and rupee economies is surmounted only very rarely by people from the rupee economy; at the same time, the support provided by the rupee economy in the form of cheap services and cheap produce remains reasonably secure. The dollar economy can continue hiring sophisticated manpower at lower-than-international salaries; their cut-price dollars command enormous purchasing power in the stagnant and held-down rupee economy. A layered national economy is the result. The dollar economy – our metaphor for the more visibly globalized and expanding sectors, commanding the bulk of the newly created purchasing power – is at the top of this heap, but by all accounts it consists of no more than 10 per cent of all Indians and probably no more than only 4 or 5 per cent.[6] The rupee economy makes up the bottom, even though its peasants and labourers, small shop-keepers and service providers account for the vast bulk of the country's population.

The rupee economy includes nearly all of the rural sector (except the tiny portions involved in export horticulture and other such boutique activities); most of the urban informal sector; and the lower-paid positions in the urban formal sectors, such as messengers and drivers and others who perform mostly menial jobs. There are close links between these three sectors. Over nearly all of India, as a recent government report observes, 'the slowing down and stagnation of agricultural growth has adversely affected the income and employment of a vast majority of rural people' (GOI 2007, p. 13). As a result, young people from rural areas are increasingly forced to seek places within the urban economy, and those who are lucky enough to find such places mostly do so in the informal sector or in the fringes of the formal sector.

In between these two economies lies a thin gray zone where a 'black' economy operates, where politicians and government officials, formally paid in rupee-economy terms, find opportunities to skim rents off those seeking to make profits in the dollar economy. So long as their tenuous in-between positions are secure, these officials feel comfortable protecting and policing the wall of separation between the rupee and dollar economies. Benign neglect results in keeping the rupee economy stagnant while the dollar economy grows through the provision of policies and protections.

India's dollar economy functions in several ways: as a circuit in itself, as a sub-circuit of the transnational and American dollar economies, and through interventions in the transnational dollar economy by Indian multinationals such as Tata and Mittal. As the dollar economy is internally differentiated and ranked, so is the rupee economy. The dynamics of the rupee economy tend to be subsidiary to the dollar economy. The dollar economy sets the terms and parameters within which the rupee economy functions. This applies to the technologies and prices of agricultural inputs, such as seeds, pesticides, fertilizer and irrigation equipment; to infrastructure and the transport of agricultural products; and to agricultural prices in domestic and international markets.

There are marked regional differentiations in the rupee economy: major sources of variation include agricultural productivity, and the roles of state and local government and social organization among the peasantry. Thus agricultural yields in Punjab are higher than in Bihar, Madhya Pradesh, Rajasthan and Uttar Pradesh. State government functions better and civic social organizations are more developed in Kerala than in Orissa, and so forth. Nonetheless, several trends pertain generally. Over time, notably since the 'green revolution' and the introduction of high-yield seed varieties, agriculture has become more input- and capital-intensive. The increase in agricultural productivity has come with growing input costs, financial dependence on moneylenders and suppliers and a growing role for multinational agro-industries such as Monsanto and Cargill. These circumstances have contributed to deepening crises in many rural areas (Sainath 1996; Shiva and Jalees 2006), which over the past decade have manifested themselves in the form of farmer suicides, armed uprisings and the takeover by 'naxalite' (neo-left-revolutionary) forces of about one-third of all districts in India (Bandhyopadhyay 2006). Apart from a few areas at the heart of these armed uprisings, the rural sector is not insular or cut off, but is nearly everywhere a stepchild of policy. Education has barely made a dent in the rural labour market. The same applies to innovations such as providing information and communication technology through internet kiosks in villages (Nederveen Pieterse 2005).

Hierarchical integration

The contemporary upbeat globalization stories of a 'borderless world' (Ohmae 1992) or a 'flat world' (Friedman 2005) make similar claims to postwar modernization theory – only the mechanisms described have changed. The mechanisms used to be modernization, industrialization, nation-building and trickle-down, and now the rising tide that lifts all boats is liberalization and export-oriented growth. The message remains the same: gradually, eventually, the benefits of development will embrace all. However, our reading of the relations between the dollar economy and the rupee economy suggests that inequality is not incidental but is *built into* the current accumulation model; in addition the findings imply that as long as the growth model doesn't change, this inequality is likely to be sustained.

This parallels wider trends in contemporary globalization. Multi-speed economies have been common in segmented societies and developing economies and it is through multi-speed economies that some of the successes of globalization have been achieved. Thus it is true that contemporary globalization makes the world more interconnected, but it is equally true that this interconnected world is being segmented in new ways. Uneven development is reinvented and re-inscribed in accelerated globalization. These unequal economies are both old and new. Intermediaries such as trading minorities and immigrant economies that act as go-betweens between different economic zones go way back. Contemporary globalization reworks these patterns as it interlinks and re-divides the world.

Some of today's epidemics and risks arise from glitches in the interaction of multi-speed economies. Avian flu arises from poultry reared by the poor in China, in close physical proximity with animals, and spread through contact into wider food chains. Toxins found in pet food in the US in spring 2007 originated in cheap additives (melamine, ground into a powder and added as a filler to look like protein while keeping costs low) in canned pet food in Chinese factories.[7] Thus as commodity chains traverse diverse economic zones they are exposed to the differential profitability equations that they seek to harness. Cost-cutting pressure by American buyers and importers precipitates these shortcuts, such as using lead-based paint in toys made in China.

There are several approaches to these configurations. One of the bywords is *glocalization* as anthropologists and geographers discuss the relations between the local and the global. Rosenau (1997) refers to contemporary globalization as a process of '*fragmegration*', a combination of integration and fragmentation. An account that is gaining ground in international relations is *neo-medievalism*, or the re-emergence of 'overlapping jurisdictions and crisscrossing loyalties' (Winn 2004).

While these approaches indicate general trends they don't capture the unevenness of power that characterizes the new configurations. The dollar economy and the rupee economy are global-local articulated economies and also refer to overlapping jurisdictions, but more importantly, they are profoundly unequal. The classic thesis of *combined and uneven development* comes closer to capturing this; combined uneven development refers to its deployment as a factor in political economy. Doreen Massey's 'power geometry' (1993) also seeks to capture different power equations.

Jim Crow in the United States, the successor to slavery, was an instance of combined and uneven development. The south of the US continued a different political economy than the north, with low wages, low taxes, low services and no unions. In the course of the 1970s and 1980s, as companies moved to the Sunbelt, this became the American standard: Dixie capitalism first became the American model and has since been reproduced in other parts of the world through structural adjustment and neoliberal reforms (Nederveen Pieterse 2004). Thus combined and uneven development is built into existing neoliberalism. Dixie capitalism means the deployment of a powerless, rights-less workforce in modernized versions of layered and sequestered capitalism.

In Chicago, 26th Street or 'La Villita' (Little Village) mediates between the (US) dollar economy and the (Mexican) peso economy. A quarter of the enterprises on this high-traffic street are storefront banks that transfer remittances to Mexico and provide other financial services (Koval and Fidel 2006; Raijman 2001). Border economies such as the *Maquiladores* on the Mexico–US border and in the Caribbean, and factories on the border of Thailand and Burma, are premised on profiting from the conjuncture of low wage, low organization, rights-less labour and modern infrastructure and technology. Special economic zones follow similar logics. While free-trade zones rank as leading instances of border-crossing capitalism they are heavily guarded by security measures and their production facilities are under stringent labour discipline (Klein 2000). Free-trade zones represent free traffic of capital, yet restrict the movement of people precisely because they straddle development gaps. So as state borders fade for some forms of capital (finance, investment, offshore production), others come in their place, such as the well-guarded fences, actual or metaphoric, erected around special economic zones, permitting only regulated flows in either direction.

The grossly unequal distribution of opportunities in India is the dark side of 'Shining India'. Relations between the dollar economy and the rupee economy and between formal and informal sectors are in flux and opaque; they are not transparent, and hidden recesses and crevices in this relationship enable various intermediaries to prosper and flourish. This section explores three ways of capturing this general configuration: asymmetric inclusion, enlargement-and-containment, and hierarchical integration, each of which seeks to capture different nuances of the contemporary political economies of inequality.

Asymmetric inclusion rejects the notion of *exclusion* – long a fashionable trope in policy and academic studies. The idea is that if the population in question (backward area, minority or least developed country) would be *included* in the modern sector or in fast-lane capitalism, it would experience the benefits of economic growth. In effect this perspective is a spatialized version of trickle-down theory. What it overlooks is that these populations have been included *already*, are already within the reach of international financial regimes and national policy, but have been included on asymmetric terms. This asymmetry is not just a minor quirk but a constituent part built into the overall equation. This also applies at the macro level with the financial drain from poor countries to rich continues, even as the international financial institutions and the Millennium Development Goals proclaim assorted targets of poverty reduction (Stiglitz 2006).

An alternative perspective is *enlargement-and-containment*. The terms are borrowed from American foreign policy. Enlargement was the overarching theme of the Clinton administration foreign policy and containment refers to US foreign policy during the Cold War. This explicitly political terminology captures another dimension of combined and uneven development – the enlargement of the influence of the US, G-8 and NATO, of transnational regimes from the WTO, IMF and World Bank to multinational corporations, oil companies, banks and hedge funds. And, on the other hand, the containment of risks that emerge in the process – from ecological spillover, toxins and diseases, popular resistance, ethnic and religious conflicts to international crime and terrorism. Thus enlargement-and-containment concerns a two-way movement. Consider ethnic cleansing. Local ethnic conflict often occurs downstream of enlargement politics: it emerges after the end of the Cold War, follows the implementation of structural adjustment programmes (as in former Yugoslavia and Rwanda) or the momentum of European unification (as in the re-Balkanization of the Balkans).

The reactions to the attacks of 11 September 2001 represent a new round of enlargement-and-containment: the enlargement of American military presence and influence in the Middle East and Central Asia and containment of the security risks and ideological fallout from this projection of power. Analytics that seek to come to terms with enlargement-and-containment are the Copenhagen school of securitization, including the securitization of migration, and work on states of exception inspired by Giorgio Agamben and induced by security operations (Ong 2006). A counterpoint is the immigrant rights movement (Doty 2007).

Enlargement-and-containment refers to top-down processes of contemporary hegemony as operations of divide-and-rule. Thus as some external borders lose salience new internal frontiers emerge, carving up social space by reworking the existing boundaries of class and status. This integration-and-fragmentation of social space also occurs in advanced societies. Stratification takes many forms. Office buildings in world cities are occupied by day by high-income earners and by night by low-wage immigrant or minority cleaning and security personnel (Sassen 1998). In the United States the development of gated communities and the privatization of space and security stand in a structured relationship to the ghettos and the society of incarceration and the criminal-industrial complex (Wilson 2007). Urban riots in Britain and France are part of the field of integration-and-fragmentation. Riots in the urban ghettoes in the UK and the *crise de banlieues* in France contest the terms of inclusion.

The overall perspective that may diagnose these relations is *hierarchical integration*, in which integration refers to increasing border crossing and borderlessness and hierarchy involves the upkeep of old borders or boundaries and the institution of new ones (Nederveen Pieterse 2001, 2002). Thus societies and parts of societies the world over are both brought closer together *and* separated in new ways. As value chains lengthen and economic and political cooperation and regulation widen in tandem with different regimes of accumulation (as in production chains, structural adjustment programmes and free-trade agreements), the newly included renegotiate their status through reworking codes of class and cultural difference (such as ethnicity, religion and status signifiers) and redrawing boundaries in space (as in resource and niche conflicts). These dynamics unfold across economic, political and cultural levels and domains. That the world is becoming smaller *and* more stratified explains the phenomenon of lessening diversity across places and increasing variety within places (Storper 2001, p. 115).

It raises the question, integration into what? Expansion by means of the 'incorporation' of less developed regions is a fundamental modality of capitalism. According to world-system theory, the modern world-system incorporates peripheries into its operations. In this perspective what takes place is *incorporation*, rather than integration. It is an extension of Marx's notion of the incorporation of labour into the workings of capital. Surely this forms part of hierarchical integration. However, as a general perspective incorporation is too system-centric and West-centric; it overlooks countercurrents and flows that run sideways (such as East–South and South–South). In contrast, hierarchical integration refers to multiple crisscrossing hierarchies and stratification systems, in a layered set of processes. In this understanding, integration, in contrast to incorporation, is not just vertical but also horizontal. Hierarchies arise not just between North and South but also between East and South, within the South, and so forth.

Studies in advanced countries document segmented labour markets with different wage rates and work conditions for minorities and immigrants (for example, Bonacich and Applebaum 2000). Accompanying notions are segmented assimilation (Portes et al. 1999) and flexible acculturation (Nederveen Pieterse 2007). We can view India's dollar economy and rupee economy as overseas extensions of segmented labour markets. It follows that not just the dollar economy but also the rupee economy should be included in mapping global value chains. The rupee economy affects the price of the outputs of India and other low-wage economies and price is obviously a variable in global value chains, particularly in buyer-driven chains (see Gereffi and Korzeniewicz 1994; Gereffi et al. 2005). The informal economy figures in treatments of subcontracting and of twilight economies such as sex tourism (Clancy 2002) and illegal trades such as the global cocaine commodity chain (Schaeffer 1997). The present research suggests that the informal economy should be methodically included in analyses of international competitiveness and global value chains.

Hierarchical integration is not merely a political economy but also a cultural politics. Marketing messages reach all but only call those who can afford the gate fee. Ads for credit cards, business-class travel, five star hotels, luxury watches and fashions, cruises, rental cars and so on all convey an aura of unrestricted mobility while at the same time establishing purchasing power thresholds. Since hierarchical integration combines bifurcating economies in which luxury consumption and bargain-basement consumption are growing side by side, it builds bridges while it erects barriers. The polarization between the hyper-rich and the growing number of the poor prompts a new private security industry. Besides the 'paper walls' that surround the advanced countries, photo IDs, surveillance cameras and security personnel erect other thresholds. Surveillance technologies such as database marketing and data use in credit and insurance implement *social sorting* (Lyon 2003, 2007). In urban studies this has given rise to the intriguing theme of *medieval modernity* (Alsayyad and Roy 2006).

Some frontiers are intangible and consist of subtle codes such as dress codes in restaurants and clubs, membership rules in country clubs, housing estates and condominiums, and new codes in relation to gender difference (Ainley 1998). They extend to politics of looks (lookism) and body politics of weight-watching (matching anorexic fashion styles), plastic surgery and cosmetics. At one end of the spectrum is the cultivation of bodies for libidinal display, as in California body culture, and at the other are the hunger, weakness, exhaustion and sickness that beset the bodies of the poor for whom strength and health are basic tools of survival. 'For many poor people, the body is their main asset. For some, it is the only asset they have' (Narayan et al. 2000, p. 95). And this asset often turns into a liability because of illnesses and ever more expensive cures that have worked cumulatively to drive millions into poverty (Krishna 2005, 2006).

Widespread, from South Asia across the Middle East to the Caribbean (Thompson 1999), is a politics of complexion that values light complexion and 'European features'. A saying in Brazil is that 'money whitens'. Thus aesthetics, too, serves as a frontier ranging from physical features and looks to new totems of style, designer clothes and labels (Maffesoli 1988). Style 'profiling' (besides 'racial profiling') is part of the social sorting of surveillance and status society.

The new fault lines of globalization take various shapes. The salience and ease of border crossing vary across domains. It becomes more difficult as we move from capital to labour and from intangible (finance, cyberspace) to tangible assets (goods, investments). As some state borders lose importance (as in offshore tax havens, special economic zones, free-trade agreements and regional co-operation), others retain their force (such as those which straddle the boundary between economic or developmental zones such as South Africa and neighbouring countries, or straddle conflict areas such as Israel's borders) or new ones emerge. As some national borders lose importance (as in the European Union) external regional borders gain weight (as in 'Barbed Wire Europe'). As some external borders lose importance, internal frontiers gain importance, such as ethnic and religious differences and frontiers of class, status, consumption and style.

Conclusion

The description of contemporary globalization as an epoch of the breaking down of boundaries is an ideological posture rather than an empirical account. Understanding contemporary globalization calls for new border theories. This treatment finds that the dialectics of contemporary globalization takes the form of a patchwork of contradictory moves. We present three perspectives to analyze these dynamics. Asymmetric inclusion critiques the social exclusion approach. Enlargement-and-containment highlights the political genealogies of new divisions. Hierarchical integration is the overarching account of uneven globalization and refers to specific processes such as segmented labour markets as part of global value chains. Rather than uncritically praising globalization or condemning its results, it is essential to learn more about the *terms of integration* of different strata and segments in layered and sequestered capitalism. What explains the longevity and the revival of these asymmetries in some cases and their mutation and flux seen in other cases?

One hypothesis is that asymmetric trends are related to ethnic and cultural difference and political representation. In brief, as cultural heterogeneity rises, political representation falls. Research in the US indicates that as cultural diversity rises, support for public spending falls. 'About half the gap between Europe and the United States in public spending on social programs could be explained by America's more varied racial and ethnic mix' and much of the rest results from stronger left-wing parties in Europe (Alesina and Glaeser 2004, quoted in Porter 2007). In India cultural heterogeneity includes caste and communalism. By this reasoning, then, contemporary globalization benefits from straddling different economic and cultural zones because cultural heterogeneity weakens political representation. To be precise, what matters is not cultural or ethnic difference *per se* but how it is represented, coded, put into discourse. Thus, research in the US also indicates that 'ethnic diversity doesn't inevitably reduce spending on public goods. Rather, spending tends to fall when elected officials choose to run and govern on platforms that heighten racial and ethnic divisions' (Porter 2007).

After the chilling of the American housing market, the subprime mortgage lending crisis and the ensuing credit-confidence crisis in 2007, the dollar is not what it used to be. This also affects the relationship between the dollar economy and the rupee economy. The rupee has proved to be a steady currency and tourists are now asked to pay for entering tourist sites such as the Taj Mahal not in dollars but in rupees. Yet, since the dollar's decline in value occurs mainly in relation to the euro rather than Asian currencies, the overall equation of the dollar economy and the rupee economy remains intact.

An understanding of globalization that doesn't include the dark side of 'Shining India' is not complete. A proper understanding of globalization must include the rupee economy as one of the lowest rungs of global value chains. This includes the creativity and resilience of the rupee economy and the global poor. Without its lowest rungs the ladder of globalization would not stand up.

Notes

1. Original empirical results reported here were supported in part by a research grant awarded to Anirudh Krishna by Ford Foundation, New Delhi (grant number 1045-0527). The authors gratefully acknowledge the comments of referees of *Development and Change* on a previous version of this article.
2. For the large literature on economic dualism we refer to the comprehensive overview by Fields (2004).
3. For instance, the role of women's work as 'the underbelly of the tiger' in East Asian economies and as part of lean Asian welfare states (Truong 1999).

4. An in-between sphere can also be distinguished, made up of government employees and pensioners who live in large cities (more on this sphere later).
5. Soon after a rash of bomb attacks on commuter trains in India killed 200 people and injured thousands more, the Indian Finance Minister referred optimistically to price trends on the Bombay Stock Exchange, asserting that 'India's growth story is intact'. Indian and foreign newspapers reported this statement widely. See for instance, www.thehindubusinessline.com/bline/2006/07/13/stories/2006071304000900.htm.
6. For example, Krishna and Brihmadesam (2006) calculated a range of 4 to 7 per cent for the proportion of Indians who have made it as software engineers over the past 10 years.
7. In June 2007 China announced a new five-year food-safety plan.

8
Inequality, Culture and Globalization in Emerging Societies: Reflections on the Brazilian Case[1]

Joanildo A. Burity

Introduction

A key issue in the global debate is inequality. There is nothing new about the existence of it as a persisting feature of capitalism. Despite the historic compromise achieved after the Second World War that led to higher integration of workers into the social and economic orders of capitalist societies in Western Europe, the system fell short of promoting equality of conditions, beyond the formal legal status of all citizens in liberal democratic polities. In the so-called periphery of the capitalist world, inequality remained as the unbending rule of protracted processes of uneven and combined development which prompted sociologies of underdevelopment, marginality, dependency and so forth. The promise was that by accelerating the pace of economic growth and technological innovation, the peripheral countries would all attain the bright future of modernization. Despite all the criticism – both theoretical and practical – met with along the 1970s by such ideological representations of capitalism as a historic form able to produce widespread prosperity and social integration, the rise and global expansion of neoliberal discourse and policies reinforced the conventional association between the adoption of market economies and better opportunities for all.

From the mid-1990s a growing number of voices began to be heard that pointed towards the increase in inequalities worldwide as a result of the implementation of neoliberal and Third-Way policies. Data on the spread or intensification of inequalities over recent decades are simply breathtaking: it has increased rather than diminished (see Green 2008, pp. 2–6, 180–1, 186–90, 224; Ipea/IBGE 2004, pp. 14–21, 36–42; UNDP 2005). It has increased in several contexts even though extreme poverty has decreased since the 1990s. This means that the old story that more wealth and skin-deep social policies do not translate into less inequality holds true. This contrasts with all the alluring promises of a deeper interconnectedness among economies, societies and cultures for furthering wellbeing, freedom, choice and progress. Persistent inequality also flies in the face of hopes for the concrete possibility of the global economy to actually end poverty, thus highlighting the inevitable ethical and political intimations to seriously respond to the challenge.

The period mentioned above coincides with a process of emergence of new candidates to the select team of global capitalist players, attributed at first to economic performance – societies with huge and underexplored internal markets, abundant and cheap labour, a relatively sophisticated technological base, that were going through market reforms and taking advantage of the global scenario. Only slowly and unevenly some awareness developed as regards both the multidimensional character of globalization and the extent to which the new partners could not and would not reiterate the paradigm of modernization. Accordingly, assessments of perspectives opened up by global flows, despite attempts by hegemonic forces to round everything up under the spell of economic interests and dynamics, led to the diversification of trajectories, allowed for non-economic actors to also become active in the global debate and made more complex the relation between national and local contexts and global processes.

Thus, there is more to emergence than mere economic performance. What has emerged in the past two decades of frantic experimentation with the discourse[2] of globalization are social formations with particular histories and cultural identities. One feature of these, to keep to my opening *fil conducteur*, is the ingrained dimension of inequality that has historically characterized them. It has been deepened but not initiated with neoliberalism. And some signs already show that political and cultural change is essential to the task of reducing inequality at a significant pace. How can one make sense of persisting inequalities over the long-term process of integration to capitalism in these societies,[3] with short periods of reversal but hardly being able to recast the pattern in the long run? Is there a reverse process whereby the current outlook of emerging societies sheds light on the situation in advanced capitalist societies? Can there be any learning from the efforts taking place in such emerging societies to overcome the perverse connection of economic performance, technological advancement and persisting injustice? This chapter, and others in this book, asserts the need to frame the notion of emergence in terms that go beyond economic and geopolitical logics of explanation, the need to incorporate reflection on sociocultural tenets. It is not framed within a politico-institutional or an economic perspective, but insists that critical analysis cannot shy away from the political character of any process of social institution. This does not mean approaching the question of emergence in terms of 'power politics' or international geopolitics. However, it does imply that the political operates within every social dimension and cannot be removed from analysis with impunity.

There has been, to that effect, an ambiguous but extensive acknow-ledgement of the cultural dimension of these processes – not only in terms of cultural heritages and forms of experiencing and facing up to the challenge of inequality, but also in terms of increasingly resorting to culture as a remedy or strategic weapon against the effects of glob-alization *cum* growing inequality. This recourse to culture is ambiguous because it brings to the fore antagonistic demands for inclusion, justice and/or reparation from groups defined on the basis of cultural traits (eth-nicity, gender, age, religion, language, sexuality, territorial autonomy), while culture also becomes an object of hegemonic struggle as an instru-ment of more effective market strategies, or the management of conflicts and social disintegration (see Yúdice 2004).

So, the question of inequality is at once material and symbolic, eco-nomic and politico-cultural.[4] It calls for historical sensitivity (in other words, attention to particularities and trajectories, but also to contin-gency in how structural features have evolved into their present form) and for a global/local nexus. In the context of globalization, it is a question of *how different modes of articulation have varied as a function of local circumstances*. Through resistance, translation or failure, global capitalism has been altered as it is iterated.[5] And over the past decades, as a partial outcome of global trends, the trajectory of emerging soci-eties render all too explicit the contradictory and hardly predictable forms in which modernization, capitalism and globalization intermin-gle. Whether one speaks of China, India, Brazil, Mexico or South Africa, for instance, inequality is a prominent feature of their history, past and present, though with different characteristics. And perhaps, because globalization is not a one-way process, one can say that their story is fast becoming, retroactively, the story of the advanced societies of the North as they grapple with the combined effects of neoliberal or Third Way politics, increased non-Western immigration and the rise of right-wing or conservative-liberal ideologies.

I wish to argue in this article that the manifold patterns of globaliza-tion in relation to inequality can give rise *both to the emergence of economic powers (again) rooted on widespread or deep social inequalities, and to transversal forces – that cut across social domains (such as the economy, politics or cultural life), national borders, and social groups or classes – seeking to reinforce or to overturn those inequalities.* This requires a broader approach that encompasses various dimensions of social life that are crucial to understanding and acting upon inequality. Emerging countries such as those mentioned above experiment strong, sometimes lacerating, tensions between opening and closing themselves to external forces; modernizing and resisting the exclusionary dimensions of modernity; relinquishing collective commitments to welfare and tackling mounting violence; joining the discourses on macroeconomic stability and responding to abject poverty; bringing to light cultural diversity, protecting it from dissolving into consumer culture and checking prejudice and intolerance. They also seem to portray the kinds of social arrangement that globalization, as it is currently evolving, is likely to produce in most parts of the world – social and economic exclusion, ethnic clashes, racial prejudice and violence, alongside startling affluence, consumerism and technological sophistication – while also allowing for cross-border articulation of social movements and progressive organizations, the dissemination of imagery of resistance and new repertoires of action which may assist local dissenting groups.

Moreover, these societies' cultural formation increasingly accounts for significant variations they have displayed in the course of their becoming global players (or being perceived to do so), but also for some of the lasting aspects of subordination and oppression that have marked modernization processes both in advanced capitalism and in the emerging semi-periphery of the capitalist world. This calls for heightened attention to the processes whereby difference is asserted *vis-à-vis* the dominant side of globalization as well as to the movements which, across borders, and mobilizing various values, social identities and repertoires of action, voice the need for equality and justice to prevail within and among nations.

In order to pursue this line, I take the Brazilian case not only to illustrate the process, but to raise a claim that goes in two directions: 1) several of the current trends in the process of globalization are not entirely unheard-of in societies which have for a long time been part of the world created after the 16th-century colonial and the 19th-century imperialist expansions of Western European countries, the former episodes of globalization;[6] 2) intermediary societies, located in the semi-periphery of the capitalist world, can be privileged points to make sense of several of the new developments introduced by the intensification of the global trends. Confronted with the Euro-American-centric paradigm of modernization and advanced capitalism (see Lander 2005, pp. 21–53; Quijano 2005, pp. 227–78), emerging societies fall far behind the social levelling (welfare) enjoyed by the majority of citizens in those societies included in the paradigm. They seem to be too marked by particularism to qualify for the new position.

However, as Santos argues, for those countries showing an intermediary level of development, 'working out the calculus of hegemonic globalization is much more complex. To start with, there is at once some capacity to capitalize on the advantages and a reasonable vulnerability as regards the risks' (2002, p. 12). He mentions Ireland, Spain, Portugal and Greece in Europe, Mexico, Brazil, Chile and Argentina in South America, and adds, '[i]n the semi-peripheral countries, the conflicts and disjunctions provoked by the hegemonic globalization thus tend to be more intense and have more unpredictable effects' (ibid.).

Global/local dynamics and the place of culture

According to Santos (2002), in our transitional global system conflicts and the unequal exchanges that express and result from them criss-cross. Thus, questions affecting the relative position of nation states, questions relating to the appropriation or valuation of mercantile resources between the global capitalist class and the nationally based classes, and *questions regarding the recognition of the appropriation or valuation of non-mercantile resources such as ethnicity, identities, cultures, traditions, sense of belonging, imaginaries, rituals or literature* give light to composite, hybrid or dual conflicts. Among these questions, the last mentioned has manifested itself prominently for some time now. Whether evolving as a result of the global/local frictional logic leading to numerous forms of resistance, or being expressed through the dissemination of struggles for the recognition of subaltern identities, culture has become a catchword for the forms of politics that can redraw the boundaries of the political in our time. Thus, it is crucial for the analysis of the processes of globalization that one focuses on the *global/local dynamics* in order to capture such a cultural dimension. It has traditionally been through the metaphor of 'the local' that *culture* has been understood – whether academically, politically or in the eyes of tourists and businesspeople – and when talking about globalization many voices seem to point to a tension between global and local, while other voices celebrate the sheer diversity that global travels and media images disclose and bring near.

It can be easily shown that global and local are not irreconcilable poles. As several authors have already singled out, not only is every successful globalization *rooted* in a localism (Anglo-Saxon neoliberal discourse, for instance), but also globalization *presupposes* localization (that is, produces it elsewhere, through hierarchization or time-space compression) (Santos 2002, pp. 63–5; Burity 2001, pp. 156–73). The global metaphor or global concrete events (for example, the announcement of a new policy; the negotiation of financial support for projects or to tackle crises; or a global meeting promoted by the UN, or the World Economic or World Social Forums) work as *tertiums* between inside and outside, near and distant, one's own and alien, and so on,[7] thus articulating the two poles. The *tertium* does not require the end of local references, but reinscribes them on to a terrain in which they can no longer be defined in isolation or by mere appeal to territorial or politico-cultural closure. Therefore, globalization both forms and distorts, requires and resists the singularity of the local (as community or nation, municipality or region). In turn, this *tertium* de-territorializes and de-institutionalizes the stability of the frontier between those reference points, though in manners fraught with paradoxes and ambiguities.

However, if it is true that a clear implication of the operation of the *tertium* of globalization is that *the local counts*, we must supplement the *de-territorializing* emphasis, and perhaps the impression left by the argument so far, in order to give due consideration to *(re)territorializing* practices. A good case for this is made by Arturo Escobar (2005, pp. 133–68), whose *demarche* also leads back into the theme of culture that lies at the heart of the analysis proposed here (see Santos 2002, pp. 72–5; 2003). Escobar (2005, pp. 134–5) argues that the weakening of place in the discourses on globalization has brought serious consequences to our understanding of culture, knowledge, nature and the economy and that it is time to balance it.

Rather than essentializing the local as the decisive and unambiguous site of transformation, Escobar draws attention to the concrete social contexts in which the effects of globalization are *translated – but also reconstructed – into vernacular cultures*, and which also demand to be heard in their own terms. He also highlights the need to counter the view that the only form of relation to reality in global times is through de-territorialized identities – privileging travel, mobility, nomadism, dislocation and diaspora and overlooking the rootedness of the majority of the people everywhere in the world (even those who migrate to other countries). For him, place is 'a form of lived and rooted space', 'the location of a multiplicity of forms of cultural politics, that is, of the cultural becoming politics, as evidenced in the tropical forest social movements and other environmental movements' (2005, pp. 151–2).

Now, it is not hard to see how this move toward place, as an instance of the local, brings us close to notions of *culture and identity*. For many social groups, communities, cities, regions or even nations in the world affected by the spread and grip of globalization or global-talk, the transformations they have to negotiate or live with have a direct bearing on their forms of life and the way they perceive themselves and others. Global values and practices have often meant uprooting the local as a reference, weakening social bonds, introducing demands for which most people find themselves structurally incompetent or unable to meet, and draining in a perverse way their chances of sustainable living conditions.

On the other hand, global events or the effects of global flows in these contexts raise or prompt the awareness of cultural difference, thus imaginarily awakening, reinforcing, recreating or splitting particular identities, as well as giving rise to new ones. This is not just something that happens to local communities or social movements and organizations from the outside. It is in the frontier(s) drawn by the differentiation or antagonism prompted by the global/local 'encounter' that a sense of belonging, of particularity and of project emerges.[8]

There is, nonetheless, a second form in which culture – in between local and global – can also qualify what emerges in the global scenario as a force. It could be called the cultural rooting of capitalist development. Recognition of this goes back a long way and different theoretical perspectives have been brought to bear on this (see, for example, Amin 1989; King 1991; Wallerstein 1993; Putnam et al. 1993; Appadurai 1996; Robbins 2004; Eisenstadt 2002). As I see it, this is a route of dissemination (Derrida), running both toward disavowing the theory of reproduction (according to which capitalism spreads and repeats itself 'at its core' wherever it goes) and toward asserting the modern character of capitalism in the so-called periphery. Cultural determination of the form and content of capitalism is not, therefore, a particularism of the periphery, but is a defining trait of the phenomenon as a whole. The view according to which emerging societies' distinctive capitalist development is both a function and expression of their cultural specificity proves ethnocentric: globalization helps highlight the cultural rooting of Western capitalist societies as they encounter competition and resistance from other (subaltern) capitalist societies.

This form of expression of culture allows us to see in the historical process of capitalist development, and its hegemonic global configuration, both the element of dissemination and the element of cultural particularism – understood not as an idiosyncrasy but as the outcome of symbolic disputes for the definition of the real among social actors – whereby the former is 'translated' and reshaped. In the global juncture, when there are signs of new powers emerging as 'national' variants of global capitalism, this second form of cultural expression can be illuminating of trends that – following our point about the de-territorialization and de-institutionalization of the frontier between global and local – are in operation in the global scenario, in different ways. As well it helps to perceive the cultural dimension of exploitation, subordination and inequality that is often overlooked by analyses of globalization focused on economic dynamics. Culture, here, both illustrates how capitalism takes root and how its intimations are invariably negotiated by local elites or consumer publics and adapted to local mores, whether reinforcing asymmetries or contributing to dislocating them.

Let us now see, in the Brazilian case, how this double dimension of resistance and conformity in regard to the links between global and local operates.

Brazil: conservative, selective modernization and the naturalization of inequality

Brazil, as one in the list of emerging societies/economies/political powers, is a telling example of the meanderings of modernization in a postcolonial situation. Let us take a quick look at this by means of a cultural approach that highlights the ways in which modernity was historically constituted there. This will be done in two stages: first, by assessing in this section the way in which the legacy of slavery – and the enormous difficulty for modern Brazil to integrate its Afro-descendant population into the social, economic and political mainstream – qualifies a double feature of the process: elitism and social exclusion; and second, in the next section, by looking at public policy in order to see how contests for the definition of inclusion have, from the 1990s, involved both cultural demands and appeals to globalization.

A startling trait of this emerging society is the clear contrast between its economic complexity, cultural diversity and vexing social inequality. It is a clear case of the non-necessary correspondence between economic growth and sophistication and a fair share for the common citizens in their country's wealth. Brazil exhibits the kind of articulation that risks becoming the stable outcome of current forces driving globalization. In witness to how insane it is, as Jessé Souza argues,

> to imagine that economic growth can do now what it has failed to accomplish over 50 years. In all countries that homogenized their classes [...] – England, the United States, France – the driving force was not economic growth. In capitalist systems, growth generally produces more inequality. It has been religious, cultural, moral and political demands that extended the model of being bourgeois toward the lower classes (Souza and Pinheiro 2003).

I am not endorsing Beck's image of the 'Brazilianization' of the world, as if the whole story were about the Brazilian failure to promote social integration and pacify everyday life. I am rather making a point about the articulation of economic modernization with social inequality as a ubiquitous mark of hegemonic globalization as portrayed in the trajectory of Brazilian capitalism (see Nunes 2002, pp. 301–44).[9] As argued by Jessé Souza, a leading Brazilian social theorist, the decisions resulting in the particular form taken by the capitalist order in Brazil, particularly from the late 19th century, were not a surrender to a pre-modern personalistic and patrimonialistic Iberian tradition, but already an outcome of deep processes of modernization:

> ... the naturalization of social inequality in peripheral countries of recent modernization, such as Brazil, may be more adequately perceived as a consequence, not stemming from an alleged pre-modern and personalistic heritage, but precisely the opposite, that is, as resulting from an effective process of modernization of great proportions which increasingly takes over the country as from the early 19th century. In this sense, my argument implies that our inequality and its everyday naturalization is modern, for it binds the efficacy of modern values and institutions based on their successful import 'from outside in'. Thus, rather than being personalistic, it [such inequality, JAB] draws its effectiveness from the 'impersonalism' typical of modern values and institutions (Souza 2003, p. 17).

In that case, any application of the notion of 'Brazilianization' to the global context would have to do with the recognition of the modern and indeed contemporary character of inequality in these semi-peripheral capitalist societies. That would work more as a mirror than as a threat of a fallback into the pre-modern past.

The roots of Brazilian inequality have a long provenance. Let me step back to the last years of the Brazilian Empire, and start with the important political manifesto 'Abolitionism', written by Joaquim Nabuco in 1883 (Nabuco 2000 [1883]; see also Mello 2000). Nabuco is one of the first interpreters – and political actors – in Brazil to confer the theme of slavery a central place in his analysis of the country's historical formation and also of its social and political destiny (see Mello 1999; Carvalho 2000). There were very few of them in his own time and even in the next generation, when he is only matched by Gilberto Freyre, in the 1920s, though the latter drew out other conclusions, contributing to articulating the myth of racial democracy that became part of the 1930s state ideology. Souza comments that the importance of the institution of slavery in Brazil is strikingly overlooked by many interpretations of Brazil, focused as they have been on determining the conditions and hindrances for the transplantation of European capitalist and liberal democratic modernization. He comments:

> This aspect is symptomatic for, after all, that is the only institution that managed, in such a young nation, to last almost 400 years and disseminate, though under peculiar forms, to every region, encompassing the whole of a huge territory. It has been the interests organically linked to slavery that allowed for maintaining the unity of the vast Brazilian territory and it has also been slavery ... that determined even the mode of living peculiar to the Brazilian free person (Souza 2003, p. 103).

On the first pages of 'Abolitionism', Nabuco stresses that the abolition would be only the immediate task of the movement, whose much more demanding responsibility was to reverse the effects of over three centuries of slavery in Brazilian society (Nabuco 2000 [1883], p. 4). An indication of the long-term difficulties facing the movement was already given in the very attitude of the country's political elite in not tackling slavery. Though acknowledging its immorality and economic inefficiency, the elite did not promote the immediate extinction of slavery, rather announcing incremental legal measures (the first of which dated from 1850, 38 years before abolition!) which left the former nearly untouched (ibid., pp. 15–18, 51–6). Nabuco is explicit about the reach and depth of slavery in the making of society's ethos, in all areas:

> The same as with the word *abolitionism*, the word *slavery* is used in this book in its broad sense. The latter does not only mean the

relation of slave and master; it means much more: the sum of power, influence, capital and clientèle of all masters; feudalism, established in the hinterland; the dependency in which commerce, religion, poverty, industry, the Parliament, the Crown, the State, find themselves before the aggregate power of the aristocratic minority, in whose lodgings [*senzalas*] thousands of these human beings live, brutalized and morally mutilated by the very regime that subjects them; and last, the spirit, the vital principle which animates the institution as a whole, especially as it starts to fear the loss of the immemorial property rights it is entitled to, a spirit that has been throughout the history of slave-holding countries the cause of their backwardness and ruin (2000 [1883], p. 5).

Nabuco's greatest fortune was that, while writing in 19th-century England and drawing ethical inspiration from its abolitionist movement, he was not 'up to date' with the scientific racist theories of the time in continental Europe (Morton's, Lombroso's or Gobineau's, for instance), that explained and forecast the road to modernity as an intrinsic attribute of the white, Western culture – thus ruling out any possibility for a country of mixed race(s) to be capable of such a feat. This allowed him to give due appreciation to *the indissoluble link between the destiny of blacks and freedom for all* in Brazil. His straightforward Hegelianism emerges in his assertion that the identities of masters and slaves were mutually dependent:

The question in Brazil is not, like in the European colonies, that of a generous movement on behalf of men [*sic*] victim of unjust oppression in far-away shores. The black race is not for us an inferior race either, alien to communion or isolated from it, and whose wellbeing affects us in the same way as any indigenous tribe ill-treated by the European invaders. For us, the black race is an element of considerable national importance, strictly bounded by infinite organic relations to our constitution, an integral part of the Brazilian people. On the other hand, emancipation does not mean only to bring to an end the injustice of which the slave is a martyr, but it is also the simultaneous elimination of both opposing types, who are at bottom the same: the slave and the master (2000 [1883], p. 10).

Current indicators show Nabuco's fears and inclusionary views to be warranted. Official data from the Brazilian Monitoring Report of the Millennium Development Goals point out that between 1992 and 2002, the share of national income of the poorest 20 per cent rose from 3 per cent to 4.2 per cent. However, in the same period, their remoteness from the wealthy hardly changed: 'In 1992, the wealthiest 20% had 55.7% of the national income. In 1996, they had 55.8% and in 2002, 56.8%.' If one controls these figures by ethnic origin, the blacks stand out as the worst off: 'The distribution of these groups within the poorest 10%, on the one hand, and within the wealthiest 1%, on the other, shows that 86% of those in the most privileged class were white, while 65% of the poorest were blacks or mulattoes' (Ipea; IBGE 2004, pp. 15–16). In terms of education, '[y]oung whites aged 15 to 17 in secondary education have almost double the attendance of young blacks and mulattos. In higher education, this difference increases fourfold. And this same picture is found in all the regions in the country' (p. 26). From the income perspective

> even among those with 12 or more years of schooling, the white population had an hourly wage almost 40% higher than that of the black and mulatto population with the same schooling level. In addition to the discrimination that is expressed by the occupation of posts requiring similar schooling levels with lower remuneration, the explanation of this phenomenon is also related to the issue of occupational segmentation. Thus, being a woman and part of the black and mulatto population makes it harder to earn higher wages (p. 38).

The Brazilian dilemma, in this light, according to Jessé Souza, is not the permanence of residues of personalistic power within an evolving modern order. It is not a case for personalism, patrimonialism or the persistence of pre-modernity within the post-1889 Republican order – as many sociological interpretations insist. For him, the dilemma is *how the impersonal capitalist moral order, finally hegemonic in the 1930s, manages to constitute itself on the basis of a naturalization of inequality*. Having imposed the institutions of the modern world – state, market, individualism, impersonal institutional relations, competition, citizenship – as ready-made products, without also disseminating a moral understanding of social relations that both legitimated the limitation of the rulers' personal power and generalized a 'basic' human type as a general reference of social recognition and a condition for the full operation of the competitive order, the Brazilian modern capitalist order condemns to oblivion and exclusion millions of its citizens – particularly its Afro-descendents (see Souza 2003, 2007).

Since the early 1800s, a process of 'Europeanization' was set in course, inciting a special attraction toward anything British or French, rather than Portuguese, as Souza highlights, following the arrival of the royal family in Brazil, fleeing from Napoleon's armies. The process also ushered in women's visibility in the private realm (freeing them from total subjection and isolation), and the growing prestige of knowledge and individual talent. This process was virtually accomplished in the 1930s, with the adoption of Italian-inspired corporatism, the political inclusion of the middle classes and the (legal and political) incorporation of urban workers (see Souza 2003, pp. 137–48; Carvalho 1997; Vianna and Carvalho 2000). Meanwhile, associated with the image of inferior, non-European races by the creators of the republican order, blacks and the poor in general were abandoned to themselves, deemed less human than integrated citizens, irrespective of any deliberate feeling of rejection the latter might personally entertain against any of the wretched ones – which is how the contours of an impersonal order emerged!

So, the generalization of the non-recognition of the poor – particularly the blacks – as full human beings and full citizens is a distinctive mark of Brazilian specificity in relation to so-called advanced societies (see Souza 2003, pp. 170–80). Brazilian modernity was constructed by articulating external models (institutions and values) to the moral matrix of slavery. Given the social attitudes of indifference, disgust and intolerance (Christophe Dejours's 'banalization of injustice') that have proliferated in many countries where the combined effects of neoliberalism and globalization have bedded in and given the growing number of people counting for nothing in the new economic order, one can argue that such a trait loses its particularism in present-day global contexts and articulates a sombre warning as regards the combination of capitalism and naturalized inequalities.

Some indicators of mounting inequality and manifestations of rejection for the poor, immigrants and ethnic minorities can be easily found in any perusal of academic or official literature. Take the 2005 UN Human Development Report. From the start, the message is clear: 'The world's richest 500 individuals have a combined income greater than that of the poorest 416 million. Beyond these extremes, the 2.5 billion people living on less than $2 a day – 40% of the world's population – account for 5% of global income. The richest 10%, almost all of whom live in high-income countries, account for 54%' (UNDP 2005, p. 4; see, for perceptions of the early 2000s, Sen 2002 and Weisbrot 2002). The report forecasts that if current trends persist, the gaps will only grow. In relation to the Millennium Development Goals (MDG), such trends show that by 2015, there will be 'more than 41 million children who will die before their fifth birthday from the most readily curable of all diseases – poverty'. In relation to poverty, there will be 'an additional 380 million people living on less than $1 a day'. As regards primary education, 47 million children will still be out of school in 2015 (UNDP 2005, p. 5). The report is skeptical about the effects of globalization on inequality:

> [W]hen it comes to income, global integration has ushered in a new era of convergence. At best, the sentiment is weakly supported by the evidence. Poverty is falling, but slowly since the mid-1990s. Meanwhile, global inequality remains at extraordinarily high levels.
>
> In the aggregate the past two decades have witnessed one of the most rapid reductions in poverty in world history. However, any assessment of trends in income poverty has to take into account large variations across regions. [...]
>
> The worrying trend for the future is that overall progress is slowing. Much of the success in pushing back poverty over the past two decades was achieved in the 1980s and the first half of the 1990s. Since the mid-1990s $1 a day poverty has been falling at one fifth the 1980–96 rate. This is despite the fact that average growth for developing countries picked up in the 1990s, increasing at more than double the per capita rate of the previous decade (pp. 33–4; see also pp. 36–7).

There have been counter-evidences to that pessimism, as will be seen below. Lower levels of poverty in the context of rather conventional social policy instruments are certainly connected to different political choices implemented from 2003 which only very recently can be detected in official statistics. They demonstrate the options available even when political agency is not bold enough to confront the pro-market orthodoxy. But the general trend is clear: we are still dealing with one of the most unequal societies in the world, that has remained consistently so while experiencing deep advances of market logic and a decisive integration into contemporary global economic, political and cultural flows.

Global pressures, global articulations and cultural awareness in public policymaking discourse

If the argument offered above seems to hide a certain asynchronism with the sophisticated features of technological innovation and social discourses of competition, free markets, mass consumption and pluralism under the current phase of globalization, the 1990s brought this disjunction to a moot point. With the election of Fernando Collor de Mello in November 1989 and his inauguration in January 1990, Brazil definitively joined the neoliberal doxa, starting with a series of liberalizing measures which gave great emphasis to open markets for foreign competition and the whole range of modernizing strategies associated with big corporations. Many companies closed down, many jobs were lost. Technological and managerial changes came in and the wonders of being (after all!) attuned to 'modernity' were loudly and relentlessly voiced by political, intellectual and entrepreneurial elites.

This is then the time when everyone everywhere seemed to have found one word to sum up the changing times: globalization. As in every case of dissemination of new imaginaries, it was not so much shared content or precise definitions that mattered, but the imaginary and non-systematic connections made by users between the issues they were struggling with and the general motif of a majestic external force prescribing (more) modernization as the only future ahead for (semi-)peripheral societies. To be sure, very few people knew what they were talking about, but they seemed all hard pressed to include references to globalization in any talk about the world newly emerging from the exhaustion of military-led developmentalist projects, the worsening social conditions under the post-1985 civilian government, and the crisis of really existing socialism. In all this, media discourse played a major part in popularizing ordinary talk of globalization and multiplying information and images from near and far that seemed to escalate into a broad picture of a process that could not be resisted *because* it was 'happening everywhere'.

A different matter is the direct incorporation of neoliberal theoretical and practical arguments about the need for downsizing the state, freeing it from the 'authoritarian' legacy of interventionism, high taxation, administrative inefficiency and social spending. For this, consultants were hired, studies were conducted, visits were planned, a new breed of public servants was trained, and an articulate political project was drafted. In 1994, the election of Fernando Henrique Cardoso, in the wake of the most successful anti-inflation policy ever implemented in Brazil, gave rise to a distinctive 'third-way' discourse, combining neoliberal emphases on competition, free markets, privatization and managerialism with social democratic trappings relating to commitment to fairness, care for the poorest among the poor, limited income redistribution and more participation by beneficiaries in public policymaking. During two terms in office, Cardoso initiated a number of reforms that included structural-adjustment policies and a changing social policy profile that valued elements such as 'active citizenship', 'partnership with civil society', 'focus on outcomes rather than bureaucratic processes', the development of a 'culture of evaluation', and recognition of identity, culture and pluralism in the definition of policy goals and procedures (see Burity 2006b).

In all this, the typical note is the reference to globalization as the horizon from which those changes drew their intelligibility. The irreversibility of the process was said to dictate the adoption of proposed measures regardless of ideological orientation. The economistic logic expanded towards the whole range of processes of deliberation and decision-making at the policy level, justifying 'the bitterness of the remedy' in the name of effecting a cure for the evils of backwardness and statism. Nobody could dare opt out of the only way forward (*pensée unique*). As the Minister for Administration and State Reform, Luiz Carlos Bresser Pereira, bluntly put it before a beleaguered nationwide audience of Brazilian social scientists in October 1995, who rejected his reasons for reforming public administration and withdraw the state from direct implementation of social programmes: 'It is a pity you're choosing to miss the train of history!'

The 1990s brought together several developments which, though not necessarily requiring a reference to globalization, nonetheless tended to draw legitimacy from it, thus reinforcing its justification. As regards practical politics and political culture, one can mention the dissemination of pro-market values and policies, intolerance towards ideas that privileged or prescribed state regulation and direct provision of public goods and, paradoxically, intense state activism (particularly from the executive) in promoting changes to the institutional and legal frameworks in order to accommodate the new capitalist culture. Simultaneously, there was an emphasis on proactive civil society initiatives in finding solutions for the problems that either could no longer be resolved by the state or should not be left to it, as well as a heightened sensitivity toward an agenda of civic activism and identity issues coming from the global circulation of such discourses that originated in the advanced societies' new social movements and NGO networks. Many cultural and identity demands were transformistically incorporated by international financial institutions in the period, leading to a legitimation of them which caused these demands to become part of the conditionalities imposed on countries that sought funding for projects, crises or debt alleviation.

Social movements organized around identity issues – gender, racism, access to culture, religion – slowly articulated a discourse in which their demands expressed the multidimensional character of exclusion and inequality as well as the persistence or slow improvement with which these demands were met *vis-à-vis* the advances in economic performance.

Such discourse also highlighted the extent to which there were cultural reasons behind the paucity of significant alleviation of the problems faced by those movements' participants (see Alvarez et al. 1998; Avritzer 2002; Gohn 1997; Scherer-Warren 1999).

Several public policies introduced bits and pieces of this new social movement agenda, as long as they fitted government views: in land reform, health, education, social welfare, and environmental programmes, issues of gender, race, ethnicity, religion, sexuality and multiculturalism became part of deliberations and shaped some decisions. Brazil actively participated in the UN conference cycle that started with Eco-92 in Rio, and voiced on those different occasions rather progressive official positions on women's, blacks', indigenous people's and environmental rights; the cultural dimension was incrementally accepted into development views and strategies. Cultural policy proper has clearly moved towards adopting discourses of cultural pluralism or multiculturalism – even though several of its components actually clash or sit uneasily with the historic trajectory of multicultural relations in the country, which is strongly oriented toward syncretism and hybrid identities and is not as monocultural as European and American identity politics. This was not unrelated to the dissemination-effect of transnational organizations, international cooperation for development and the first echoes of an emerging global civil society in domestic governmental discourse.

On the other hand, culture and globalization also became part of counter-hegemonic discourses. Brazilian social movements and the increasingly significant field of non-governmental organizations truly globalized from the early 1990s, and slowly incorporated the new cultural discourse, bending it toward calls for solidarity and global mobilization in order to resist the dark side of the neoliberal hegemonic project and challenging the obtuseness of conservative elites or even the prevailing general culture regarding workers' and minorities' rights, not to mention human rights as an indivisible set of rights and social obligations. As most of the groups that appropriated such vocabulary in the articulation of their demands operated locally and in small-scale projects, the impact over a decade of this new discursive context can already be discerned by reviewing their public statements, project drafts and internal discussion documents. Even the labour union movement has moved in that direction and is firmly involved in providing space for cultural demands in the conduct of its cadre formation policy and in its participation of networks where such demands are crucial (see Burity 2006a, 2006b).

In all these developments, the role of globalization, as rhetoric or in terms of the real effects of its flows and its concrete actors' interventions, has marked the new face of Brazilian society, particularly within its political and economic elites, since the 1990s: still unable to sort out its huge inequality record, prey to a certain fatalistic realism about the possibilities of change in the global scenario, Brazil gladly joins the chorus of those who regard recent trends to be the final accomplishment of the unfinished project of modernity. The past few years have witnessed some degree of self-assertion in Brazilian foreign policy and the grip of global discourses has become subject to more complex negotiations in public policy. Some authors and official data have drawn attention to falling rates of inequality and poverty, but are cautious regarding its sustainability (see Néri 2007; Góis 2007; Brazil – Presidency of the Republic 2007, pp. 12, 27–30).

The previous two sections allow a number of points to be made. It would be foolish to deny the long-term roots of unequal social relations in the constitution of modern Brazil. Although it sits increasingly out of joint with the advances in social organization of the subaltern groups, the social, political and cultural background of present-day ills persists, reproducing a pattern of non-recognition of the poor, women, blacks and other discriminated-against groups that is reflected in the figures for inequality. After the wane of slavery, millions of Brazilian former slaves and their descendents formed a mass of invisible citizens, to whom civil rights and social integration were denied through their confinement in urban slums, without schools, health care and decent jobs. The path of embracing globalization has not altered these circumstances. On top of economic deprivation, because most of the present-day Brazilian poor are Afro-descendents – and represent over 45 per cent of the population – they have also had to face racial discrimination that no examples of upward mobility for a few successful ones has been able to appease. Gender and racial exclusion still combine to victimize black women even more deeply.

Naturalized inequality, which in Brazil has been coupled with an enduring bias against its Afro-descendent population that gives a racial twist to poverty, educational and income levels, job availability and even political representation, converged with the global/local post-1989 dynamics. The drive toward competition, efficiency, market relations and disarticulation of the nation state's regulatory powers generated and spread demeaning corporate, political and social attitudes towards unemployed, illiterate or under-schooled people. Several forms of everyday derogatory or stigmatising discourse formerly used to express racial prejudice returned, apparently without the racial sting, in order to label the new order's outcasts or misfits.

However, if the global lesson of Brazil's rise is the dire need to reconcile global demands with social demands, there are counter-tendencies in action. The setting of globalization is wider and more complex than mere economic readings would suggest. In different and interwoven ways, the rise of new social movements have intersected with the translocal enactment of globalized networks for equality, justice, peace and environmental awareness, and with pressures from powerful international organizations (in turn prompted by governmental and non-governmental demands) for the adoption of complex forms of social equality. Part of this process has involved a double mobilization of cultural resources: on the one hand, by revealing the symbolic dimensions of exclusion, poverty, violence, the operation of political institutions and procedures, and the values and imaginaries on which they are produced, sustained or confronted; on the other hand, by constituting new forms of identification on the basis of identity traits other than class or socioeconomic conditions.

Such a mobilization has led to several outcomes: the widening of social demands beyond material distribution of resources; the acknowledgement that cultural constraints on social development, represented by entrenched forms of life or identity claims, can not be uprooted with impunity without damaging valuable means ordinary people have to cope with major social changes while retaining their protagonist role in the process; and the fact that, while global flows may serve local struggles for democracy and social justice, they are still biased towards a certain conception of market freedom that is as particularistic as any local road to development. In order to articulate or further claims, a global/local dialectics was put to work in contextual ways. With and against each other, local and global actors produced a tangle of initiatives that has cut deep into the fabric of the contemporary Brazilian social formation.

Whether Brazil, as an emerging power, for all its complex articulation of local and global features, economic advance and social unevenness, can meet the challenge of contemporary discourses on social and environmental justice and match some of the well-established global partners is a matter of political action as much as of social and cultural change. However, its rise in the present juncture is telling, both for its reiteration of the lasting failure of capitalism to harmonize economic freedom with social equality, revealing to what extent globalization can give us more of the same, and for showing what role cultural politics – understood as symbolic disputes over the meaning and direction of social situations and processes, as well as the political mobilization of identities as symptoms of social failure to produce inclusion and justice – can play in the present and the future.

Culture counts, because there is no social process without symbolic, signifying practices, and because many of the contemporary points of political antagonism turn around cultural differences. Fighting inequality, therefore, involves both cultural struggles and cultural sensitivity but cannot take place outside political agency. This is still what the emergence of the so-called global South (one more sweeping phrase meant to encompass such distinct cases) keeps in reserve: it is a promise of alternative paths, with some steps taken, but the assessment of where it is going must make room for hegemonic stalemates and political drawbacks along the way.

Notes

1. The author wishes to thank the National Council for Scientific and Technological Development (CNPq, Brazil) for the research grant that has made this work possible.
2. I use the concept of discourse here in the sense attributed to it by Laclaunian post-structuralist theory. Influenced by Wittgenstein's idea of language games, French discourse analysis's conception of discourse as a material force, and pragmatic linguistic definitions of discourse, Laclau stresses that discourse necessarily implies language and action, and linguistic and non-linguistic dimensions (see Laclau and Mouffe 1989; Laclau 2005; Howarth and Glynos 2007).
3. Latin American societies are part of the constitutive moments of the world capitalist system, as colonies of the Iberian powers, although their integration as independent nations dates from as early as the 1820s. The timing and modes of integration for contemporary emerging societies varies extensively, but one could say that the period from the 1930s can roughly be taken as a marker of the intensification of such a process.
4. This is view is put forward in passing by Amartya Sen, in his discussion of India's global insertion. He both acknowledges the point that the key debate on globalization has to do with inequality and that how unequal the world is or has become is the object of heated dispute (see Sen 2006, pp. 341–2).
5. I allude here to Derrida's conception of iterability, which can help us deal with the question of repetition (or system expansion) without recourse to notions of reproduction or evolutionary understandings of change (see Derrida 1982, 1990; Burity 1994).
6. This is not new as a general point, having been put forward by various analysts of globalization, such as Tilly, Robertson or Sen, who insist on the existence of previous processes of globalization. What I add to their view is the point that the colonial and postcolonial conditions 'allowed' the subaltern societies to

experience and develop responses, from the very beginning of their encounters with the West, to several features of present-day globalization, though this *avant-la-lettre* experience has taken place amidst the contradictory and unevenly developed dimensions of economic, social, political and cultural life that have marked those nations as 'underdeveloped', 'poor' or 'non-modern'. For several reasons, some of which will be spelled out here, such distinctive marks of postcolonial, subaltern societies have been seen to revolve around the trappings of *cultural difference*, whereas in Western capitalist societies the process was for a long time credited to world-historical laws of development dictated by reason and progress. Recent changes to this process, pointing to a decentring of the West, leading to the emergence of new loci of power outside Europe and America, have been responded to as a threat or civilizational crisis.

7. This image of the 'third' can be found in several contemporary authors, such as Bhabha, Laclau, Soja or Derrida, with different applications and implications. In all of them, there is a clear discomfort with and disengagement from dualistic and binary thinking.

8. A good example of such a complex take on the importance of locality (which must be understood both in spatial and symbolic terms) is the discussion offered by Silva (2006) on the adoption and implementation of affirmative-action policies in Brazil and South Africa in favour of black (and poor) students in public higher education.

9. As regards Brazil, the process has been variously designated. Two of the more forceful arguments have developed around the concepts of 'conservative modernization' and 'selective modernization'. Both emphasize the singularity of Brazilian modernization and, by the same token, insist on it being a case of modernity rather than a deviation from or a falling short of it (see Domingues 2002, 2006; Souza 2000, 2007).

Part III
Engagements

9
Africa's Engagement with China: Perpetuating the Class Project?

Sanusha Naidu and Johanna Jansson

Introduction

This chapter develops ideas proposed in earlier article that was published in the journal *Futures* (Naidu and Mbazima 2008). In the period since that article was written, the African engagement with China can be deemed to be maturing, at least in terms of the euphoria that initially surrounded the engagement. Nevertheless the criticisms still remain between those who interpret the Chinese engagement as an imperialist, neo-colonial exploitative agenda and others who argue that China provides a much-needed impetus to Africa's development prospects through large-scale infrastructure, trade and investment projects (see Ampiah and Naidu 2008).

In the earlier paper we focused on how China may have to consider Africa's fragile political, economic and social landscape when trying to fit in. We concluded that as much as China can be seen as offering a new continental impulse to Africa's engagement with traditional external partners, Beijing itself may eventually also come to behave like Africa's traditional development partners, especially as it begins to realise that the state-to-state engagement needs to take into consideration different power configurations which involve non-state actors, particularly where economic interests are at stake. Moreover we cautioned African leaders against replacing one external power with another benefactor since this does not increase the continent's leverage. Rather it makes Africa adopt a double standard that defeats the principles of good governance and democratic accountability. We finally highlighted that the 'All Weather Friend' is a sovereign state guided by national interests and domestic considerations. Therefore African leaders must come to realize that Beijing is not going to be the panacea of their development challenges. We remain committed to these conclusions.

Using the previous article as a framework for this chapter, we would like to contend that the Africa-China engagement produces a new set of challenges. This can be felt within African societies. While the earlier paper focused on new power configurations in Africa created by the emerging China Policy, it only briefly touched on the societal and class impacts that are produced through the Africa-China engagement. And this is where the current debates in the literature have been lacking.

Many of the debates in the current Africa-China discourse have centrally focused on or are essentially preoccupied with the politics and economics of the relationship. In essence these debates have been mainstreamed in traditional political science thinking of power politics and balance-of-power theories. On the other hand economists have also been divided between liberal thinking and mercantilist ideas of the China-Africa engagement. With these views dominating the current thinking, there have been very few studies disaggregating the impact of the China-Africa engagement in relation to the class debate it provokes within African societies, especially around the construct of emerging societies. In instances where there has been some reference to the class impact this is referred to in economic terms of displacing local producers, poor working conditions, dismal wage packages and rising unemployment. Mohan and Power rightly point out that the China-Africa engagement embodies 'new African choices' amongst which is 'differentiating the generic impacts from country specific' studies, that take into consideration the 'changing class dynamics' this creates and the implications this has for 'organised civil society based politics' (2008, p. 38).

Based on these considerations, this chapter will attempt to provide some contextual overview of the class dynamic that underlines the Africa-China engagement. The purpose of the chapter is to provide an alternate view of the Africa-China relationship and to raise other significant issues that come to the fore now that China is an established actor within the international system and across Africa. Moreover, the issue of emerging societies is a relevant construct in the Africa-China engagement as an outcome of the South-South cooperation dynamic. Essentially this paper will ask the following questions: How does the Africa-China engagement benefit African societies? Are African leaders perpetuating another form of risk and hence dependency with China? If so, what are the implications? And finally, who are the winners and losers of the engagement? We will return to these questions in the conclusion, but first the chapter will contextualise the Sino-African engagement through the lens of the factors that influence the current relationship.

Contemporary Sino-African relations

During President Jiang Zemin's 1996 tour of Africa, a 'Five Point Proposal' was presented which established the terms of a new relationship with Africa (Alden 2005, p. 147). The new relationship emphasized reliable friendship, sovereign equality, non-intervention, mutually beneficial development and international cooperation. While the foundations of President Jiang's five points echoed a realignment of Beijing's foreign-policy principles following the crackdown of the democratic student protests at Tiananmen Square, it also signified a new economic impetus towards Africa that was devoid of Mao's historical ideological leanings.

Four main rationales can be identified in China's current engagement with Africa. Advocated by Chris Alden, these are: the need for new markets and investment opportunities; resource security; symbolic diplomacy and development cooperation; and, finally, the forging of strategic partnerships (2005, p. 248).

The need for new markets and investment opportunities

The economic reforms of the post-Maoist era (after 1978) had paid substantial dividends for Deng Xiaoping, China's pragmatic economic leader. His socialist modernization project, aimed at reorienting the economy through massive injections of foreign direct investment and technological innovation, provided the foundation for Beijing's current phenomenal growth rates. Between 1983 and 2003 China's GDP grew by 9.7 per cent annually. Over the past 25 years China's economy has grown at an annual growth rate of more than 9.5 per cent (Kaplinsky 2006, p. 12). The OECD estimates that by 2016 China will be the world's second-largest economy (Goldstein et al. 2006). Between 1978 and 2002, poverty reduction amongst China's largely rural population was an extraordinary success. During the period approximately 222 million people were lifted out of poverty – an 88.7 per cent decrease (Angang et al. 2003, pp. 1f).

During its modernization project, China attracted high levels of FDI. This, together with a centrally directed economic development policy focused on industrialization, resulted in gross domestic oversupply, increasing the need to export manufactured goods to international markets. As a result, China developed a massive foreign exchange reserve (Bello 2008; Figure 9.1). In March 2008, China's foreign exchange reserves – excluding gold – stood at $1.7 trillion (Chinability 2008). This has enabled China to become an exporter of foreign direct investment, not least to Africa where Beijing offers African countries concessional

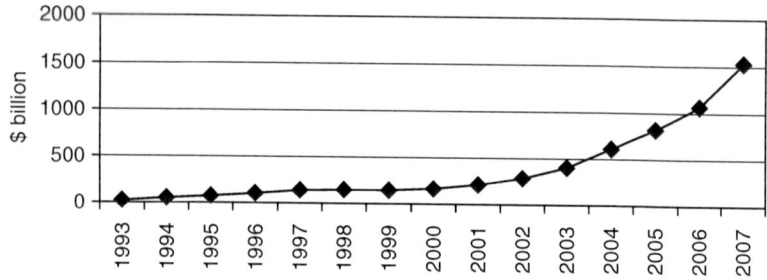

Figure 9.1   China's foreign exchange reserves 1993–2007
Source: State Administration of Foreign Exchange, People's Republic of China.

loans and other preferential credits. Wong and Chang illustrate that 'from 1979 to 2000 the total flow of utilised FDI amounted to $568 billion' (2006, p. 273).

China's foreign exchange reserve is indicative of the financial muscle wielded by Beijing. Not only does it enable China to become an attractive trade partner but it also provides it with financial power to become an alternative lender to low-income countries who do not satisfy or qualify for financial assistance from the IMF, World Bank and Western donors. This is discussed further below in the section on development assistance.

In 2001, the Chinese government initiated the 'Going Out' strategy, encouraging its corporate sector to transform into multinational companies and invest overseas. The rationale for this was to make Chinese corporations gain experience and thus become more competitive (Barboza 2005; Kaplinsky et al. 2007). Currently, more than 800 Chinese companies operate in Africa in various sectors and countries; roads or railways in Ethiopia, Rwanda and Sudan, the reconstruction of Angola's shattered economy, the expansion of telecommunication businesses into 39 sub-Saharan Africa countries by Huawei Technologies, the rehabilitation of power stations in the Niger Delta, or the construction of a hospital and oil pipelines in Sudan (Mills and Thompson 2008).

Also, African markets have become lucrative for Chinese exporters of consumer goods. Kaplinsky notes 'that China-sourced imports ... have substituted traditional suppliers, often providing much cheaper and more appropriate products than those sourced from high-income economies of Europe, North America and Japan' (Kaplinsky 2006, p. 15). Chinese products are thus affordable also to those with very little disposable income. Also, the success of Chinese consumer goods on the African continent is to a great extent made possible by the countless

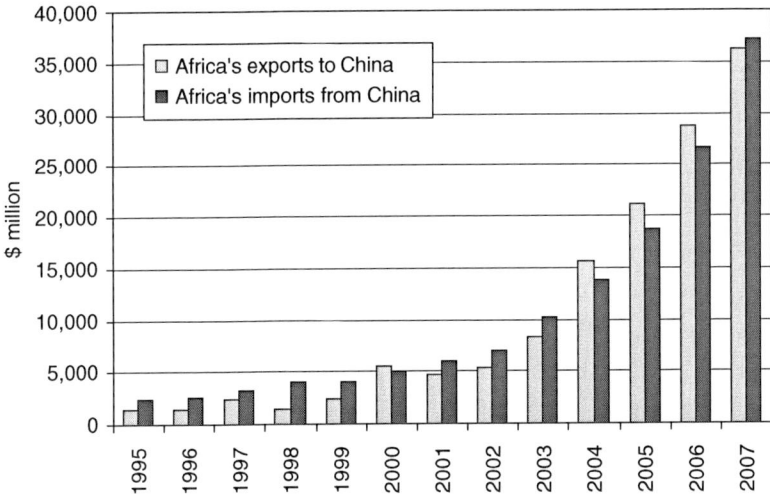

Figure 9.2 China's trade with Africa 1995–2007
Source: World Trade Atlas/Tralac.

Chinese entrepreneurs and petty traders that run so called 'China shops' all across the continent (see for example Dobler 2005).

Another important motivator for China's interest in Africa is the linkage of its markets to the US and the EU through partnership agreements; the African Growth and Opportunity Act (AGOA) and the Economic Partnership Agreements (EPA). Through these, exports take place at concessional rates to the US and the EU markets, something that has spurred Chinese firms to enter into joint ventures with local companies in export-oriented sectors like textiles and agroindustry.

Relations between China and Africa have definitely gained momentum over the past decade, and trade between the two has seen an unprecedented boom. During the 1990s, Sino-African trade grew by 700 per cent (Savant 2005). From 2000 to 2007, it grew from $10.5 billion to $74 billion (see Figure 9.2). In December 2005 Premier Wen Jiabao announced that trade with Africa is set to rise to $100 billion by 2010.

The development of China's relations with Africa is multifaceted. Private Chinese companies and small-scale entrepreneurs are economically active on the continent along with the Chinese state-owned enterprises (SOEs), the powerful tools for the Chinese government's economic policy.

As much as the trade between the two seems exponential, in real terms it remains nominal when compared to Africa's traditional trade partners

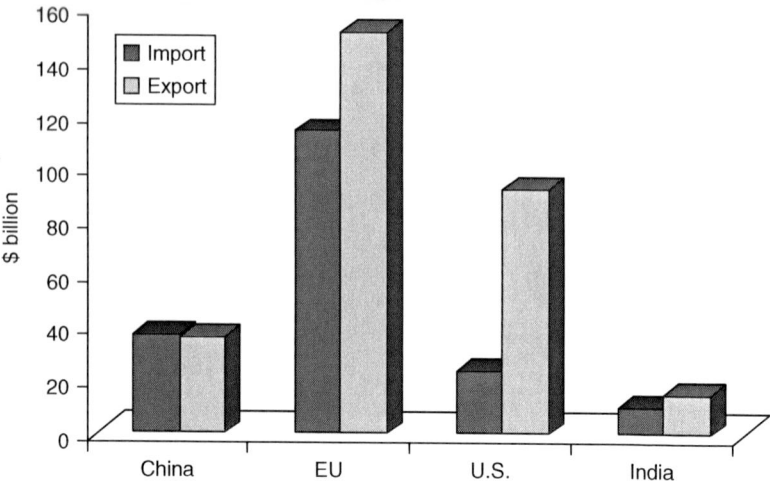

Figure 9.3   Selected trade statistics for Africa 2007
Sources: World Trade Atlas (China), EU Commission, US Census Bureau, Tralac (India).

such as the US and the EU. Moreover, Africa remains one of China's smaller trading partners (see Figures 9.3 and 9.4).

Resource security

An important part of China's imports from Africa consists of raw materials. China's thriving economy and rampant industrial growth require access to natural resources to sustain performance. China has been a net oil importer since 1993 and is currently the world's second largest consumer of oil. The volatility in the Middle East currently creates uncertainty in the global oil supply chain and jeopardizes sustainable long-term access to crude-oil provisions. The importance of Africa in China's energy security strategy has therefore grown immensely, and Africa is now established as an important source for China's oil imports. In 2006, Africa provided China with 32 per cent of its oil imports (ICG 2008, p. 40).

While oil clearly dominates the relationship with Africa (see Figure 9.5), other natural resources such as iron ore, cobalt, platinum, timber and copper also form part of China's crucial imports from Africa. For example, Africa is China's main supplier of cobalt, with 85 per cent of imports coming from only three countries: the Republic of Congo, the Democratic Republic of Congo and South Africa (Trinh and Voss 2006; Naidu and

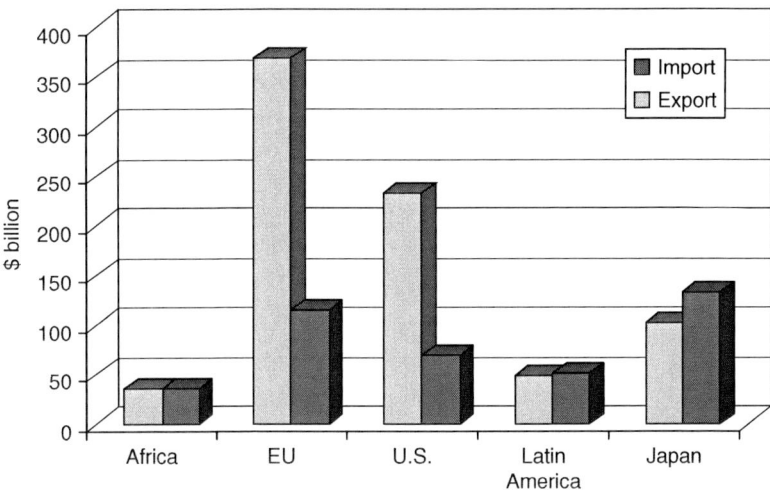

Figure 9.4 Selected trade statistics for China 2007
Sources: Tralac (Africa), EU Commission, US Census Bureau, UN Comtrade (Latin America and Japan).

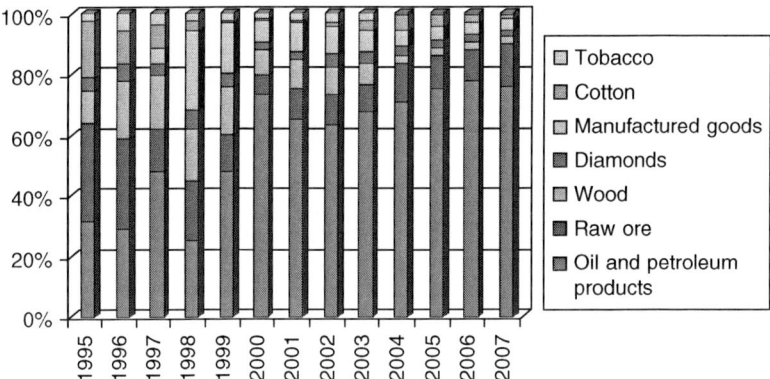

Figure 9.5 Composition of China's imports from Africa 1995–2007
Sources: World Trade Atlas/Tralac.

Davies 2006). In 2006, South Africa was China's fourth-largest supplier of iron ore while Cameroon, Equatorial Guinea, Gabon and the Republic of Congo accounted for 14 per cent of China's rough wood imports. In Mozambique's Zambezi province logging is the main industry and has become the principal export to China.

In line with the 'Going Out' strategy, the oil and exploration rights controlled by China's three big National Oil Companies (NOCs – CNOOC, CNPC and Sinopec) are important. Chinese SOEs are active in resource extraction across Africa in countries such as Sudan, Angola, Nigeria, Equatorial Guinea, Gabon, Libya, Niger, Central African Republic, the DRC and the Republic of Congo in a variety of activities ranging from building pipelines to oil and gas exploration and extraction. West African oil is particularly appealing to the Chinese companies because of its high quality – light, waxy and low in sulphur – which is similar to the grade used in its domestic oil market (Burke et al. 2007, p. 84).

Alden and Davies note that 'China's approach to Africa [and] the role of Chinese MNCs . . . in particular those in the petroleum and gas industry as well as related infrastructure development, had become a significant feature of the African investment and development landscape' (2006, p. 90). Interestingly however, it can be noted that in relative terms, China's NOCs are actually small players on the African continent. Downs notes that 'the commercial value of the oil investments in Africa of China's NOCs is just 8 per cent of the combined commercial value of the IOC's investments in African oil and 3 per cent of all companies invested in African oil' (2007, pp. 43f).

Angola is, together with Saudi Arabia, one of China's leading oil suppliers. In March 2004 the China Export Import (Exim) Bank extended a $2 billion oil-backed loan to Angola for the postwar refurbishment of infrastructure. In 2006 the loan was doubled to $4 billion, which was subsequently increased by a further $500 million in 2007. The oil-backed loan may seem disadvantageous to China's interests in the short term, yet Chinese construction companies will benefit from the lion's share of contracts for national reconstruction. According to the terms of the loan, Angolan companies can only tender for 30 per cent of the infrastructural projects while the other 70 per cent are set aside for Chinese companies. General China Export Import (Exim) Bank requirements state that for projects funded by China Exim Bank, 'Chinese enterprises should be selected as contractor/exporter' (Exim Bank 2008). In addition, a minimum of 50 per cent of technology, material and equipment should be sourced from China.

This has been one of the most criticized features in the discussion around China's engagement with Africa. The policy inevitably means that Chinese workers are brought in to carry out work in African countries, although the Chinese companies also employ a certain number of local workers. On that note, this is a practice used not only by China Exim Bank: 'About 80 per cent of US grants and contracts to developing countries must be used to buy goods and services from US firms and NGOs. Some 90 per cent of Italy's aid benefits Italian companies and experts; 60–65 per cent of Canada's aid and much of that of Germany, Japan and France is tied to purchases from those states' (Sautman and Hairong 2008, p. 104).

In exchange for the low-interest loan, Angola will export 10,000 barrels of oil per day to China over a period of 17 years. By April 2006, $1.8 billion of the loan had been utilized. In terms of investments, a 55/45 joint venture between Sinopec and Sonangol was formed in 2006 and by means of the joint venture, Sinopec acquired a 27.5 per cent stake in offshore block 17; 40 per cent in block 18 and 20 per cent in block 15. Also, the joint venture negotiated to build a new $3.5 billion refinery in Lobito. However the negotiations for the refinery broke down in March 2007 and thereafter Sinopec was excluded from the project (Corkin 2008a, pp. 7ff). In July 2008 it was announced that China Exim Bank is to contribute an additional $135 million towards the refurbishment of Angola's electricity, road and water systems (Reuters 2008).

In Nigeria, an $800 million crude-oil sale deal was struck in 2005 between PetroChina and the Nigerian National Petroleum Corporation to supply 30,000 barrels of crude oil per day to China (*Vanguard* 2005). Kenya granted China's CNOOC exclusive rights for offshore exploration in six out of 11 available and hotly contested blocks in April 2006, covering 44,500 square miles in the north and south of the country. Some of these exploration rights were subsequently sold off in February 2007 (*The East African Standard* 2006; allAfrica 2007).

In Gabon, China National Machinery and Equipment Import and Export Corporation (CMEC) has signed an agreement to mine 30 million tonnes of iron ore annually for 25 years in the Belinga iron deposits (*China Daily* 2008). In May 2006 it was announced that China National Petroleum Corporation (CNPC) and Madagascar Petroleum International would jointly explore a large onshore oil field discovered on the island (Dow Jones Newswires 2006).

In Zambia, where the Chambishi copper mine closed its doors in 1988 due to financial mismanagement, the mine has been reopened as a result of Chinese investment and management. Today, it is a bustling centre of activity and will become China's first Special Economic Zone (SEZ) where duty waivers and tax incentives will apply. An initial investment credit of $800 million has been made available for Chinese firms that wish to establish themselves in the zone, whose main investment will be a $250 million copper smelter (Davies et al. 2008, p. 26).

The latest significant development in the area is the $9 billion deal announced in May 2008 between the government of the Democratic Republic of Congo (DRC) and Exim Bank. According to the terms of the deal, the DRC's state-owned mining giant Gécamines will form a 32/64 joint venture with China's Sinohydro and China Railway Engineering Corporation (CREC). By means of the agreement, the DRC will receive well-needed infrastructure refurbishment; 3,125km of railways from the southern mineral-rich Katanga province to the Atlantic port of Matadi; more than 6,000km of roads; hospitals; health centres; hydro-electric dams and airport infrastructure (*International Mining* 2008). In exchange, the mining joint venture has received the right to mine 10.6 million tonnes of copper and 626,000 tonnes of cobalt. The deal has received severe criticism from the Congolese opposition, which claims that the deal is worth substantially more than $9 billion for the Chinese partners to the deal, and the by the International Monetary Fund (IMF), which argues that the deal risks to create macroeconomic imbalances as a result of its sheer size (Guèye 2008; Bridge 2007).

According to forecasts, China's import-demand growth rate until 2020 will remain 'in lower double digit territory ... for most commodities' (Trinh and Voss 2006). Related to import demand is also the issue of food security, with China becoming a net importer of food in 2003. Projections are that the Chinese population is expected to increase in the future while the loss of significant agricultural land to the booming economy has compounded the situation. To this end the Chinese state has encouraged investments in agriculture, fisheries and related secondary facilities in Africa. For instance, in Gabon, Mozambique and Namibia, joint ventures have been set up in fish processing and in Zimbabwe, Zambia and Tanzania, agricultural land has been leased to Chinese companies. Moreover, China is also increasing its reliance on the export of fresh fruit, vegetables and livestock from Southern Africa (Alden 2005, p. 249; Chen 2007; Anderlini 2008). At the Forum for China-Africa Cooperation meeting in Addis Ababa in 2003, a 2004–5 work plan for agricultural cooperation was presented, including agro-infrastructure development; farming, breeding and aquaculture; exchange and transfer of applied agriculture technology; skills transfer and technical assistance; manufacturing of farm machinery; and processing of farm produce (Edinger 2008, p. 7).

Symbolic diplomacy, development assistance and cooperation

Symbolic diplomacy plays a significant role in China's contemporary African relations. Crudely, it can be termed a new form of dollar diplomacy where investments in public infrastructure projects of great symbolic value are seen as vital in developing closer relations with African governments and in strengthening trade ties. The most prominent example to date is the Tazara railway project described in the introduction. More recent examples include the funding of sport stadiums in Gambia, Mali and Sierra Leone, government buildings in Mozambique, Angola, Uganda and Djibouti, road construction in Kenya and Ethiopia, and dam projects in Ghana and Ethiopia (Davies et al. 2008). Also, China had plans to build a conference centre for the African Union headquarters in Addis Ababa (PRC 2006).

The use of symbolic diplomacy is not new. In 1971 Chinese efforts to garner African support in the UN General Assembly were successful and it received the support of the African bloc in its successful claim to the permanent seat in the Security Council in preference to the Republic of Taiwan. In the contemporary situation, little has changed in terms of the aims for the symbolic diplomatic efforts; an ambition of its leadership to secure long-term strategic influence and facilitate the entry of Chinese corporations so that they can position themselves in the African market.

This symbolic diplomacy is further complimented by China's development assistance to and co-operation with African governments, which is considered an important avenue of mutual strategic interests. Premier Wen Jiabao, during his June 2006 tour to six African countries, stressed that some 900 projects of economic and social development in Africa had been completed, the provision of scholarships for 18,000 students from 50 African countries to study in China had been undertaken and the deployment of 16,000 medical personnel to 47 African countries, who have treated 240 million patients, had been recorded (Xinhua 2006).

Moreover, under the African Humanitarian Resource Development Initiative, Beijing has forgiven about $1.3 billion in debt of at least 30 African countries, trained more than 10,000 African personnel in both civilian and security sectors, and sent more than 700 teachers to work in rural schools across Africa. In addition, Beijing has also become a serious partner in the UN's peacekeeping operations in Africa, contributing several hundred peacekeepers to operations in the DRC and Liberia.

More recently, through a Memorandum of Understanding signed with the NEPAD Secretariat, the Chinese government made a $500,000 donation to the Secretariat for medical purposes. Such linkages are set to increase following the 2006 FOCAC Summit where President Hu Jintao promised to double China's development-aid package to Africa by 2009. The multi-billion dollar development package included the following: $3 billion in preferential loans and $2 billion in preferential buyer's credits over the following three years; the doubling of its 2006 aid assistance by 2009; initiating a China-Africa development fund that will reach $5 billion to encourage Chinese companies to invest in Africa and provide support to them; increasing the preferential zero-tariff treatment of more than 440 products (up from 190); the training of 15,000 African professionals; the setting up of 10 agricultural technology demonstration centres in Africa over three years; the building of 30 hospitals and $37.5 million in grants to help fight malaria; the dispatching of 100 senior agricultural experts; the building of 100 rural schools; the increase in the number of Chinese government scholarships from 2,000 to 4,000 by 2009 for African students to study in China; and the write-off of all interest-free loans that matured at the end of 2005 owed by the most heavily indebted and underdeveloped African nations (Hu 2006).

Certainly, to some African leaders the lacklustre approach by certain other donor countries to deliver on their aid promises certainly pushes them further into China's ambit. However, as much as China can increase its aid packages to Africa through what has become a massive foreign exchange reserve, there are concerns about whether this can be viable in the future given the looming pension and healthcare crisis, and the widening inequality the Chinese leadership faces at home.

But apart from such widely acceptable modes of interaction, Beijing is also using military engagement as a form of deepening co-operation with Africa. In some instances this level of collaboration has rendered the relationship controversial, especially with states like Zimbabwe and Sudan, which has led to accusations that China is intensifying the conflict in war-torn societies for the purposes of its own national economic interest and cushioning the power base of undemocratic regimes. Examples include the supply to the Mugabe regime of military hard and software such as fighter jets and the technology for jamming radio signals and filtering the internet; helicopters, anti-personnel mines and ammunition to the Khartoum government; or fuelling the 1998 Ethiopia-Eritrea conflict by selling arms to both sides. It is also asserted that Beijing has equipped its contract workers with weapons to protect pipelines and oil investments in southern Sudan.

The criticism levelled against China is valid, as Beijing, while under the banner of non-interference, in fact interacts with oppressive regimes in Africa. However, it is not the only great power to do so. It is commonly recognized that the international community has for a long time faced a situation where the most powerful actors are also the most 'ordinanced'. Besides China, the United Nations (UN) Security Council harbours four of the world's other great arms dealers, whose share of global arms transfers are as follows; the United States (31 per cent), Russia (25 per cent), France (9 per cent) and the United Kingdom (4 per cent) (SIPRI 2008, p. 14). China's dealings with rogue regimes and undemocratic leaders could therefore be mentioned along with phenomena such as US support, as part of its 'war on terror', to Ethiopia in terms of weapons supply and military advice during its attack on Somalia's supposedly Al-Qaeda-supported government in late 2006 (Slavin 2007). Many times, the most important difference between the major Western powers and China is the way they manage their public relations. Millward (2008) notes that 'much could be gained if China only learned how to do a better job talking to outsiders about China. China has a plausible rationale for its actions, and need neither look like a bully nor feel beleaguered'.

The rationale for China to maintain these controversial diplomatic ties is the ambition of its leadership to secure long-term strategic influence. This facilitates the entry of Chinese corporations so that they can position themselves in the African market to take advantage of future opportunities in countries where the economic activities of the North are supposedly subject to sanctions, in countries such as Zimbabwe and Sudan. However, also in this case, China is not the only country to use this strategy; despite sanctions, companies from both Western and African countries are active both in Zimbabwe and in Sudan.

In Zimbabwe, many South African companies maintain their activities in the country, arguing in a similar fashion that if they pull out now, it will be difficult for them to re-establish themselves again once the situation stabilizes. A cross-section of South African blue-chip companies and a number of smaller enterprises is still economically active in Zimbabwe. For example, South African Impala Platinum is Zimbabwe's largest foreign investor through its subsidiary Zimplats, and has no intention of closing down its operations in Zimbabwe. On the contrary, it expects its operations in the country to increase four-fold by 2010. South African Standard Bank is another of the most important South African companies, trading under its Zimbabwean name Stanbic (Khumalo 2008). Also, Anglo Platinum is currently investing $400 million in Zimbabwe's Unki platinum mine that is scheduled to come into operation in 2010. Anglo Platinum has argued that the investment does not breach any sanctions and that the project was being developed 'because we have responsibility to our employees, contractors and the local community' (*Trading Markets* 2008).

China's involvement in Sudanese oil production has been the subject of much criticism, not least through the American 'Genocide Olympics' campaign, which claimed that China ought to use its leverage in Khartoum to stop the violence in the Darfur region. Interestingly, however, more than half of the oil that China extracts in Sudan is sold on the international market (Downs 2007). It is ironic that the buyers of the oil are probably many of the countries that criticize the Chinese presence in the war-torn country. Also, many more actors than just China are active in Sudan. India has since 2003 held a 25 per cent stake in the Greater Nile Petroleum Company, a joint venture in which China's CNPC is also involved (Beri 2005, p. 13). Although at the time, US sanctions against Khartoum were being implemented over Darfur, and despite threats from Sudanese rebel groups, the Indian government chose to get involved in the Sudanese joint venture (Biswas 2007, p. 8). Moreover, gum arabic, used in foodstuff and pharmaceuticals production, is exported to the United States from Sudan, a trade valued at several billion dollars a year (Cecil 2005).

Forum on China-Africa Cooperation

The establishment of the Forum on China-Africa Cooperation (FOCAC) in 2000 has clearly become the vehicle that has institutionalized this symbolic diplomacy. Since its inception, FOCAC has cemented and expanded political and economic ties between Beijing and Africa's leaders and has provided the impetus to become an alternative development paradigm of engagement to the G-8's Africa plan and the Washington Consensus. With 48 African countries having formal diplomatic relations with China, Beijing is now seen as a valuable alternative partner that can help Africa reverse its underdevelopment challenges. For example, South Africa's former President Thabo Mbeki, who until recently was considered by the West to be influential and a visionary leader in addressing Africa's governance and development problems, has acknowledged that China's rising importance in the global economy compels Africa to calibrate its interests with China given the fact that both share a common bond of interests with regard to their position and understanding of the development crisis in the South. This was noted in a speech that then-President Mbeki made at Tsinghua University in Beijing during his 2001 visit to China:

> The world and all of us are defined by the divide between rich and poor, the haves and the have-nots, the developed and the underdeveloped [...] It constitutes the difference between the countries of the North and those of the South [...] Together with China, we are

commonly defined by our situation as belonging to the South (Mbeki 2001).

The forging of strategic partnerships

Concern over the current unilateral character of dominance in the international system has prompted Beijing to seek greater alignment with strategic partners. Washington's growing use of unilateral force and aggression in its war on terrorism after 9/11 – the invasions of Afghanistan and Iraq and the looming threat of conflict with Iran – has forced Beijing to consider how Washington's hegemony may impact the One China policy. With Hong Kong and Macau returning to Beijing's fold, Taiwan's de facto independence frustrates the completion of Greater China, and this is an important rationale for China's forging of strategic partnerships. Even though Taipei's diplomatic recognition has declined, especially in Africa (where only four countries have formal ties with Taiwan[1]) it is still a factor that informs China's strategic political and economic relations with African governments. This is because the more Beijing is able to isolate and frustrate Taipei's prospects of renewing ties with former friends the better are its chances in legitimising the One China policy. For China the symbolism associated with the One China policy is critical to its foreign policy engagements and enables Beijing to rightfully restore its place in the global setting.

China's response to the dominance of the United States has been the strategy of 'Peaceful Rise' and 'Peaceful Development'; to secure national interests through symbolic co-operation and to counterbalance American hegemony through the support of initiatives in multilateral agencies. In particular, showing solidarity with partners from the South, such as Africa, and in reforming the power structures of the IMF, World Bank and the United Nations Security Council, enables Beijing to court the votes of these strategic allies in pursuing its own multilateral diplomatic interests. At least this is how it is interpreted within the contours of the official rhetoric. Similarly, at a cursory level, African countries seek to assert their own independent voice and China is seen as a desirable partner in supporting such a move.

Multifaceted development?

The conundrum remains whether China is 'Africa's new partner in development' or 'Africa's neo-colonialist'. Since the diversity and complexity in the relationship is important, it is inappropriate to argue wholeheartedly for the one or the other. What is clear, however, is that China is changing the rules of engagement as it has become Africa's third largest trading partner after the US and France (see Figure 9.2). Depending how one interprets Africa's renewed geo-economic position in the global setting, it is unmistakable that China's growing geopolitical and economic influence in Africa encroaches upon what Western powers have seen as their traditional cauldron of interest and influence. From the great European Scramble for Africa through to decolonization, the Cold War and beyond, Africa has remained in the sphere of Western influence. Currently, China's deepening involvement, certainly in Africa's natural resource sector, is now beginning to become apparent – the strategic interests of major powers are clearly clashing in Africa. Undoubtedly, the competitiveness of Chinese companies has raised certain challenges for other foreign corporations, including those from South Africa, in seeking to embed themselves in the African market.

Yet it is not only the clash over energy interests that makes the concerns of Africa's traditional partners so acute. A recent report by the *Asian Times* online noted that there are rising concerns in Europe about Chinese economic presence in Africa's infrastructure, agriculture and telecommunications sectors. At an urban-development conference in Germany hosted immediately after the 2006 FOCAC Summit, the German Chancellor Angela Merkel told participants that 'We Europeans should not leave the commitment to Africa to the People's Republic of China'. She also added that 'We must take a stand in Africa' and that 'European policy toward Africa should not be based on "charity arguments"', as it had been in the past, but on our 'stalwart interests' (Godoy 2006). Clearly China's growing political and economic influence in Africa has ignited a reawakening amongst Western donors that Africa's leverage is also growing and providing a new impetus for engagement.

As Palat (Chapter 2 in this volume) notes, Africa will not necessarily gain leverage from China in its relation to major Western powers, as 'neither the Chinese corporations nor the Chinese government has done anything to benefit trade unions or social justice movements in Africa'. To demonstrate the 'leverage' argument further, it is imperative to deconstruct the concept 'Africa' and distinguish the actors we are discussing; African leaders, women, soldiers, businessmen, children, workers, rich people, poor people? Apart from such vertical differences within African society, horizontal differences also have to be taken into consideration, as Africans from various countries certainly do not have the same experience of interacting with China.

In the case of African leaders, it is undeniably so that China's interest in their economies provides them with increased leverage in their dealings with Western countries. In the case of Gabon, Burke et al. argue that the country increasingly sees China as a tactical partner to offset France's influence in the country, and that some of the concerns voiced by Western powers such as France in relation to China's engagement with Gabon stem from a perception of threatened commercial and geostrategic interests (2007, p. 75).

Another example is Niger, the underdeveloped but uranium-rich country that in the wake of exponential rises in oil prices and subsequently renewed interest in nuclear energy currently finds itself courted by various global actors. The country has traditionally been very much in France's sphere of interest, and Maitre and Massalatchi note that the French nuclear giant 'Areva had for more than 30 years enjoyed a monopoly on uranium mining in Niger, but in the last two years the government has issued dozens of uranium exploration permits to companies from China, Canada, Britain, South Africa and elsewhere. It says it is planning to issue many more' (2008). In 2006, Niger signed agreements with three Chinese companies; Trendfield Holdings, China National Nuclear Corporation (CNNC) and ZXJOY Invest (Michel and Beuret 2008, p. 332). Furthermore, in November 2007, permission to mine the Azelik deposit was granted to Sino-Uranium (China Nuclear International Uranium Corporation), a subsidiary of the state enterprise China National Nuclear Corporation (CNNC) (Bednik 2008). On that note, Bednik concludes that 'the French monopoly in Niger is over' (ibid.) because the increased demand for uranium has given the Niger government increased leverage in its negotiations with French Areva.

This is definitely not just a result of China's interest in Niger's uranium; oil prices and general global demand for uranium indeed play their role. However, it is clear that China's interest and readiness to sign up for exploration licences has given the Nigerian government a good negotiating position; in January 2008, as Areva renewed its uranium mining license for the Imouraren site, it agreed to pay the Nigerian government 50 per cent more as a result of increases in prices of the ore (Maitre and Massalatchi 2008). Michel and Beuret note that Areva now had to pay more to the Niger government: 'Autrement dit au président Tandja et à son entourage' ['In other words, to President Tandja and his entourage', author's translation] (2008, p. 197).

Michel and Beuret's comment aligns with Palat's argument: that the leverage African leaders enjoy does not necessarily translate into general leverage for ordinary Africans. The heritage of neo-patrimonialism and clientilist practices, defined by Van der Walle as 'the style of rule that emerged combined the authoritarian legacy of the colonial administration and village traditions of patrimonialism' (2001, p. 116), remains deeply rooted in many African countries. Van der Walle notes that in a neo-patrimonialist system, centralized personal rule combines with a modern rational-legal bureaucratic state, and the access to state resources renders the expansion of clientelist practices possible (2001, pp. 118ff). Certainly, this is still the status quo in many of the African countries that China interacts with. Beijing's demand for Africa's resources generates enormous revenues for African governments, yet there is no automatic link guaranteeing that China's disbursements will go towards socioeconomic development and improvement of living conditions for the average African.

However, this applies equally to resource payments made by Canada, the US, France, India or any other major power on the world's resource market. Although the exponential demand in China's resource imports is conspicuous, it would be incorrect to assume that China is the only global actor fuelling neo-patrimonialist tendencies in Africa. Certainly, the West also interacts with leaders such as President Omar Bongo of Gabon or President Denis Sassous N'Guesso of the Republic of Congo, both currently appearing in a lawsuit filed by Transparency International France accusing them of large-scale corruption (Samuel 2008). Unfortunately, the logic of the globalized economy is advantageous for elites, as noted by Palat: '[t]he opening to the market in most countries has, however, only benefited narrow elites' (2008, p. 21).

Nonetheless, the question that needs to be asked is whether China's activities on the African continent have the potential to benefit Africa's peoples? Certainly the provision of affordable and accessible consumer goods and the prompt delivery of infrastructure such as roads, houses and hospitals has had a positive impact at the grassroots level, especially in connecting people to markets and providing the impetus for new markets along transport corridors. At the same time the flood of cheap Chinese goods certainly may have displaced local African producers, but the total impact is difficult to assess, certainly in terms of indirect effects such as the altering of global value chains and commodity prices as a result of China's expansion (Kaplinsky et al. 2007, p. 7). Of course, judging the impact is also made more uncertain by the fact that Africa has a weak manufacturing base.

Conclusion

China is no longer the new game in town, or the new kid on the African block. Therefore the contradictions, threats and tensions in China's relations with Africa are obvious, as they are with other external partners dealing with the continent. The most obvious challenge is the asymmetrical nature of engagement between China and Africa. This is evident in the disparate way African countries exploit their interests *vis-à-vis* China's sovereign engagement, which is further exemplified by the unequal trade relationship: primary exports versus value-added imports. To this end Clapham notes that 'there is no African economy that can even begin to engage with China in the way that China is engaging with Africa; and the size of South Africa's economy – by far the largest and most developed in Africa – is trivial by comparison with that of the East Asian leviathan' (2006, p. 3).

While the aforementioned issues are critical in contextualising the more practical elements of the China-Africa engagement, it also significantly raises the issue of whether the relationship with China creates an enabling environment for development or perpetuates a class conflict and widening inequalities within African societies.

Returning to the questions raised in the beginning of this chapter, it is apparent that the China-Africa engagement embeds a class dynamic. The very nature of the state-to-state engagement engenders an elite pact. In Africa the elite represents both the ruling class and the private sector. Therefore the assumption that China's engagement in Africa can lead to meaningful development tends to oversimplify the class contradictions and widening inequalities this relationship embeds. This can be felt and seen at various levels of African society.

The tensions, which have been noted in Zambia and elsewhere across the continent – the Niger Delta region of Nigeria or the oil-rich area of the Ogaden region in Ethiopia, for example, where Chinese workers have either been kidnapped or killed – has less to do with anti-Chinese sentiment but rather frustrations directed at African political and economic elites because of the skewed nature of wealth accumulation within African states. A case in point is the Angolan oil-backed deal. Corkin notes that the creation of the specialized Gabinete de Reconstrução Nacional (GRN) in the Presidency was specially established to manage the Chinese credit line and the finance of large construction projects (2008, p. 111). Yet, she highlights that there is little transparency in the management and tendering process while it is not clear how the revenues from the oil receipts are being invested to revitalize the country's ailing economy (ibid.; see also Burke et al. 2007). Speculation by international agencies such as Global Witness and non-governmental agencies in Luanda point to President Dos Santos and other political elites' expansive business interests, which include control of strategic sectors ranging from telecommunications to energy. And herein lies the dilemma: is transparent management of Africa's natural resources by political and economic elites and accountability to Africa's people regarding the revenue from these resources possible?

In their edited volume (2008), Ampiah and Naidu ask two complementary questions: 'Is China aiding Africa along the path of industrial development through the Smithian sense of "enlightened selfishness" or is it directing the continent towards further economic paralysis?' (p. 331). Their response is: How can 'enlightened selfishness' benefit Africa in the engagement with China? They conclude that 'perhaps the greatest challenge facing African governments as they engage the world's next superpower is to see how they can ensure that Smith's theory of 'enlightened selfishness' brings maximum good for Africa's people' and not what seems to be the current state of play of minimum benefits for the few 'enlightened political and economic elites' (p. 338).

Furthering Ampiah and Naidu's argument, we note that in so far as African policymakers 'seem to be following the trail of what may well be the relocation of the centre of capitalism to East Asia' (p. 333), this does not extend to African societies. As much as African and Chinese leaders may be fraternizing with each other under the rubric of South-South cooperation as a means of absorbing the exigencies of globalization, the community of the global South remains fragmented and concerned with national issues of socioeconomic development. And this is where the emerging communities of the South remain differentiated from each other. This becomes apparent under the WTO Doha Development Round where national issues tend to take precedence over global trade issues of the South. The 2008 breakdown of the talks in Geneva reflected this. Therefore, as China seeks to create harmony in its own society by redressing widening inequalities between rural and urban centres, and interior and coastal provinces, Beijing will face increasing pressures for the redistribution of wealth despite its rhetoric of trying not to infringe or undermine Africa's development prospects.

While at a cursory level African and Chinese citizens share the same interests in seeking social justice and a greater share in the redistribution of national wealth, it does not always mean that their approaches will synergize or assist each other. As the introduction and other chapters in this volume reflect, the new and emerging engagement with China tends to reinforce the class project in Africa while at the same time exacerbating polarized growth in many African countries. Perhaps the greatest dangers lurking in the Africa-China engagement are a renewal of the dependency relationship, the strengthening of a Southern comprador class and the marginalization of Africa's people from prospects of sustainable development.

Note

1. African countries that currently recognize the Republic of China (ROC) are Burkina Faso, Gambia, São Tomé och Príncipe, and Swaziland.

10
The Renaissance of Society: From Emerging Powers to Emerging Societies in a European Perspective

Hermann Schwengel

The fine art of periodization is booming again. The crisis of the financial markets, of energy and food supply as well as the public feeling that economic and political leadership able to control the turbulences seems not to be available, favour the desire for periodization. From 1932 to 1968 and from there to 2008, the rise, fall, and rebirth of the socially embedded economy and other models of historical time were or will be debated. The results of analysis are often ambivalent: indeed, there is not much doubt that globalization is slowing down. But this could mean declining connectivity or more intensive connectivity, because societies as societies have to be involved much more in global exchange and networking.[1] The fact that the global order has been challenged by new economic and political powers such as China and India and that these nation states are at the same time global regions and old civilizations matches the diversification of capitalism within the North, within the South and between them, creating a new Second World of semi-central instead of semi-peripheral societies. But the concept-metaphor, to give this process an intellectual face, is not defined yet and needs clear intellectual work and debate. Additionally, food, energy, resources and industrial production have gained ground against the service-led economic evolution directed by self-regulated financial markets. The emergence of a new Second World coincides at least with the revaluation of the Second Sector, threatening the post-industrial economic and political ideologies of the last decades. The United States has not become the new global informational empire nor have the knowledge multitudes found their voice. So the as-if-Marxism of the Southern attack on Northern hegemony and the as-if-liberalism of the ruling elite in Davos have lost their momentum. The Third Way discourse was not able to preserve its own political quality between the populist demand for global justice and the liberal demand for global wealth.

To understand the transformation of emerging powers to emerging societies may contribute to lifting the debate to a new level, especially if this transformation is a learning process rethought by the actors themselves. 'Emerging powers' is a concept-metaphor with implications other than those of the concept-metaphor 'emerging societies'. Concept-metaphors, as the anthropologist Henrietta Moore interprets the idea, maintain attention between pretentious universal claims and particular contexts and specifics.[2] They are linked to pre-theoretical commitments, they are part of the life-world of practising academics as well as political actors and they constitute an image of a system and of parts that together make sense within a whole. Emerging powers mean such an image. If one compares the contemporary literature on emerging powers with the work of the 1970s dealing mainly Japan and China as emerging powers for different reasons (for example, Mueller and Ross 1975), one gets an idea of the changed particular contexts and specifics even if one tends toward universal claims. Introducing emerging societies will change the concept-metaphor again.

The idea and process of emerging powers has to be unfolded from the image of the great shift as the great, irresistible, transformation Karl Polanyi had in mind, to the dialectic of emerging powers. The step-by-step process of a 'learning experience' then leads to the transformation of emerging powers into emerging societies, changing at the same time the design of the social sciences. Europe as an association of societies could become a mediator of emergence itself, as well of emerging societies. The transformation of the concept-metaphor of emerging powers to the concept-metaphor of emerging societies may provide a Machiavellian moment for the social sciences, although it is much too early to expect that they would take this opportunity.

The dialectic of emerging powers

Emerging powers are structurally diverse: firstly, there are nation states and societies as vast as continents and civilizations such as India and China, associations of regional states as in the European Union, Southeast Asia and South America, and all the varieties of reflexive territorialism that lie between them. Secondly there are networks of global firms and technology hubs, the nodes of capital markets and knowledge systems, constituting a new economic archaeology of power. There are, thirdly, Appadurai's (1996) widespread media-, techno-, ideo-, religious, and cultural scapes, including the old and new ecumenical spheres, diasporic locations, and islands of meaning with their flows of images, text, sound and artefacts. Last but not least, there are global cities no longer defined only as financial headquarters, by historical-political functions, and as homes for the creative classes, but by their participation in the permanent struggle for centrality in the global landscape of power (Sassen 1995). Emerging powers work from above and from below, from within global societies and within their inter-dependency: people see, hear, taste, feel and smell this emergence, as public discourse proves. There is the misleading division of labour between political scientists talking about rivalries of new and old powers, the desire of philosophers to reconstruct the normative codes global actors are using, the efforts of sociologists to explore the sociocultural dimensions of differentiation and integration and the search of the media to find the connectivity between the global and the local, the village and the globe. This is probably the main message – that centrality is no longer the property of any given hegemonic structure but the object of permanent competition and conflict.[3] Introducing the term emerging societies will develop this concept-metaphor even further.

There is a certain realignment literature describing the rise of the new global regions as a great historical shift (Dicken 2003), that is, a change from quantity to quality in which the extension of markets, value chains and economic power creates a new framework. To start with a number of undeniable facts (Prestowitz 2005): there is the entry of some 20 to 25 million workers from these economies into the labour market each year, but even more important, the expansion of industry is not related to lower-value goods but increasingly to high-value goods, providing China with an export profile much more advanced than the given income structure should allow. China and India do not only produce an enormous number of engineers and software specialists and invest in their higher qualifications but take part in the competitive structure of defining quality. There are amazing figures concerning the share of China and India in the location of global research and development facilities and engineering services, so that Thomas Friedman can speak about 'roundsourcing' instead of outsourcing, expecting a further integration of global enterprises. Additionally, foundation agencies are spreading. Nevertheless, as Ravi Arvind Palat (Chapter 2 in this volume) writes, China's transformation into the world's workshop has not come at the expense of its neighbouring states, as it attracts imports for final production in China, and offers Singapore, Hong Kong, and others the opportunity to be active in more advanced services.

This list of achievements could be extended, but criticisms of the simple idea of the great shift are equally obvious. The earlier advanced globalization literature already felt the necessity to elaborate a more comprehensive account, as Barrington Moore did for the modernization literature some time ago (Mittelman 2000). Emerging powers produce side-effects: financially risky exchange structures; export-driven growth accompanied by the erosion of balanced social structures; unrest in agrarian areas; and deepening inequalities. The highest quintile of the population in terms of income is best off in societies such as Brazil and South Africa. China is following and India leaves still more shares to the majority of the population than others. To sum up: in many respects the rise of the emerging powers looks more like expectation than fact; the historical time needed to complete the shift is difficult to calculate; the inner contradictions within the emerging powers – from poverty and damaged environment to the lack of education and broad technological experience – may prove to be increasing rather than decreasing; the political capacity of leadership to manage this transformation is limited; and the relative differences in productivity and infrastructure are so enormous that they may even grow due to structural effects rather than disappear. One needs extraordinary political imagination to believe in such a shift.

To understand this process as a step-by-step transformation of emerging powers to emerging societies, however, is more promising, as failure at any step can always be expected. Historically it would be much more illuminating to compare our contemporary global constellation with the problems of the three decades preceding the First World War, when at the same time the managerial habits of the new middle classes and the desires for solidarity of the new working classes were attracting and opposing each other (Joffe 2006). Additionally, in this period the idea of society – in Max Weber's perspective, distinguished from the social relations of struggle and of community – gained the power of imagination that we now know. In the period of imperialism the constellation of emerging powers could not really occur and if we speak of today as the renaissance of society, then that period was something like the antiquity of society.

For the design of a learning process it is not useful to speak of one step forward and two steps back (Palat, Chapter 2 in this volume) or two steps forward and one step back, as I would prefer to suggest, but to create a new model for emergence: the *first* step emerges with a new flexible capitalism that has been given several names – post-Fordism, disorganized capitalism or post-industrialism – all of which have a point. The nodes of global economic networks lose their mere accidental political character as the superstructures of a fundamental mode of production; they are defined much more by their technological, social and cultural capacity to govern their own political universe, making financial and information markets the heart of any industry beyond postwar corporatist arrangements. Flexible accumulation was accompanied by new nodes of global cultural systems, making new types of knowledge brokers, information elites and managerial leadership rather than enlighted liberal capitalists, civic elites and modernist educated classes the heroes of their time. Even regional states in Europe, with their strong roots in the European 19th century, not to mention the Southeast Asian and Southern American associations of states, lost their postwar ground, becoming more deregulating powers then regulators, and preferring intergovernental contracting as the appropriate way to accompany and strengthen opening to markets. The general trend towards money markets post-Bretton Woods, the early rise of media politics and self-conscious professionalism, and the new urban elites opened the historical space for what we call today emerging powers. Nobody expected this dynamic and structural change, which had its beginnings in the early 1970s. It has been, so to speak, an unintended consequence of the evolution of capitalism and political power. But the structural effects of this transformation remained unspecific, the varieties of capitalism and certainly the varieties of welfare state regimes were not reduced and the occidental perspective was still dominant.

The *second* step began with the rise of East Asian commercial city-states such as Singapore and Hong Kong, and in societies such as South Korea and Taiwan confronted with specific historical conditions like separation or civil war pushing them forward. These four so-called Tiger economies specified and orientalized the emergence of new powers although they learned structurally from earlier 'emerging powers' such as Japan and postwar West Germany. Massive investment in education, infrastructure and science were at least as important as market-driven innovations. Of course, as the societies were acting fully under the umbrella of American hegemony, they were not identified as emerging powers in the sense of the transformation we are experiencing today, but they gave important lessons, especially in reviving the role of the state. The specification of flexible accumulation by the Tiger economies was nearly forgotten in the mood of the great shift some years later when Japan came to be seen as a kind of Asian Switzerland – small, aging, rich, and a bit insular – and when corporatist Germany post-reunification seemed similarly exhausted – the continental 'sick man'. The ideological struggle around the specification of flexible accumulation continued in Europe right up to the first half of the present decade, with liberal political leaders suggesting little more than adaptation to global markets as the new ruling idea. But their efforts failed in Italy and Germany as well as in Spain and in France. The process of emerging powers took a different path.

This second step, of unfolding flexible accumulation by Tiger economies, found its equivalent in Eastern Europe, but it was accompanied by the emergence of economies such as Finland, The Netherlands and Austria among others, as well as by key European economies, led by Germany and France. Smaller economies used their flexible coherence to bridge to larger societies through the organized complexities of their societies and social structures. This 'emergence' was merely reflected in the ideology of the great shift, but the idea of different societies and associations of societies becoming similar and having to actively define their place in the world was already born. The idea that cultural resources are necessary to manage diversity without losing a sense of identity was already gaining ground against the idea that open markets alone would provide enough space for innovation and experiment. Even the postwar catching-up experience of Japan and Germany eventually became re-evaluated as Japan's sophisticated 'postmodernist' cultivation of seemingly traditional experience and Germany's cultivation of differentiated regional, local and urban responsibilities came to be regarded as useful resources. Even the persistence of an industrial reflexivity not relying solely on the promises of service societies gained ground after a period of nothing but liberalization and privatization. The introduction of 'knowledge societies' ultimately proved to be competitive, if knowledge is fairly defined both in service and industrial terms. After the enthusiasm about the opportunities presented by emerging information societies, and the division of labour and work between the brain industries in the centre and more simple hard- and software enterprise in semi-peripheral regions, social and industrial fantasies again became much broader and culturally deeper-rooted in historically informed professional experience, increasingly finding their place in Europe. The question of where the creative class (Florida 2006) would really find their place became an open one again, to be decided by cultural dissemination and within the structural competition between societies or associations of societies and not solely by global markets, transnational corporations and governments.

To sum up, the second step of the emerging powers was much more specific, located in many places, and not to be identified as one 'tiger effect'.

It is only if we understand the rise of China and India as a *third* step in this historical upward ladder and we realize the change from quantity to quality, that we can become able to estimate risks and opportunities and become ready to develop the appropriate political categories to give advice to actors and people. It is only in this context that we can see the rise of China and India as the very reason that the rise of Brazil, South Africa and Southeast Asia can not be interpreted in terms of a second generation of East Asian Tiger economies, but in terms of the first generation of globally emerging powers. As European diversity, from Ireland to Poland and Finland to Germany, *was* already taking place among emerging powers, the ongoing change of the European Union from a postwar political order for peace and wealth to a global actor cooperating with the emerging powers had some ground to take off from. It was only in the context of this global emergence that Europeans could slowly begin to suggest deliberately new institutional settings and ways of life not defined by the Europeans themselves, but negotiated in global social structures. That is a difference that will make a difference. It is only if we take the dialectic between these three steps and their own diversity into account that the gap between expectations and facts concerning emerging powers might be closed. Nevertheless, the ideological gap between these new historical realities and the persistence of old thoughts is enormous. Most of all, the geopolitical limits of this learning process cannot be neglected. Although the idea of a global market politically guaranteed by the United States as an equally Pacific and Atlantic power and as a benevolent empire is no longer globally accepted, neither by the elites nor by the common people, no other geopolitical force or rule-making institution exists to provide the public goods of global security and economic leadership. There is a certain geopolitical irony in the take-off of emerging powers using the capacities of smaller city-states, challenged nations, postwar societies and reinvented industrial traditions under the umbrella of American hegemony; the US is now confronted with the results of its own caretaking.

If this dialectic of emerging powers is true, the key concept-metaphor of the last two decades, globalization, is beginning to look pale. The concept of globalization – as nothing else but globalization – has reached the point where its success as a discourse no longer matches its capacity to explain what is going on in the world. After rethinking the dialectic of emerging powers one should at least distinguish three periods of contemporary globalization experience which overlap and confuse public opinion. The first, the monetary and political postwar regime from the early 1970s, which lasted until 1989 when the economic division of the world finally collapsed, already included elements of emerging powers and the steady rise of flexible accumulation, although it was still dominated by the institutions of the bipolar world. The second step, from 1989 to the early 21st century, proved to be an intermediary period in which the process of emerging powers unfolded, but without an appropriate institutional framework. Now we are in a third period of, so to speak, 'inner' globalization, in which societies as societies have to properly define their place in the whole spectrum between local accumulation, regional clusters, national frameworks, continental densities and global expectations. To speak of nothing but globalization no longer makes sense for the social sciences (Therborn and Khondker 2006) as historical and political-geographical metaphors move between the continents and such transnational political ideas as cosmopolitanism attract attention (Delanty 2006). The early criticism applied to the concept of globalization – that it does not incorporate the experience of older concepts and of industrialization – seems to be true. The later utopian alternative concept-metaphor of *Weltgesellschaft* seems still more to exist within the history of ideas rather than being related to empirical power analysis. Some fascinating ways out of this impasse have been articulated, such as in the debate among progressive economists on global value chains opening up space for the location of emerging powers. The nodes of these global business networks can be described without making too-premature judgments on their institutional chances and open space for varieties of political framing (see Leoncini and Montresor 2007). Such an idea seems interesting because other popular political metaphors, such as empire and counter-hegemonic movements, do not have the persistent intellectual power to determine the global debate.

The concept of society at least provides the space to reintroduce the social distinctions between work and labour, between agricultural, industrial and service sectors and between access to labour markets and quality of work and livelihood (for Germany, see Atzert and Müller 2004). But as this happens under the conditions of globalization, society is now directly related to the reconstruction of the global order.

Again it is useful to remember that this intimate relation between society and global order did not exist in the antiquity of modern society. Social differentiation and integration was much more separated from the process of global order-making, although industrialization, information technology, migration, labour movements and elite communication had already prepared some ground. At that time this process was guided by the British Empire, although only for a limited historical time, caged and caging in colonialism, unable to develop sustainable global trade structures and not offering enough access for new players and competitors. Some emerging powers of that time, Germany and Japan, for example, had even weaker answers to this global constellation. It would be extremely interesting to reconstruct how the emerging powers of that time were integrated into imperial structures – from Russia to Austria-Hungary, from Germany to Japan, even from France to Italy – making them unable to leave structurally the world of the 19th century. It was only the United States, with its deep experience of a Gilded Age as well as political unrest, populism as well as progressivism (Priester 2007), European immigration and structured diversity, that in the long run became prepared for global leadership. In the dialectic of accumulation and innovation, finally it was innovation that became the decisive resource for leadership. This shift had already begun in Europe, but was better institutionalized in the United States, making all counter-projects of the 20th century fail. It was no accident that the concept of society was institutionalized and made more sophisticated under American leadership. Talcott Parsons succeeded Max Weber. At the end of the 1960s, however, a merger between the European and the American ideas of society seemed inevitable.

Between 1968 and 2008 – to use the now-popular periodization – both the Atlantic merger and a sense of the meaning of society eroded. Because of this erosion and the rise of the emerging powers there is a growing expectation that for technological, environmental and social reasons the shift towards American leadership has come to an end. Historical comparisons always lack some dimensions, but the dialectic of emerging powers and reconstruction of society is more promising than any notion of the antagonism between capitalist hegemony and popular resistance. Class compromise at the beginning of the 20th century was only imaginable within the ruling occidental societies and, at a cost to the exploited oriental members of the global community. It will be the key issue for any global democracy. Emerging powers and global balance will have to be mediated in a decisively new manner that the elites and the public are only beginning to imagine. Therefore it is misleading only to look just now at what is happening in the global mediating institutions, such as the IMF, the World Bank, the WTO and the OECD; one must also understand the sometimes still hidden dynamics of this process which will lead to changed power relations. Not so hidden is the experience negotiating powers had after the conference of Cancún and the failure of the Doha Round. American and European negotiators underestimated the changes in power relations and the political environment and how complex these might be. Europeans did not exploit the historical moment to move faster to global compromise. Of course they were afraid of their agricultural constituents, the lobbying power of farming industries and the ambivalence of the public over these questions. But the fact is that the societies as a whole are not involved in this process, which is also the case in Indian politics in relation to the status of their small farmers. Both, in defending particular positions, do not realize the necessity of negotiating a historical compromise as decisive as the historical compromise between classes in industrial societies. But the failure of the Doha Round makes obvious that the emerging powers are beginning to prefer their own unity over the advantages some could have gained alone in the manufacturing or informational sector. Although this alliance is far from becoming solid, Western negotiators will never again be in the same unassailable position. Already this expectation is changing the global conditions for structural change. If Europeans want to be mediators of emerging powers, defining Europe itself among emerging powers, they have to accept this change, especially if they take the future of energy and food supply into account. But the acknowledgement of facts does not provide the design for the further management of emerging powers, but only strong ideas rooted in European global history. The emerging powers in China, India, South Africa and Brazil do the same as they mobilize their own postcolonial history, the cultural resources of their societies, and their vitality to shape their emergence.

Europe mediating emerging powers

The position of a mediator is a complex and difficult one, most of all demanding a decent attitude in the mediator itself. There are good reasons why Europeans experienced the double character of power as both asymmetrical, as Max Weber characterized it, and creative, that is, requiring the ability to do something with somebody else, as Hannah Arendt stressed, very intensively in their own modern history. But the history of the beginning of this century is tangled and has to be rewritten to become a tool in global negotiations. The European cultural memory may have moved beyond Braudel's world of traditional empires and their global economies, it may have moved beyond the worlds of national states and their international economy and beyond the world of the liberal empire and its global economy, but this transformation is not enough for the world no matter how dramatic it seems to Europeans themselves. Europeans do not own the reflection of the singular world-system; they have to think through their histories of rising, rivalling and declining power in a collective psychoanalysis in order to contribute to and mediate the antagonisms of a true global world-system. After their centuries of religious civil war, and reason, revolution and development, life and difference – Helmuth Plessner has suggested the sequence of reason, development and life for the European centuries – the process of modernization emerged in the first half of the 20th century as the only mediator between universalism and the balance of power, industry and commerce, pluralism and belief now defined by the American experience. As the challenge of socialism offering a Second World on a superior level disappeared in the second half of that century, and the aspirations of the Third World remained limited because the constitution of many independent states was not embedded in an institutionalized global economic order, for a moment in history the American unification of modernity and globality even seemed to be the end of history; globalization would finally get an American face. Any historical criticism seemed to have no choice than to discover earlier and earlier take-offs of conquest, discrimination and misleading development to explain the present. But only a few years afterwards the hard questions of the one-world system returned, more open than ever before. If Europeans are entering the contemporary struggle and competition for the mediation of the emerging powers of globalization, they do not only have to understand the shift of economic, political and cultural power to the American project of global modernization during the last century, but maybe even more the global limits of their own postwar European project which, from a contemporary perspective, proves to be much more inward-looking, historicist and passive than most of them believe.

After the postwar recovery, in the crisis of the 1970s, Europeans became conscious of their reflexive capacities and developed some sublime feelings of superiority over the 'cold' liberal project of modernization. Although at the end of the century most of these feelings proved to be illusions, software without hardware, this amalgam of reflexive social capacities and sublime illusions is still a severe obstacle to any global mediating role giving globalization a European face. Europe loved to see some civilizational advantages resulting from a longer and more intensive period of industrialization creating the appropriate institutions and the appropriate behaviour of mass society, sophisticated organization and democracy. More than this, European urban experience seemed to preserve an idea of public life, depth of collective experience and vital senses that supported the division of meaning between urban and rural landscapes. Some people even thought that the European experience of family, marriage and intensive bonds between individuals had the better historical prospect of being cultivated and extended (for the debate, see Kaelble 1987). When, three decades ago, the first waves of our contemporary globalization arrived, many Europeans arrogantly believed that they were better prepared by their mature historical institutions, the complexities of their urban life and their differentiated family life for the uncertainties of modernity. Indeed, the American way of life had been Europeanized by war, consumerism, welfare statism and communication. American hegemonial overstretching and overconsumption led to the global crisis of the 1970s.

But by turning this decline upside down, hegemonic American liberalists – and their British followers – firstly learned from their Japanese and German competitors and then used the new opportunities of globalization, information industry and global media-scapes to make their project of modernization reflexive, raising productivity, incorporating vital parts of European and Asian societies into their realm again. The seemingly civilizing European advantages were then doubted. The long and extensive experience of industrialization could also be a disadvantage in flexible high-tech production or high-quality services structured by global tertiarization. The European urban experience, with its historical-cultural core, might not be open enough for the productive effects of migration, transnational media experience and anthropological reflexivity. Even the often-quoted stability of personal bonds, reciprocity and public life expressed in public places, theatres and museums could be doubted as too slow, too homogeneous and too inflexible for a vital postcolonial world of intensive differences. The European face at once seemed to be looking old, not only compared to the new America but compared to the new eastern Europe and the emerging powers of India and China, and of South African and South American states and societies (see Bankoff et al. 2004). Europeans seemed to be equipped for leading the debate on global vulnerabilities but not for the governance of technological, monetary and communication interdependencies.

At the end, however, in these days it proved to be clear that neither the old nor the new Europe, neither the old nor the new America, neither the First nor the Third World, were able to face up to the questions of our time. When after 1973 economic globalization began to recover from the deglobalization of two world wars, when after 1989, with the collapse of the Berlin Wall and peaceful reunification, the 'German question' was over, and when after 2005 the new constitution in Europe failed, people finally became aware of its limits in relation to globality, Europeans found themselves, surprisingly, among emerging powers. This approach to Europe as mediating emerging powers and mediated by emerging powers differs sharply from two other visions that take both the relative weakness of Europe in military-political terms and its strength in soft power into account, but differently. Although Europe is wealthy, with a population of nearly half a billion, it is no strategic player because it is no *e pluribus unum* and will not be for a long time (Joffe 2006). Therefore, in strategic terms, the first view says Europeans should focus on their junior role within a global G-2 coalition. This is the opinion the majority of elites shared in the West until recently, even if the neoconservative misshaping of the American creed came to an end. The other idea, ironically, also suggested mainly by American liberals (such as Jeremy Rifkin) but of a different species, believes in the cultivation of European soft power in industrial and social relations, the anchoring of sustainability in economic and cultural mentalities and the enhancement of responsible individualistic values developed through the interaction of old and new social movements over the past decades. Our idea of mediating emerging powers is not compatible with both visions. The advocates of American *realpolitik* underestimate the economic and political capacities Europeans have developed over the same period in the context of less spectacular growth and the political inclusion of Eastern Europe. The advocates of soft power overestimate the cultural contribution Europeans can give to the world, as the arts, the humanities and moral institutions are only beginning to take the oriental challenge seriously. This European cosmopolitanism is not anchored in mentalities yet, it still has the quality of leisure travel, chatting and stylish people; the realities of the global division of labour, technology and cultural trade are different. The progressive space between these poles of American *realpolitik* and European *kulturpolitik* is smaller than the Third Way proponents of the mid-1990s thought in their cloudy rhetoric, and that is the reason they failed. But the space is not as small as European sceptics, from Britain to Poland – in contrast to Stockholm or Milan – think. The cartharsis through which European thought is undergoing now following the 'No' vote by the French, Dutch and Irish to the European Constitution may clarify the future or at least prepare the ground for European global sensitivity to the emerging powers. One key question would be how the global division of labour – better to say the division of work – connects the global tertiarization of welfare, housing and education with the specific cultural production of societies in the South as well as in the North (Graßl 2000). Europeans seem better prepared than Americans to negotiate global ways of life with emerging powers – at least at this moment – and even stubborn majorities of the American population might become open to the 'reflexivity' of European modernity.

But, after all, the common ground of the world of emerging powers cannot be the 'rise of the West' or the eternity of modernity. The historical 'great divergence' (Pomeranz 2000) between the West and the others was later, shorter and less deep – a contested divergence – than Western-ers themselves thought for a long time. Johann Arnason (2006) has given the best sketch of this contested divergence, which will probably be with us for decades. Thus, in this concept, society is equipped to play the role of an intermediary power between the different social actors and groups, families and individuals on the one side and globalized markets and institutions on the other. In the times of national welfare states, inter-mediary powers were the associations of employment and labour, social and cultural agencies, welfare organizations and private-public endeav-ours between state and markets. Societies as a whole could begin to play this role in the interaction of global markets, multi-level politics and livelihood in complex cultural settings. Globalists have to accept that it is not enough to enable individuals and their families to make their life in only minimally regulated globalization. Advocates of bringing back the state have to learn that even the modernized state as a clearing agency between different levels of social interaction is not equipped with the necessary capacities to civilize mobility and migration, to let tolerance for religious and cultural diversity grow and to provide comprehensive education. For that reason any status in the society has to be re-evaluated in terms of the position of the society in the global context. This is as dif-ficult for the Northern as it is for the Southern societies, but both could identify a common ground. Managing inequality will remain different in different parts of the world, but the ways of management are inter-related. European subsidies for certain agricultural status groups interact with the defence of Indian small peasantry and both societies have to manage this interaction in global politics. Political and economic elites, trade specialists and expert negotiators will be flat out carrying out this task in societal institutions such as parties, movements, trade unions and civil society groups. State agencies often prefer elite conversation with experts because communication in the society seems too risky and to bring poor results. But in relation to the necessities for long-term change this elitist political professionalism is too narrow. This is more or less equally true for environmental necessities, demographic change and the struggle against poverty. Any category of social structure and any category of social action are modified by this intensive globalization, however slowly it may develop in the next years.

Obviously, societies are not the only nodes in global networks and interactions. Global cities or mega-cities and their networks are them-selves playing the role of 'society' to a certain degree. Transnational corporations are creating an economic universe of their own, creat-ing economic 'societies' around them much more than the traditional transnational firms did and becoming decoupled from the checks and balances of the classical society. And indeed, if society is rearticulated only in terms of status and class relations as we know them from the heyday of industrial society in the postwar period, then the decoupling of economy and society will advance further. Enterprises, cities and technological hubs create places where ways of life are socially as well as technologically experienced; from Los Angeles to Bangalore, from Chinese foundation agencies to European networks of excellence, the global creative class is moving between them. But although this is 'society' it will not become society as an intermediary power mediating between the dimensions and levels of global social life. Yet-to-be-born 'sociocultures' (Rehbein 2007), with their own original patterns of life, will remain only loosely connected to global connectivity, and globalist bohèmes' understanding of themselves as the body of global life may grow further, but both are not essentially part of what we are used to understanding as 'society'. While a valuable contribution to global life, functionally they are not able to play the role of an intermediary power. But to repeat: the traditional national society is even less prepared to do this job. There are promising learning zones between the societies of the emerging powers; the Chinese, Indian, South African and Brazilian elites not only explore the space between their own development and the West, but more and more take the interdependencies of their own Second World experience into account. This is a major contribution to the renaissance of society, not devaluating the sole experience, but putting it into the new context of emerging powers.

Theories and politics

There is no doubt that the dialectic of emerging powers will vitalize the debate on society but not allow classical or neoclassical social theory just to do business as usual. High-technology enterprises, media and culture industries provide too many framing opportunities, desires, life chances and intellectual models. The agenda politics for globalized 'societies' are not easily performed. The power of academic theory can no longer be understood as given, but has to compete with other modes of managing diversity. So the intellectual mediation of emerging powers is nothing the world is waiting for. The European intellectual voice is additionally limited by the lack of economic unity, the difference between Scandinavian, Anglo-Saxon, and continental welfare regimes and the uncertainty over whether there is still a European social model. From the glorious times of European modernity there might remain a distinguished sense of global complexities, the fluidity of objects and subjects between words, history and experiences, there may be still a cultivated sense of the dignity of places, persons and artefacts, but the reinvention of society does demand something more. Nobody knows today whether the European crisis eventually will give birth to a perspective of Europe among emerging powers. The emerging world order is an opportunity for Europe but at the same time Europe needs this ideology for herself, that is, not only cultural memory and economic success but a set of goals, tools and futures. As academic theory no longer provides clear-cut differences, but a wide range of choices and theoretical options, the work of ideology will be done by concept-metaphors, more open than the classical ideologies such as liberalism and Marxism in the 19th and early 20th centuries and more cohesive than post-colonial fragmentation, postwar modernism and post-totalitarian difference. As often in history, Europeans could prove to be the most universal and the most particular human beings at the same time. They are born to invent the idea of *Weltpragmatismus* – a possible ideology for the societies of world society – but could also become lost between the history and the questions of this time and this space. Again, the difference between emerging powers and Europe among them – in the double sense of leaving the old role behind and gaining a new one – and the rise of the West is important. Arnason (2006) has discovered in Samuel Huntington's work that the rise of the West is 'a confusing notion: It lumps together two very different things, the original constitution of the West as a distinctive civilization and the temporary advantage which the West derived from its pioneering role in a process that ultimately re-empowers its adversaries.' But there is no innocent rise of the West called the 'civilizational project of modernity', only a process intertwined with the taking of temporary advantage by the West and the re-empowerment of its adversaries called modernization. Although this deeply normative aspiration exists, success is only possible in the real emancipation of the former 'Orient', contributing essentially to a global order of things and the maturation of the old 'Occident' into societies packed with reflexivity, tolerance of ambivalence and respect for life, offering imagination for others.

In times of dramatic geo-economic and geopolitical change, when given truths are weakened and the new truths are not established – to put it in Gramscian terms – there is a certain desire to return to some old truth. Against the pluralism of the multiple-modernities concept that has been gaining ground in sociology over the past decades (Eisenstadt 2000) the idea of varieties of modernity – getting its inspiration from the varieties-of-capitalism paradigm guiding the new political economy literature – is reintroduced because it seems to have a focus on institutions, rather than the vague, barely explicated notions of culture and cultural difference in the multiple-modernities concept (Schmidt 2006). But, of course, there have been not only decades leading to multiple modernities but also decades of institutionalist thinking theoretically exhausted to an equal degree and waiting for the next Kuhn-like paradigm revolution. Probably it would be wise to leave the debate on modernity untouched for a while and not rely on the necessity of long experience in modernity to participate in global structuration and, even more, to refrain from seeing modernity in early axial ages of civilization, as Eisenstadt (2000) suggests.

As an alternative to varieties of modernity, there is a second, seductive, point of view. Because it looks convincing to speak of 5,000 years of globalization rather than 500 years, as André Gunder Frank (1998) has suggested, the global universe after modernism will not be defined by any postmodernism we can concieve but by the return to the very long waves of globalization from the archaeological structures of trade, diasporas and distant parity interaction[4] to the world of empires and their world economies, and from there to the world of nation states and their global economy. But this second set of theories is not really equipped to answer some harsh contemporary questions: whether the dynamics towards universal nations or the balance of strategically acting powers, and the commercial and credit institutions of economic power or the professional and industrial commodification of labour are shaping life, and whether the institutionalized coexistence of beliefs, traditions and cultures, or the mediation of different human experiences in a single universe of science, ethics and aesthetics, makes the world go round. The challenge of Immanuel Wallerstein's world-systems theory, to speak of a singular economic world-system, is indeed obvious in the world of emerging powers, but the theoretical dimensions have to be reshaped in the light of contemporary experiences. Otherwise the given constellation will continue; an open theoretical analysis is only superficially completed by political statements and observations already published in weekly newspapers and magazines and not really bridged to the premises and logic of the theory. Of course, this gap between grand theory and quotidian newspaper knowledge indicates the political weakness of intellectual scenarios. Colin Crouch (2004) has described this 'black hole' of society and social sciences as post-democracy. The main reason for the decline of democracy is the imbalance between the interests of corporations and the interests of all other groups of a society. This leads to the mode of politics in which the political affairs again become only the task of closed-shop elites without access for any other group. The effects of this mode of politics penetrate not only the interaction of economy and politics but are – even more importantly – modifying the way in which public goods are provided and how the priorities of government are set. In the context of globalization this reduction of the meaning of politics is widening the gap between the necessities of global arrangements and the capacities of social majorities to understand their place in and between societies. But because of this gap the necessity of bringing the state back in creates the necessity of bringing society back in. Crouch suggests mobilizing new identities, making people aware of their status as outsiders and getting them to reflect on the way that people are part or parts of globalization processes. Mobilizing new identities of democracy competes, of course, with the power of populism, which is no longer the hallmark of certain historical-political areas such as South America, but is beginning to characterize generally globalized societies. And in the attraction-environment of populism, media are playing the central role in distinguishing the mobilization of democracy from populism without looking at populism with an attitude of liberal snobbery.

We move closer to our contemporary media and event world if we interpret the overall change through globalization as the world 'becoming flat', in Thomas Friedman's (2005) globally communicated image (the opposite of Crouch's point of view). After intensive consideration of the phenomenon of Bangalore, the Indian Silicon Valley, and thinking through the rise of other Asian societies, Friedman posits the theory of a flat world led by the emerging powers – global data flows and value chains make the idea that the world is round, that is, determined by political-geographical structures and historical mentalities, look old. Walls are falling down and windows have been opened as new networks connect the world, make computers into managers of time, and make use of the competences of older communities in new types of connectivity. Friedman is a Ricardian free-trader, but one aware of the risks and depths of Ricardian issues. While there are comparative advantages in free-trade dynamics, there are also drawbacks, from lower wages to pressures on the pure necessities of subsistence, but he is nevertheless devoted to the geopolitical conviction that for America and the world there is no serious alternative to this flat interdependence. After all that has been said about the contradictions of emerging powers here, one may doubt that the world is flat. The inspirational qualities of this concept-metaphor – it is less an ideological idea than a public media construction – do not make room for the well-known images of resistance – landscapes of Northern oligarchy and power, deserts of Southern poverty, deep rivers of capital flows and oceans of exploitation. In the war of images the flat world is strong, but it would be better that we speak of the hilly world, as I would like to suggest, in a new metaphorical approach (Schwengel 2007). After three decades of outer globalization we are moving towards a long period of inner globalization in which societies begin to identify, invent and establish themselves within the connectivity of emerging powers. The hilly world may not be attractive for the revolutionaries in the West and East, but may attract powerful European and Asian reformism and be a real challenge to the old IMF-Wall Street-Treasury complex. Societies define themselves in this perspective not against or without globalization but by globalization. Inner globalization takes historical time into account, thinks in terms of differentiated spaces and different types of elites and masses, expressing political futures in cohesive, either progressive or conservative codes. This is a world of concept-metaphors beginning to bridge the world of intellectual research and media politics.

Conclusion

In contemporary global capitalism global value chains meet global concept chains. The rules of the game have been changed by the process of emerging powers which did not arise with the re-entry of China and India into global history but with a turn in their dialectic provoked by their entry. With globalization emerging powers have many faces: from powerful transnational cooperations and their internal transnational transactions to innovative local and regional contexts, global cities and cultural contexts. Additionally, from global networks and global clusters to public organizations and institutions equipped with the right tools for this new game, the unity of contradictions – to put it in Hegelian terms – is reshaped. To repeat, Europe is among these emerging powers. The diversification of Europe – letting the French look much more again to the Mediterranean, the Germans more to Eastern Europe, the Austrians to the southeast, and so on – is no disadvantage to locating Europe among emerging powers. The next historical occasion will be the negotiations on the future political structures of the Near and the Middle East and Central Asia. Europe will neither seek the role of a new great power nor remain constrained to nothing but soft power, which is merely the ideology of the great powers turned upside down. But this can only happen if the Europeans understand themselves as an association of societies in which the forces of social assemblage are encouraged to experience, in Europe, the society of societies itself. You can offer a global model only if you live it yourself.

For the social sciences there have obviously been Machiavellian moments in the past, in which their necessity became obvious. This was firstly the case around the turn from the 19th to the 20th century, when sociology was part of the challenging triangle of socialism, social politics and social sciences in a world already beginning to be globalized but separated by imperialism, colonialism and orientalism. A second moment appeared in the 1960s when sociology and the social sciences turned from the virtues of electoral democracy to studying the state and its relation to classes, social movements as vehicle processes, and the deepening of democratic participation. The sociology of work turned its focus from processes of adaptation, as Michael Burawoy has put it, to the study of domination and labour movements, and the study of stratification shifted its focus from social mobility within a hierarchy of occupational prestige to the examination of changing structures of social and economic inequality, class, race and gender. The sociology of development abandoned modernization theory for underdevelopment theory, world-system analysis, and state-orchestrated growth (Burawoy 2005). This second Machiavellian moment cast a long shadow, and guides many social scientists up to this day. With the topic of emerging powers, a third Machiavellian moment is approaching the professions, the institutions and the public. As a part of this Machiavellian moment the concept of society will, I believe, experience a renaissance. As mentioned above, any renaissance has its antiquity and society had this antiquity a century ago. As intellectual history tells us, one should not overstress analogies but as a tool they are useful in defining the historical and intellectual frame in which we are arguing. For decades, the very concept of society lost ground against the diversity of social action, against the different arms of social movements and social organizations, against the impact of migration, mobility and cultural diversity, community life, and many other valuable social questions. Finally, with a very late echo of the former wave of sociological thinking, the idea that sociology should move as a third sociology towards a sociology of event, the concept of society was in danger of losing any common ground. This risk is disappearing. Between antiquity and renaissance of societies there have been no dark centuries as there is in the classical metaphor of antiquity and renaissance, but dark times there have been. With the process of emerging powers the global division of labour, the empowerment of mobile capital against immobile labour, of qualified professional work against nothing but labour, of formal members against informal members, of insiders against outsiders, the concept of society as a living, acting and reflecting body will be reconfigured. Societies have to locate themselves within the global division of labour, they have to relate their own social structure to long-term change in the global social structure, and they have to communicate this change within their own conflict structures and between transnational classes, groups and professions.

Geopolitical dynamics are working in favour of the social sciences again in this context – something that has not been the case for decades – but only if the social sciences capture their historical moment over the next years. There are some key areas in which the social sciences have to prove their ability to contribute to a constitution of globalization; they have to bridge the reflection of inequality within societies and between societies more carefully than economists, leaving some old dichotomies of markets and states behind. They have to challenge the notion of political ideologies as being only the liberal superstructure of dominating elites, and they have to define the experimental conditions in which globalized societies are constituting themselves. After decades of methodological individualism and the powerless opposition of methodological communalism, labourism and cosmopolitanism they have to think through some methodological constitutionalism for the world of emerging powers. If the idea of public sociology is to gain any ground, the configuration of these questions will be essential (Schwengel 2006b). It is not so that the social sciences have not accumulated sophisticated knowledge in the past decades for this task of constituting globalization, in the same way that we may think of Bruno Latour's radical rethinkings of connectivity, Hardt's and Negri's imagination of multitude, Urry's elaboration of global complexities, the sophisticated work of urban and cultural studies and the huge body of literature in the meantime globalized as *Theories of Globalization* (Rehbein and Schwengel 2008), as well as many others. Nevertheless those political opinions articulating and distinguishing the long waves of social evolution between 1932 and 1968 and from then to our day are fundamentally correct. Either you understand Machiavellian moments or you do not.

Notes

1. In Freiburg, this debate was inaugurated with the conference on 'Long Waves of Globalization' in October 2005, intensified during the World Congress of Sociology in Durban in 2006 with myself as convenor of a panel on emerging powers, and a panel at the Congress of the Indian Sociological Association in Chennai in December 2006. It will find its full expression in a European research project. For an introduction, see Hermann Schwengel (2006a).

2. Moore is suggesting that globalization research should take metaphors from bio- and computer technology, physics or mathematics into account; see Moore (2006). For the use of concept-metaphors in cultural anthropology, see Kumoll (2007).
3. This is probably the most important contribution of Michael Hardt and Antonio Negri (2000).
4. For the interesting archaeological debate see Stein (1999).

Bibliography

Agtmael, A. van (2007) *The Emerging Markets Century* (New York: Free Press).

Ainley, R. (ed.) (1998) *New Frontiers in Space, Bodies and Gender* (London: Routledge).

Ake, C. (1996) *Democracy and Development in Africa* (Washington DC: Brookings Institution).

Alden, C. (2005) 'China in Africa', *Survival*, 47 (3), pp. 147–64.

Alden, C. and M. Davies (2006) 'A Profile of the Operations of Chinese Multinationals in Africa', *South African Journal of International Affairs*, 13 (1), pp. 83–96.

Alden, C. and M. A. Vieira (2005) 'The New Diplomacy of the South: South Africa, Brazil, India, and Trilateralism', *Third World Quarterly*, XXVI (9), pp. 1077–95.

Alesina, A. and E. Glaeser (2004) *Fighting Poverty in the United States and Europe* (New York: Oxford University Press).

allAfrica (2007) 'Kenya: China Selling Off Oil Rights It Got for Free'. Nairobi: 25 February. Sourced 14 July 2008 from http://allafrica.com/stories/200702260008.html

Alsayyad, N. and A. Roy (2006) 'Medieval Modernity: On Citizenship and Urbanism in a Global Era', *Space and Polity*, 10 (1), pp. 1–20.

Alternative Economic Survey (2007) *Pampering Corporates, Pauperizing Masses* (New Delhi: Daanish Books).

Alvarez, S. E., E. Dagnino and A. Escobar (eds) (1998) *Cultures of Politics, Politics of Cultures: Re-Visioning Latin American Social Movements* (Boulder: Westview).

Ames, R. T. (2004) 'Indigenizing Globalization and the Hydraulics of Culture: Taking Chinese Philosophy on Its Own Terms', *Globalizations*, 1 (2), pp. 171–80.

Amin, S. (1989) *Eurocentrism* (New York: Monthly Review Press).

Ampiah, K. and S. Naidu (eds) (2008) *Crouching Tiger, Hidden Dragon? Africa and China* (Scottsville: University of KwaZulu Natal Press).

Anderlini, J. (2008) 'China Eyes Overseas Land in Food Push', *Financial Times*, 8 May 2008, sourced on 16 July 2008 from www.ft.com/cms/s/0/cb8a989a-1d2a-11dd-82ae-000077b07658.html

Angang, Hu, Linlin, Hu and Zhixiao, Chang (2003) 'China's Economic Growth and Poverty Reduction (1978–2002).' Paper presented at the Conference *A Tale of Two Giants: India's and China's Experience with Reform and Growth*, co-organised by International Monetary Fund and the National Council of Applied Economic Research, November 14–16, 2003, Taj Mahal Hotel, New Delhi, India. Sourced on 9 July 2008 from www.imf.org/external/np/apd/seminars/2003/newdelhi/angang.pdf

Appadurai, A. (2004) 'The Capacity to Aspire: Culture and the Terms of Recognition', in V. Rao and M. Walton (eds) *Culture and Public Action: A Cross-Disciplinary Dialogue on Development Policy*, pp. 56–84 (Palo Alto: Stanford University Press).

Appadurai, A. (1996) *Modernity at Large: Cultural Dimensions of Globalization* (Minneapolis: University of Minnesota Press).

Arendt, Hannah (1958) *The Origins of Totalitarianism* (New York: Meridian Books).

Arnason, J. (2006) 'Contested Divergence. Rethinking the "Rise of the West"', in Gérard Delanty, *Europe and Asia Beyond East and West* (London and New York: Routledge), pp. 77–91.

Arrighi, G. (1994) *The Long Twentieth Century* (London and New York: Verso).

Arrighi, G. (2007) *Adam Smith in Beijing* (London and New York: Verso).

Arrighi, G. and Lu Zhang (2007) 'From the Washington to the Beijing Consensus and Beyond', Department of Sociology, Johns Hopkins University, unpublished paper.

Arrighi, G., Po-keung Hui, Ho-fung Hung and Mark Selden (2003) 'Historical Capitalism, East and West', in Giovanni Arrighi, Takeshi Hamashita and Mark Selden (eds) *The Resurgence of East Asia: 500, 150 and 50 Year Perspectives* (London and New York: Routledge), pp. 259–333.

Asfaw, A. and J. Braun. (2004) 'Is Consumption Insured Against Illness? Evidence on Vulnerability of Households to Health Shocks in Rural Ethiopia', *Economic Development and Cultural Change*, 53 (1), pp. 115–29.

Atzert, T. and J. Müller (eds) (2004) *Immaterielle Arbeit und imperiale Souveränität. Analysen und Diskussionen zu Empire* (Münster: Verlag Westfälisches Dampfboot).

Avritzer, L. (2002) *Democracy and the Public Space in Latin America* (Princeton: Princeton University Press).

Bajpaee, C. (2008) 'The Indian Elephant Returns to Africa', *Asia Times* online, 25 April.

Balakrishnan, P. (2005) 'Macroeconomic Policy and Economic Growth in the 1990s', *Economic and Political Weekly*, 3 September, pp. 3969–77

Bandhyopadhyay, D. (2006) 'Is the Institution of District Magistrate Still Necessary?', *Economic and Political Weekly*, 41 (47), pp. 4847–9.

Bankoff, G., G. Frerks and D. Hilhorst (eds) (2004) *Mapping Vulnerability. Disasters, Development and People* (London: Earthscan).

Barboza, D. (2006) 'Some Assembly Needed: China as Asia's Factory', *New York Times*, 9 February. Globalization and Development: Debates in China 389.

Barboza, D. (2005) 'China Seeks Known Brands to Go Global', *International Herald Tribune*. June 30, sourced 7 October 2008 from www.iht.com/articles/2005/06/29/business/brands.php

Bardhan, P. (2005) 'China, India Superpower? Not So Fast!', *YaleGlobal Online Magazine*. Available at: http://yaleglobal.yale.edu/ (accessed 25 October 2005).

Bardhan, A. D. and C. A. Kroll (2003) 'The New Wave of Outsourcing', Fisher Center for Real Estate and Urban Economics, Berkeley, California.

Barrett, C., Marenya, J. McPeak, B. Minten, F. Murithi, W. Oluoch-Kosura, F. Place, J. Randrianarisoa, J. Rasambainarivo and J. Wangila. (2006) 'Welfare Dynamics in Rural Kenya and Madagascar', *Journal of Development Studies*, 42 (2), pp. 248–77.

Barrett, C., T. Reardon, and P. Webb (2001). 'Non-farm Diversification and House-hold Livelihood Strategies in Rural Africa: Concepts, Dynamics, and Policy Implications', *Food Policy*, 26, pp. 315–31.

Bartke, W. (1992) *The Agreements of the People's Republic of China with Foreign Countries 1949–1990* (Munich: Saur).

Baulch, B. and B. Davis (2007) 'Poverty Dynamics and Life Trajectories in Rural Bangladesh.' Paper prepared for the Wellbeing in International Development Conference, 28–30 June 2007, University of Bath, UK.

Beck, U. (1992) *Risk Society: Towards a New Modernity* (London: Sage).

Beck, U. (2005) *Power in a Global Age* (Cambridge: Polity).

Becker, E. and E. L. Andrews (2004) 'IMF Says Rise in US Debts is Threat to World Economy', *New York Times*, 1 August.

Bednik, A. (2008) 'Radioactive Land is Real Price of Uranium; Niger's Mine War', *Le Monde Diplomatique*, 1 July.

Bello, Walden (2005) 'The Real Meaning of Hong Kong: Brazil and India Join the Big Boy's Club', Focus on the Global South, retrieved 27 December 2005, (http://www.focusweb.org/content/view/799/36/).

Bello, W. (2008) 'Chain-Gang Economics: China, the US, and the Global Economy', in Dorothy Grace Guerrero and Firoze Manji (eds) *China's New Role in Africa and the South. A Search for a New Perspective* (Cape Town, Nairobi and Oxford: Fahamu).

Beri, R. (2005) 'Africa's Energy Potential: Prospects for India', *Strategic Analysis*, 29 (3), July–Sept.

Bhide, S. and A. K. Mehta (2004) 'Correlates of Incidence and Exit from Chronic Poverty in Rural India: Evidence from Panel Data', New Delhi: Indian Institute of Public Administration and Chronic Poverty Research Centre, Working Paper 15.

Birdsall, N. (2006) 'Stormy Days on an Open Field: Asymmetries in the Global Economy', Working Paper Number 81 (Washington DC: Center for Global Development).

Biswas, A. (2007) 'India's Engagement in Africa: Scope and Significance.' Paper delivered to the CODESRIA–HSRC Workshop on South Africa in Africa, Gold Reef City, Johannesburg, October.

Bonacich, E. and R. Applebaum (2000) *Behind the Label: Inequality in the Los Angeles Apparel Industry* (Berkeley: University of California Press).

Bond, P (2004) 'US Empire and South African Subimperialism', in L. Panitch and C. Leys (eds) *Socialist Register, 2005: The Empire Reloaded* (London: Merlin), pp. 218–38.

Bond, Patrick (2006a) *Looting Africa: The Economics of Exploitation* (Pietermaritzburg: University of KwaZulu-Natal Press).

Bond, Patrick (2006b) *Talk Left, Walk Right: South Africa's Frustrated Global Reforms.* (Scottsville: Univ. of KwaZulu-Natal Press).

Bradsher, K. (2006) 'From the Silk Road to the Superhighway, all Coin Leads to China', *New York Times*, 26 February: Weekend p. 4.

Bradsher, K. (2009) 'China Losing Taste for Debt from the US', *New York Times*, 8 January, pp. A1–10.

Brazil – Presidency of the Republic (2007) *Millennium Development Goals:* National Monitoring Report (Brasília: Ipea/MP, SPI), September.

Breen, R. and C. Garcia-Penalosa (2005) 'Income Inequality and Macroeconomic Volatility: An Empirical Investigation', *Review of Development Economics*, 9 (3), pp. 380–98.

Bridge, S. (2007) 'IMF wary of China's DRC loan' on Fin24.com, 10 April 2007, sourced on 14 July 2008 from www.fin24.com/articles/default/display_article.aspx?ArticleId=1518- 1783_2195763

Buckler, W. A. M. (2005) 'Global Report', *Privateer*, 518, January, pp. 1–12.

Burawoy, M. (2005) 'For Public Sociology', *Soziale Welt*, 56, pp. 347–75

Burity, J. A. (1994) 'Iterability, Contexts, Globalization: Notes on Latin American Social Movements, Religion and Democracy', *Essex Papers in Politics and Government*, 4, pp. 1–21.

Burity, J. A. (2001) 'Globalização e identidade: desafios do multiculturalismo', in V. Gico, A. Spinelli and P. Vicente (eds) *As Ciências Sociais: desafios do milênio* (Natal: Edufrn/PPGCS), pp. 156–73.

Burity, J. A. (2006a) 'Identidades colectivas en transición y la activación de una esfera publica no estatal', in C. W. Lubambo; D. B. Coelho and M. A. Melo (eds) *Diseño institucional y participación política: experiencias en el Brasil contemporáneo* (Buenos Aires: Clacso), pp. 74–124.

Burity, J. A. (2006b) 'Reform of the State and the New Discourse on Social Policy in Brazil', *Latin American Perspectives* 33 (3), pp. 67–88.

Burke, C., L. Corkin, and N. Tay (2007) 'China's Engagement of Africa: Preliminary Scoping of African Case Studies. Angola, Ethiopia, Gabon, Uganda, South Africa, Zambia.' November. Sourced on 7 October 2008 from www.ccs.org.za/downloads/RF_Paper_Final.pdf

Callahan, W. A. (2002) 'Civilization and Transnational Relations: Critical IR Theory and Chinese Foreign Policy', paper presented at the conference on 'International Relations Theory: A Sino-British Dialogue', School of International Relations and Public Affairs, Fudan University, Shanghai, 25–26 April.

Cammack, P. (2004) '"Signs of the Times:" Capitalism, Competitiveness, and the New Face of Empire in Latin America', in L. Panitch and C. Leys (eds) *Socialist Register, 2005: The Empire Reloaded* (London: Merlin Press), pp. 256–70

Carter, M. and J. May. (2001) 'One Kind of Freedom: Poverty Dynamics in Post-apartheid South Africa', *World Development*, 29 (12), pp. 1987–2006.

Cartier, C. (2004) 'Engendering Industrialization in China Under Reform', in Chiao-min Hsieh and Max Lu (eds) *Changing China: A Geographic Appraisal* (Cambridge MA: Westview Press), pp. 269–90.

Carvalho, J. J. de (2005) *Inclusão étnica e racial no Brasil: a questão das cotas no ensino superior* (São Paulo: Attar).

Carvalho, J. J. de (1997) 'Mandonismo, Coronelismo, Clientelismo: Uma Discussão Conceitual', in *Dados – Revista de Ciências Sociais*, 40 (2), DOI: 10.1590/S0011-52581997000200003.

Carvalho, J. J. de (2000) 'Saudade do escravo', in *Folha de São Paulo*, Caderno Mais!, 2 April, 2–1.

Cecil, C. O. (2005) 'Gum Arabic', in *Saudi Aramco World*, March/April, pp. 36–9. Sourced 23 April 2008 from: www.saudiaramcoworld.com/issue/200502/gum.arabic.htm

Central Intelligence Agency (2004) *World Factbook 2004* (Washington DC: CIA).

Chambers, R. (1997) *Whose Reality Counts? Putting the First Last* (London: Intermediary Technology Publications).

Chan, Kam Wing (2003) 'Migration in China in the Reform Era', in Alvin So (ed.) *China's Developmental Miracle: Origins, Transformations, and Challenges* (New York and London: M.E. Sharpe), pp. 111–35.

Chandrasekhar, C. and Jayati Ghosh (2006) 'Employment Growth: The Latest Trends', at www.macroscan.com/fet/nov06/fet171106Employment_Growth.htm

Chen Zhimin (2005) 'Nationalism, Internationalism, and Chinese Foreign Policy', *Journal of Contemporary China*, 14 (2) (February), pp. 35–53.

Chen, Shun (2007) 'New Impetus to China-Africa Agricultural Cooperation', Xinhua. Published on 30 December 2007, sourced on 14 April 2008 from

www.macaudailytimesnews.com/index.php?option=com_content&task=view
&id=4720&Itemid=31

Cheng Ming (1989) (Hong Kong), 10 October 1989, cited in *Foreign Broad-cast Information Service-China* (*FBIS-CHI*), 3 October 1989, quoted in Taylor (2004).

Chi, Lau Kin and Huang Pin, eds (2003) *China Reflected*, special issues of *Asian Exchange*, 18 (2) and 19 (1).

Chibber, V. (2006) *Locked in Place: State-Building and Late Industrialization in India* (Princeton: Princeton University Press).

China Daily (2005) 'Giants Cash in on Chinese Craze for Sports', 26 May.

China Daily (2008) 'Chinese Firm to Develop Iron Ore Project in Africa', 9 July, sourced on 14 July 2008from www.chinamining.org/Investment/2008-07-09/1215570253d15011.html

China Labor Bulletin (2008) *Migrant Workers in China*, at www.clb.org.Hong Kong./en/ (home page), accessed 10 July 2008.

Chinability (2008) 'China's Foreign Exchange Reserves, 1977–2008'. Data from the State Administration of Foreign Exchange, People's Republic of China. Sourced on 10 July 2008 from www.chinability.com/Reserves.htm

Chomsky, N. (2006) 'Latin America and Asia are Breaking Free of Washington's Grip', *Japan Focus*. Retrieved 20 March 2006 at http://japanfocus.org/article.asp?id=545

Chua, A. (2003) *World on Fire* (New York: Doubleday).

Clancy, M. (2002) 'The Globalization of Sex Tourism and Cuba: A Commodity Chains Approach', *Studies in Comparative International Development* 36 (4), pp. 63–88.

Clapham, C. (2006) 'Fitting China in', *Brenthurst Discussion Papers*, 8/2006 (Johannesburg: Brenthurst Foundation).

Cohen, R. and P. Kennedy (2007) *Global Sociology*, 2nd edition (Basingstoke: Palgrave).

Corkin, L. (2008a) 'AERC Scoping Exercise on China-Africa Relations: The Case of Angola', African Economic Research Consortium, January.

Corkin, L. (2008b) 'All's Fair in Loans and War: The Development of China–Angola Relations', in Kweku Ampiah and Sanusha Naidu (eds) *Crouching Tiger, Hidden Dragon? Africa and China* (Scottsville: University of KwaZulu Natal Press).

Croll, E. (2006) *China's New Consumers: Social Development and Domestic Demand* (London and New York: Routledge).

Crouch, C. (2004) *Post-democracy* (Cambridge: Polity Press).

Cumings, B. (1984) 'The Origins and Development of the Northeast Asian Political Economy: Industrial Sectors, Product Cycles, and Political Consequences', *International Organization* 38 (1), pp. 1–40.

Das, D. K. (2006) *China and India. A Tale of Two Economies* (London/New York: Routledge).

Davies, M., H. Edinger, N. Tay and S. Naidu (2008) 'How China Delivers Development Assistance to Africa', February (University of Stellenbosch: Centre for Chinese Studies).

Davin, D. (1999) *Internal Migration in Contemporary China* (Houndmills and London: Macmillan Press).

Davis, M. (2006) *Planet of Slums* (London: Verso).

Davis, P. (2007) 'Discussions Among the Poor: Exploring Poverty Dynamics with Focus Groups in Bangladesh.' CPRC Working Paper 84 (Manchester: Chronic Poverty Research Centre).

Dawar, N. (2005) 'Prepare Now for a Sino-Indian Trade Boom', *Financial Times*, 31 October, p. 11

Deininger, K. and J. Okidi. (2003) 'Growth and Poverty Reduction in Uganda, 1992–2000: Panel Data Evidence', *Development Policy Review*, 21 (4), pp. 481–509.

Delanty, G. (ed.) (2006) *Europe and Asia Beyond East and West* (London and New York: Routledge).

Deng Yong and T. G. Moore (2004) 'China Views Globalization: Toward a New Great-power Politics?' *The Washington Quarterly*, 27 (3) (Spring), pp. 117–136.

Deolalikar, A. (2002). 'Access to Health Services by the Poor and the Non-Poor: The Case of Vietnam', *Journal of Asian and African Studies*, 37 (2), pp. 244–61.

Derrida, J. (1982) *Margins of Philosophy* (New York/London: Harvester Wheatsheaf).

Derrida, J. (1990) *Limited Inc*. (Paris: Galilée).

Dicken, P. (2003) *Global Shift. Reshaping the Global Economic Map in the 21st Century*, 4th edition (London/Thousand Oaks/New Delhi: Sage).

Dilip, T. R. and R. Duggal (2002) 'Incidence of Non-Fatal Health Outcomes and Debt in Urban India.' Working Paper, Center for Enquiry into Health and Allied Themes (CEHAT), Mumbai.

Dirlik, A. (1998) *What Is In a Rim? Critical Perspectives on the Pacific Region Idea* (New York and Oxford: Rowman and Littlefield).

Disarmament and International Security (n.d.) 'Summary' Available at www.sipri.org/

Dobler, G. (2005) 'South-South Business Relations in Practice: Chinese Merchants in Oshikango, Namibia', Institute for Social Anthropology, Universität Basel, Switzerland. Sourced on 5 May 2008 from: www.eldis.org/vfile/upload/1/document/0708/DOC22353.pdf

Dollar, D. and A. Kraay (2002) 'Growth is Good for the Poor', *Journal of Economic Growth*, 7 (3) pp. 195–225.

Domingues, J. M. (2002) 'A dialética da modernização conservadora e a nova história do Brasil', *Dados – Revista de Ciências Sociais*, 45 (3), pp. 459–82.

Domingues, J. M. (2006) 'Instituições formais, cidadania e solidariedade complexa', *Lua Nova*, 66, pp. 9–22.

Doty, R. L. (2007) 'States of Exception on the Mexico–US Border: Security, "Decisions" and Civilian Border Patrols', *International Political Sociology* 1 (2), pp. 113–37.

Dow Jones Newswires (2006) 'CNPC and Madagascar Petroleum to Explore Madagascar Oil Field', 24 February, sourced on 14 July 2008 from www.gasandoil.com/goc/company/cna61070.htm

Downs, E. (2007) 'The Facts and Fiction of Sino-African Energy Relations', *China Security*, 3 (3) (Summer), pp. 42–68.

Duffield, M. (2001) *Global Governance and the New Wars: The Merging of Development and Security* (London and New York: Zed Books).

Duménil, G. and D. Lévy (2001) 'Costs and Benefits of Neoliberalism: A Class Analysis', *Review of International Political Economy*, 8 (4), pp. 578–607.

Dwyer, G. (2004) 'Winning US Presidency May Prove a Poisoned Chalice', *New Zealand Herald*, 24 September.

Dyer, G. (2008) 'China Sees Slower Growth in Its Forex Reserves', *Financial Times*, 15 July.

Eagleton, T. (2004) *After Theory* (London: Penguin Books).

Economy, E. (2005) 'China's Rise in Southeast Asia: Implications for the United States', *Journal of Contemporary China*, XIV (August), pp. 409–25.

Edinger, H. (2008) 'How China Delivers Rural Development Assistance to Africa'. Presentation at the sixth Brussels Development Briefing: 'New Drivers, New Players in ACP Rural Development', 2 July. Available at www.slideshare.net/euforic/how-china-delivers-rural-development- assistance-to-africa

Eisenstadt, S. N. (ed.) (2002) *Multiple Modernities* (New Brunswick/London: Transactions).

Elliott, L. (2005) 'America's Tricky Balancing Act', *Guardian Weekly*, 7–13 October, p. 16.

Ensor, T. and B. San. (1996). 'Access and Payment for Health Care: The Poor of Northern Vietnam', *International Journal of Health Planning and Management*, 11 (1), pp. 69–83.

EQUITA (2005) 'Paying Out-of-Pocket for Health Care in Asia: Catastrophic and Poverty Impact'. Working Paper No. 2. Available at www.equitaorg

Escobar, A. (1995) *Encountering Development: The Making and Unmaking of the Third World* (Princeton: Princeton University Press).

Escobar, A. (2005) 'O lugar da natureza e a natureza do lugar: globalização ou pós-desenvolvimento?', in E. Lander (ed.) *A colonialidade do saber. Eurocentrismo e ciências sociais: perspectivas latino-americanas* (Buenos Aires: Clacso), pp. 134–5.

Exim Bank–China Export Import Bank (2008) 'Chinese Government Concessional Loan'. Sourced on 29 June 2008 from http://english.eximbank.gov.cn/business/government.jsp

Fabricant, S., C. Kamara and A. Mills (1999) 'Why the Poor Pay More: House-hold Curative Expenditures in Rural Sierra Leone', *International Journal of Health Planning and Management*, 14 (3), pp. 179–99.

Fan, C. (2004) 'Gender Differences in Chinese Migration', in Chiao-min Hsieh and Max Lu (eds) *Changing China: A Geographic Appraisal* (Cambridge MA: Westview Press), pp. 243–68.

Farmer, P. (1999) *Infections and Inequalities: The Modern Plagues* (Berkeley: University of California Press).

Farmer, P. (2003) *Pathologies of Power: Health, Human Rights, and the New War on the Poor* (Berkeley: University of California Press).

Feinstein, C. H. (2005) *An Economic History of South Africa. Conquest, Discrimination and Development* (New York: Cambridge University Press).

Ferguson, J. (1999) *Expectations of Modernity* (Berkeley, University of California Press).

Fernandes, S. (2006) 'Trade Treaties and US Hegemony in the Americas', *Economic and Political Weekly*, 20 May.

Fields, G. S. (2004) 'Dualism in the Labor Market: A Perspective on the Lewis Model after Half a Century', *The Manchester School*, 72 (6) pp. 724–35.

Financial Times (London) (2005) 'China's Five-year Plan Will Underline Hu's Agenda', 9 October.

Fitzgerald, A. (2006) 'Petrodollars are Helping Keep US Economy Afloat', *International Herald Tribune*, 3 January.

Florida, R. (2006) *The Rise of the Creative Class and How It's Transforming Work, Leisure, Community and Everyday Life* (New York: Basic Books).

Ford, G. (2005) 'Forging an Alternative to US Hegemony', *Japan Times*, 7 February, available at http://search.japantimes.co.jp/cgi-bin/eo20050207a1.html

Forero, J. (2006) 'Chavez, Seeking Foreign Allies, Spends Billions', *New York Times*, 4 April.

Foster-Carter, A. (1978) 'The Modes of Production Controversy', *New Left Review*, 107, pp. 47–77.

Frank, A. G. (1998) *Re Orient: Global Economy in the Asian Age* (Berkeley: University of California Press).

Friedman, T. L. (2005) *The World is Flat. A Brief History of the Twenty-first Century* (New York: Farrar, Straus and Giroux).

Gan, L., L. Xu and Y. Yao (2005) 'Health Shocks, Village Governance, and Farmers' Long-term Income Capabilities: Evidence from Rural China', FED Working Papers Series No. FE20050066. Available at www.fed.org.cn

Gaonkar, D. (ed.) (2001) *Alternative Modernities* (Durham NC: Duke University Press).

Giridharadas, A. (2007) 'India's Edge Goes Beyond Outsourcing', *New York Times*, 4 April.

George, C. J. (2004) 'How to Bring Millions of Investors into Market', 27 April. www.hinduonnet.com/businessline/blbby/stories/2004042700090300.htm

Gereffi, G. and M. Korzeniewicz (eds) (1994) *Commodity Chains and Global Capitalism* (Westport: Praeger).

Gereffi, G., J. Humphrey and T. Sturgeon (2005) 'The Governance of Global Value Chains', *Review of International Political Economy* 12 (1), pp. 78–104.

Gittings, J. (2005) *The Changing Face of China: From Mao to Market* (Oxford: Oxford University Press).

Global Commission on International Migration (2005) *Migration in an Interconnected World: New Directions for Action*, at www.gcim.org./en (home page), accessed 10 July 2008.

Glyn, A. (2006) 'Finance's Relentless Rise Threatens Economic Stability', *Financial Times*, 27 April, p. 13

Glynos, J. and D. Howarth (2007) *Logics of Critical Explanation in Social and Political Theory* (London: Routledge).

Godoy, J. (2006) 'China Swaggers into Europe's "Backyard"', *Asia Times Online*, 17 November.

Gohn, Maria de Glória (1997) *Teorias dos movimentos sociais: Paradigmas clássicos e contemporâneos* (São Paulo: Loyola).

GOI (2007) *Report of the Expert Group on Agricultural Indebtedness* (New Delhi: Government of India, Department of Economic Affairs, Ministry of Finance).

Góis, A. (2007) 'Desigualdade no país pára de cair em 2006', in *Folha de São Paulo*, Dinheiro, 12 April. Available at www1.folha.uol.com.br/fsp/dinheiro/fi1204200732.htm. Accessed 15 April 2008.

Goldstein, A., Nicolaus Pinaud, H. Reisen and X. Chen (2006) *The Rise of China and India: What's in it for Africa?* (Paris: Development Centre of the OECD).

Goodman, D. S. G. and G. Segal (eds) (1994) *China Deconstructs: Politics, Trade, and Regionalism* (London and New York: Routledge).

Goodman, P. S. (2006) 'Booming Exports Boost China's Foreign Currency Reserves', *Washington Post*, 16 January.

Gosh, P. S. (2006) 'Beyond the Rhetoric', *Frontline*, 6 October, pp. 7–9.

Graßl, H. (2000) *Strukturwandel der Arbeitsteilung. Globalisierung, Tertiarisierung und Feminisierung der Wohlfahrtsproduktion* (Constance: UVK).

Gray, J. (1998) *False Dawn* (London: Granta).

Green, D. (2008) *From Poverty to Power: How Active Citizens and Effective States Can Change the World* (Oxford: Oxfam).

Growth Commission Report (2008), Washington DC, at www.growth commission.org

Gu, W. (1995) *Politics of Divided Nations: The Case of China and Korea* (Westport: Praeger). Quoted in Ian Taylor, 'The "All-weather Friend"? Sino-African Interaction in the Twenty First Century', in Ian Taylor and Paul Williams (eds) *Africa in International Politics: External Involvement on Africa* (London: Routledge, 2004).

Guèye, H. (2008) 'The DR of the Congo; The Chinese Mining Contract is Creating Division', *Les Afriques*, 26 May, sourced on 28 May 2008 from www.lesafriques.com/en/news/dem.-re-congo/the-dr-of-the-congo-the-chinese-mining-contract-is-creating-division.html?Itemid=35?articleid=0102&section id= &releasecatid=&countrytitle=

Guha, K. (2007) 'IMF Warns of Risk to Global Growth', *Financial Times*, 22 August, p. 3

Guthrie, D. (2006) *China and Globalization: the Social, Economic and Political Transformation of Chinese Society* (New York: Routledge).

Hacker, J. (2006) *The Great Risk Shift* (New York: Oxford University Press).

Haddad, L. and A. Ahmed (2003) 'Chronic and Transitory Poverty: Evidence from Egypt, 1997–99', *World Development*, 31 (1), pp. 71–85.

Hamilton, G. and Wei An-Chang (2003) 'The Importance of Commerce in the Organization of China's Late Imperial Economy', in G. Arrighi, T. Hamashita and M. Selden (eds) *The Resurgence of East Asia: 500, 150 and 50 Year Perspectives* (London and New York: Routledge), pp. 173–213.

Han Yuhai (2006) 'Assessing China's Reforms', *Economic and Political Weekly*, XLI (22), June 3, pp. 2206–12

Haq, M. ul (1995) *Reflections on Human Development* (New York: Oxford University Press).

Hardt, M. and A. Negri (2000) *Empire* (Cambridge MA: Harvard University Press).

Harris, J. (2005) 'Emerging Third World Powers: China, India and Brazil', *Race & Class*, 46 (3), pp. 7–27.

Harvey, D. (1989) *The Condition of Postmodernity* (Oxford: Blackwell).

Harvey, David (2003) *The New Imperialism* (Oxford: Oxford University Press).

Hatekar, N. and A. Dongre (2005) 'Structural Breaks in India's Growth: Revisiting the Debate with a Longer Perspective', *Economic and Political Weekly*, XL (14), 2 April, pp. 1432–5.

Himmelstein, D., E. Warren, D. Thorne and S. Woolhandler (2005) 'Illness and Injury as Contributors to Bankruptcy', *Health Affairs*, 2 February.

Hobson, J. M. (2004) *The Eastern Origins of Western Civilisation* (Cambridge: Cambridge University Press).

Holstein, W. J. (2005) 'Erasing the Image of the Ugly American', *New York Times*, 23 October, p. B9

Hsiao, H. M. and A. So (1993) 'Ascent Through National Integration: The Chinese Triangle of Mainland-Taiwan-Hong Kong', in Ravi Palat (ed.) *Pacific-Asia and the Future of the World-System* (Connecticut and London: Greenwood Press), pp. 133–47.

Hsiao-Tung, Fei (1989) *Rural Development in China: Prospect and Retrospect* (Chicago and London: University of Chicago Press).

Hsing, You-tien (1997) 'Building *Guanxi* Across the Straits: Taiwanese Capital and Local Chinese Bureaucrats', in Aihwa Ong and Donald Nonini (eds) *Ungrounded Empires: The Cultural Politics of Modern Chinese Transnationalism* (New York and London: Routledge), pp. 143–64.

Hu, Jintao (2006) 'Full Text of President Hu's speech at China-Africa Summit', 4 November, sourced on 16 July 2008 from http://news.xinhuanet.com/english/ 2006-11/04/content_5289052.htm

Hui, Wang (2003) 'The 1989 Movement and the Historical Origins of Neo-liberalism in China', in Lau Kin Chi and Huang Pin (eds) *China Reflected,* special issues of *Asian Exchange*, 18 (2) and 19 (1), pp. 211–23.

Huntington, S. P. (1993) 'The Clash of Civilizations?', *Foreign Affairs*, 72 (3), pp. 22–49.

ICG – International Crisis Group (2008) 'China's Thirst for Oil.' Crisis Group Asia Report No. 153, 9 June.

International Mining (2008) 'Massive DRC mining (and infrastructure) agreement with China', 9 May, sourced on 5 June 2008 from www.im-mining.com/2008/ 05/09/massive-drc-mining-and-infrastructure- agreement-with-china/

Ipea/Instituto de Pesquisa Econômica Aplicada; IBGE/Instituto Brasileiro de Geografia e Estatística (2004) *Millennium Development Goals – Brazilian Monitoring Report* (Brasília: Ipea), September.

ITGLWF-Africa press release (2005) 'Call for Action Against China Grows', Cape Town, 11 October.

Jalan, B. (2005) *The Future of India*, Vol. 2 (New Delhi: Viking).

Jin Canrong (2005) 'China's New Diplomacy and Sino-US Relations: Domestic Resources from a Chinese Perspective.' Paper presented at the conference on 'China and the US Mutual Perceptions and Bilateral Relations', Center for American Studies, Fudan University, Shanghai, 27–28 May.

Joffe, J. (2006) *Überpower: The Imperial Temptation of America* (New York: W.W. Norton & Co).

Johnson, J. (2006) 'Insurgency in India – How the Maoist Threat Reaches beyond Nepal', *Financial Times*, 26 April, p. 13.

Johnson, S. (2005) 'Indian and Chinese Banks Pulling Out of Ailing US Dollar', *Financial Times*, 7 March.

Kaelble, H. (1987) *Auf dem Weg zu einer europäischen Gesellschaft. Eine Sozialgeschichte Westeuropas 1880–1980*, (München: Beck).

Kang, Liu (1998) 'Is There an Alternative to (Capitalist) Globalization? The Debate about Modernity in China', in F. Jameson and M. Miyoshi (eds) *The Cultures of Globalization* (Durham NC: Duke University Press), pp. 164–88.

Kaplinsky, R. (2006) 'Winners and Losers: China's Trade and Opportunities for Africa', in Leni Wild and David Mepham (eds) *The New Sinosphere: China in Africa* (London: IPPR).

Kaplinsky, R., D. McCormick and M. Morris (2007) 'The Impact of China on Sub-Saharan Africa.' Working Paper 291, November, Institute of Development Studies, Brighton, UK.

Kappel, R., J. Lay and S. Steiner (2005) 'Uganda: No more Pro-Poor Growth?', *Development Policy Review*, 23 (1), pp. 27–53.

Kenjiro, Y. (2005) 'Why Illness Causes More Serious Economic Damage than Crop Failure in Rural Cambodia', *Development and Change*, 36 (4) pp. 759–83.

Kennedy, P. (2001) 'Maintaining American Power: From Injury to Recovery', in S. Talbott and N. Chanda (eds) *The Age of Terror: America and the World after September 11* (New York: Basic Books), pp. 53–80.

Khumalo, S. (2008) 'SA Firms Tough It Out in Zimbabwe', *Mail and Guardian*. 13 July, sourced on that date from www.mg.co.za/article/2008-07-13-sa-firms-tough-it-out-in-zimbabwe

King, A. D. (ed.) (1991) *Culture, Globalization and the World-System: Contemporary Conditions for the Representation of Identity* (Basingstoke: Macmillan).

Klein, N. (2000) *No Logo* (London: Flamingo).

Kohli, A. (2006a) 'Politics of Economic Growth in India, 1980–2005: Part I – The 1980s', *Economic and Political Weekly*, 1 April, pp. 1251–9.

Kohli, A. (2006b) 'Politics of Economic Growth in India, 1980–2005: Part II – The 1990s and Beyond', *Economic and Political Weekly*, 8 April, pp. 1361–70.

Koval, J. and K. Fidel (2006) 'Chicago: The Immigrant Capital of the Heartland', in J. Koval, L. Bennett, M. Bennett, F. Demissie, R. Garner and K. Kim (eds) *The New Chicago: A Social and Cultural Analysis* (Philadelphia: Temple University Press), pp. 97–104.

Krasner, S. (1995) 'Compromising Westphalia', *International Security*, 20 (3), pp. 115–51.

Krishna, A. (2004) 'Escaping Poverty and Becoming Poor: Who Gains, Who Loses, and Why?', *World Development*, 32 (1), pp. 121–36.

Krishna, A. (2005) 'Why Growth is Not Enough: Household Poverty Dynamics in Northeast Gujarat, India', *Journal of Development Studies* 41 (7), pp. 1163–92.

Krishna, A. (2006a) 'Escaping Poverty and Becoming Poor in 36 Villages of Central and Western Uganda', *Journal of Development Studies*, 42 (2), pp. 346–70.

Krishna, A. (2006b) 'Pathways Out Of and Into Poverty in 36 Villages of Andhra Pradesh, India', *World Development*, 34 (2), pp. 271–88.

Krishna, A. (2007) 'For Reducing Poverty Faster: Target Reasons before People', *World Development*, 35 (11), pp. 1947–1960.

Krishna, A. and V. Brihmadesam (2006) 'What Does it Take to Become a Software Professional?', *Economic and Political Weekly*, 41 (30), pp. 3307–14.

Krishna, A. et al. (2004) (with P. Kristjanson, M. Radeny and W. Nindo) 'Escaping Poverty and Becoming Poor in 20 Kenyan Villages', *Journal of Human Development*, 5 (2), pp. 211–26.

Krishna, A. et al. (2005) (with M. Kapila, M. Porwal and V. Singh) 'Why Growth Is Not Enough: Household Poverty Dynamics in Northeast Gujarat, India', *Journal of Development Studies*, 41 (7), pp. 1163–92.

Krishna, A. et al. (2006a) (with D. Lumonya, M. Markiewicz, F. Mugumya, A. Kafuko and J. Wegoye) 'Escaping Poverty and Becoming Poor in 36 Villages of Central and Western Uganda', *Journal of Development Studies*, 42 (2), pp. 346–70.

Krishna, A. et al. (2006b) (with P. Kristjanson, J. Kuan, G. Quilca, M. Radeny and A. Sanchez-Urrelo) 'Fixing the Hole in the Bucket: Household Poverty Dynamics in Forty Communities of the Peruvian Andes', *Development and Change*, 37 (5), 997–1021.

Krishna, A. et al. (2006c) (with C. Gibson-Davis, L. Clasen, M. Markiewicz and N. Perez) 'Escaping Poverty and Becoming Poor in Thirteen Communities of Rural North Carolina', Working Paper, Sanford Institute of Public Policy, Duke University. Available at www.pubpol.duke.edu/krishna

Kumar, A. (2009) '2008: a difficult year, relief not in sight soon', *The Tribune* (New Delhi), January 1.

Kumoll, K. (2007) *Kultur, Geschichte und die Indigenisierung der Moderne. Eine Analyse des Gesamtwerks von Marshall Sahlins.* PhD thesis, University of Freiburg.

Lander, E. (2005) 'Ciências sociais: saberes coloniais e eurocêntricos', in E. Lander (ed.) *A colonialidade do saber. Eurocentrismo e ciências sociais: perspectivas latino-americanas* (Buenos Aires: Clacso), pp. 21–53.

Le Monde (2005) 'En Chine, le parti communiste veut concilier 'justice sociale' et performances e'conomiques', 13 October.

Lee, Ching Kwan (1998) *Gender and the South China Miracle: Two Worlds of Factory Women* (Berkeley and London: University of California Press).

Lee, Ching Kwan (2007) *Against the Law: Labor Protests in China's Rustbelt and Sunbelt* (Berkeley and London: University of California Press).

Leoncini, Riccardo and Sandro Montresor (eds) (2007) *Dynamic Capabilities, Firm Organization and Local Systems of Production* (London/New York: Routledge).

Lim, Hyun-Chin and Jin-Ho Jang (2006) 'Neoliberalism in Post-crisis South Korea', *Journal of Contemporary Asia*, 36 (4) pp. 442–63.

Lin, T. (1996) 'Beijing's Foreign Aid Policy in the 1990s: Continuity and Change', *Issues and Studies*, 32 (1).

Lind, M. (2005) 'How the US Became the World's Dispensable Nation, *Financial Times*, 26 January.

Lipton, M. (1977) *Why Poor People Stay Poor: Urban Bias in World Development* (London: Maurice Temple Smith).

Lyon, D. (2007) 'Sociological Perspectives and Surveillance Studies', *Contemporary Sociology* 36 (2), pp. 107–11.

Lyon, D. (ed.) (2003) *Surveillance as Social Sorting: Risk, Privacy, and Digital Discrimination* (London: Routledge).

Macintyre, A. and B. Naughton (2005) 'The Decline of a Japan-Led Model of the East Asian Economy', in T. J. Pempel (ed.) *Remapping East Asia: The Construction of a Region* (Ithaca: Cornell University Press), pp. 77–100.

Maffesoli, M. (1988) *Le temps des tribus* (Paris: Klincksieck).

Magnier, M. (2006) 'US Is Watching China's Latin American Moves', *Los Angeles Times*, 15 April.

Magnus, G. (2006) 'The New Reserves of Economic Power', *Financial Times*, 22 August, p. 11

Mahadevia, D. (2006) *Shanghaing Mumbai: Visions, Displacements and Politics of a Globalizing City* (Ahmedabad: Centre for Development Alternatives).

Maitre, M. and A. Massalatchi (2008) 'Areva Renews Niger Uranium Deal, Pays 50 pct More', Reuters, 14 Jan, sourced on 16 July 2008 from www.reuters.

com/article/rbssIndustryMaterialsUtilitiesNews/idUSL149087320080114?
sp= true

Mallaby, S. (2006) 'In India, Engineering Success', *Washington Post*, 2 January.

Mallee, H. (2002) 'Taking Grain as the Key Link: Population Registration and Development Discourse in China', in Luigi Tomba (ed.) *East Asian Capitalism: Conflicts, Growth and Crisis* (Milan: Feltrinelli), pp. 419–52.

Mann, M. (1986) *The Sources of Social Power* (Cambridge: Cambridge University Press).

Marber, P. (1998) *From Third World to World Class: the Future of Emerging Markets in the Global Economy* (Reading MA: Perseus).

Marques, R. M. and A. Mendes (2007) 'Servindo a dois senhores: as políticas sociais no governo Lula', *Katálysis*, 10 (1) (January-June), pp. 15–23.

Marshall, T. (2006) 'Southeast Asia's New Best Friend', *Los Angeles Times*, 17 June.

Martin, W. G. (2008) 'South Africa's Subimperial Future: Washington Consensus, Bandung Consensus, or Peoples' Consensus', *African Sociological Review* (in press).

Massey, D. (1993) 'Power-geometry and a Progressive Sense of Place', in J. Bird, B. Curtis, T. Putnam, G. Robertson and L. Tickner (eds) *Mapping the Futures: Local Cultures, Global Change* (London: Routledge), pp. 59–69.

Mato, D. (2007) 'Cultura, comunicación y transformaciones sociales en tiempos de globalización', in D. Mato and A. Maldonado Fermín (eds) *Cultura y transformaciones sociales en tiempos de globalizatión* (Buenos Aires: Clacso), pp. 13–84.

Mazlish, B. (2006) 'Global History', *Theory Culture & Society*, 23 (2–3), pp. 406–8.

Mbeki, T. (2001) Speech at Tsinghua University, Beijing, China, 11 December 2001.

McGee, R. (2004) 'Constructing Poverty Trends in Uganda: A Multidisciplinary Perspective', *Development and Change*, 35 (3), pp. 499–523.

McGregor, R. (2006) 'Pressure Mounts on China Forex Management', *Financial Times*, 28 November, p. 6.

McKenna, B. (2005) 'With Friends Like the IMF and the World Bank, Who Needs Loans?', *Globe and Mail* (Toronto), 16 August, p. B11.

McKernan, S. and C. Ratcliffe. (2002) 'Transition Events in the Dynamics of Poverty' (Washington DC: Urban Institute). Available at www.urban.org

McMichael, P. (2004) *Development and Social Change: A Global Perspective* (Thousand Oaks: Pine Forge Press).

McNeill, W. H. (1982) *The Pursuit of Power* (Chicago: University of Chicago Press).

Mearsheimer, J. J. (2005) 'Better to be Godzilla than Bambi', *Foreign Policy*, 146 (January–February), pp. 47–8.

Mearsheimer, J. and S. Walt (2006) 'The Israel Lobby', *London Review of Books*, 23 March, pp. 3–12.

Mello, E. C. de (1999) 'O caráter orgânico da escravidão', in *Folha Online – Brasil 500 d.C.*, available at www1.uol.com.br/fol/brasil500/dc_4_3.html.

Mello, E. C. de (2000) 'Reler 'O abolicionismo''', in *Folha de São Paulo*, Caderno Mais!, 27 February, pp. 5–18.

Melville, C. and O. Owen (2005) 'China and Africa: A New Era of 'South-South Co-operation', *Open Democracy*, 8 July, available at www.opendemocracy.net/globalization-G8/south_2658.jsp#

Michel, S. and M. Beuret (2008) *La Chinafrique. Pékin à la conquête du continent noir* (Paris: Grasset).

Milanovic, B. (2005) *Worlds Apart: Measuring International and Global Inequality* (Princeton: Princeton University Press).

Mills, G. and C. Thompson (2008) 'China: Partner or Predator in Africa?', 25 Jan, sourced on 10 July 2008 from www.atimes.com/atimes/China_Business/JA25Cb 02.html

Millward, J. A. (2008) 'China's Story; Putting the PR into the PRC.' Published on *Opendemocracy.org*, 18 April, sourced on 23 April 2008 from: www.opendemocracy. net/article/governments/how_china_should_rebrand_0

Minwala, Shabnam (2005) 'Second Wave of Outsourcing', *Times of India*, 10 October.

Mittelman, J. H. (2000) *The Globalization Syndrome: Transformation and Resistance* (Princeton: Princeton University Press).

Mittelman, J. H. (2004) *Whither Globalization? The Vortex of Knowledge and Ideology* (London and New York: Routledge).

Mittelman, J. H. (2006) 'Globalization and Development: Learning from Debates in China', *Globalizations*, 3 (3), pp. 377–92.

Mohan, G. and M. Power (2008): 'New African Choices: The Politics of Chinese Engagement', *Review of African Political Economy*, Special edition on 'The New Face of China-Africa Co-operation' (guest editors: Marcus Power and Giles Mohan with Sanusha Naidu), 35 (115), pp. 23–42.

Moore, H. L. (2006) 'Global Anxieties. Concept-Metaphors and Pre-Theoretical Commitments in Anthropology', *Anthropological Theory*, 4 (1), pp. 71–88.

Moore, T. G. (2000) 'China and Globalization', in S. Kim (ed.) *East Asia and Globalization* (Lanham: Rowman & Littlefield), pp. 105–31.

Mueller, P. G. and D. A. Ross (1975) *China and Japan – Emerging Global Powers* (New York, Washington, London: Praeger).

Nabuco, J. (2000 [1883]) *O abolicionismo* (São Paulo: Publifolha). Available at www.bibvirt.futuro.usbr

Naidu, S. and D. Mbazima (2008) 'China-Africa Relations: A New Impulse in a Changing Continental Landscape', *Futures*, 40 (8), pp. 748–61.

Narayan, D., R. Chambers, M. Kaul Shah and P. Petesch (2000) *Voices of the Poor: Crying Out for Change* (Washington DC: World Bank and Oxford University Press).

Narayan, D., R. Patel, K. Schafft, A. Rademacher and S. Koch-Schulte (2000) *Voices of the Poor: Can Anyone Hear Us?* (New York: Oxford University Press).

Naughton, B. (1996) 'China's Emergence and Prospects as a Trading Nation', *Brookings Papers on Economic Activity*, 2, pp. 273–344.

Naughton, B. (1997) 'The Emergence of the China Circle', in Barry Naughton (ed.) *The China Circle: Economics and Technology in the PRC, Taiwan, and Hong Kong* (Washington DC: Brookings Institution Press), pp. 3–37.

Naughton, B. (1999) 'China: Domestic Restructuring and a New Role in Asia', in T. J. Pempel (ed.) *The Politics of the Asian Economic Crisis* (Ithaca and London: Cornell University Press), pp. 203–23.

Naughton, B. (2007) *The Chinese Economy: Transitions and Growth* (Cambridge MA: MIT Press).

Nederveen Pieterse, J. (2001) *Development Theory: Deconstructions/Reconstructions* (London: Sage).

Nederveen Pieterse, J. (2002) 'Fault Lines of Transnationalism: Borders Matter', *Bulletin of the Royal Institute for Inter-Faith Studies*, 4 (2), pp. 33–48.

Nederveen Pieterse, J. (2004a) *Globalization or Empire?* (New York: Routledge).

Nederveen Pieterse, J. (2004b) 'Towards Global Democratization: To WTO or Not to WTO?', *Development and Change*, 35 (5), pp. 1057–63.

Nederveen Pieterse, J. (2005) 'Digital Capitalism and Development: The Unbearable Lightness of ICT4D', in Geert Lovink and Soenke Zehle (eds) *Incommunicado Reader* (Amsterdam: Institute of Network Culture), pp. 11–29.

Nederveen Pieterse, J. (2006) 'Oriental Globalization: Past and Present', in G. Delanty (ed.) *Europe and Asia Beyond East and West: Towards a New Cosmopolitanism* (London: Routledge), pp. 61–73.

Nederveen Pieterse, J. (2007a) 'Political and Economic Brinkmanship', *Review of International Political Economy*, 14 (3), pp. 467–86.

Nederveen Pieterse, J. (2007b) *Ethnicities and Global Multiculture: Pants for an Octopus* (Lanham: Rowman & Littlefield).

Nederveen Pieterse, J. (2008b) *Is There Hope for Uncle Sam? Beyond the American Bubble* (London: Zed).

Néri, M. C. (2007) 'Pobreza e políticas sociais na década da redução da desigualdade', *Nueva Sociedad* (Especial em português), October, pp. 53–75. Available at www.nuso.org/esp_portugues/Cortes%20Neri.pdf, accessed on 25 July 2008.

Ngok, K. (2008) 'The Changes of Chinese Labor Policy and Labor Legislation in the Context of Market Transition', *International Labor and Working-Class History*, 73, 45–64.

Nunes, J. A. (2002) 'Teoria crítica, cultura e ciência: O(s) espaço(s) e o(s) conhecimento(s) da globalização', in B. S. Santos (ed.) *A globalização e as ciências sociais*, 2nd edition (São Paulo: Cortez), pp. 301–44.

Nayyar, D. (2006) 'Economic Growth in Independent India: Lumbering Elephant or Running Tiger?' *Economic and Political Weekly*, April 15, pp. 1451–8.

Ohmae, K. (1992) *The Borderless World: Power and Strategy in the Global Marketplace* (London: HarperCollins).

O'Neill, J. (2009) 'Why It Would Be Wrong To Write off the Brics', *Financial Times*, January 6.

Ong, A. and D. M. Nonini (eds) (1997) *Ungrounded Empires: The Cultural Politics of Modern Chinese Nationalism* (New York and London: Routledge).

Ong, A (1997) 'Chinese Modernities: Narratives of Nation and Capitalism', in A. Ong and D. Nonini (eds) *Ungrounded Empires: The Cultural Politics of Chinese Transnationalism*, (New York and London: Routledge), pp. 171–202.

Ong, A. (1999) *Flexible Citizenship: The Cultural Logics of Transnationality* (Durham NC: Duke University Press).

Ong, A. (2006) *Neoliberalism as Exception: Mutations in Citizenship and Sovereignty* (Durham NC and London: Duke University Press).

Palmisano, S. (2006) 'Multinationals Have Been Superseded', *Financial Times*, 12 June.

Pang Zhongying (2005) 'China's Changing Attitude to UN Peacekeeping', *International Peacekeeping*, 12 (1) (Spring), pp. 87–104.

Panitch, L., C. Leys, A. Zuege and M. Konings (eds) (2004) *The Globalization Decade* (London: The Merlin Press).

Parker, G. and A. Beattie (2006) 'Chinese Lenders 'Undercutting' on Africa Loans', *Financial Times*, 29 November, p. 3.

Pathak, K. N. (2005) 'Education-Time for Over All', *The Tribune*, September 24.

Patnaik, P. (2005) 'The Economics of the New Phase of Imperialism', Retrieved 30 Sept 2005 from www.networkideas.org/themes/world/aug2005/we26_Economics_New_Phase.htm

Peel, Q. (2005) 'The South's Rise is Hindered at Home', *Financial Times*, 17 November, p. 17.

Pei Minxin (2006) 'The Dark Side of China's Rise', *Foreign Policy*, 153 (March/April), pp. 32–40.

People's Democracy (2006) XXX (26), 25 June.

Perry, E. J. and M. Selden (2004) 'Introduction: Reform and Resistance in Contemporary China', in E. J. Perry and M. Selden (eds) *Chinese Society: Change, Conflict and Resistance* (London: Routledge Curzon), pp. 1–22.

Petras, J. (2006) *The Power of Israel in the United States* (Atlanta: Clarity Press).

Petrusewicz, M., J. Schneider and P. Schneider (eds) (2008) *Come Studiare i Sud* (Bologna: Il Mulino).

Pilling, D. and F. Guerrera (2003) 'We Are a Mixture. Western Style in Management But With an Eastern Touch', *Financial Times*, 26 September.

Ping, Huang (2006) 'Globalization and Inequality in Rural China', in Göran Therborn (ed.) *Inequalities of the World: New Theoretical Frameworks, Multiple Empirical Approaches* (London and New York: Verso), pp. 220–46.

Ping, Huang and F. Pieke (2003) *China Migration Country Study*, Regional Conference on Migration, Development and Pro-Poor Policies in Asia, Dhaka, Bangladesh, at www.livelihoods.org/hot_topics/docs/Dhaka_CP_3.pdf (home page), accessed 10 July 2008.

Ping, Huang and Zhan Shaohua (2005) *Internal Migration in China: Linking It To Development*, Regional Conference on Migration and Development in Asia, Lanzhou, China, at www.iom.int/chinaconference/files/documents/bg_papers/china.pdf (home page), accessed 10 July 2008.

Planning Commission (2008) 'Development Challenges in Extremist Affected Areas', April (New Delhi: Government. of India).

Pocha, J. S. (2005) 'China's New Left', *New Perspectives Quarterly*, 22 (2) (Spring), pp. 25–31.

Polanyi, K. (2001) *The Great Transformation: The Political and Economic Origins of Our Time* (Boston: Beacon Press).

Pomeranz, K. (2000) *The Great Divergence* (Princeton: Princeton University Press).

Porter, E. (2004) 'Private Investors Abroad Cut Their Investments in the US', *New York Times*, 19 October.

Porter, E. (2007) 'The Divisions that Tighten the Purse Strings', *New York Times*, 29 April, p. BU4.

Portes, A., L.-E. Guarnizo and P. Landolt (1999) 'The Study of Transnationalism: Pitfalls and Promise of an Emergent Research Field', *Ethnic and Racial Studies* 22 (2), pp. 217–37.

PRC—Embassy of the People's Republic of China in the Federal Democratic Republic of Ethiopia (2006) 'Interview with Chinese Ambassador, H.E. Mr. Lin Lin', on Ethiopian National Radio, 12 June 2006. Sourced on 16 July 2008 from http://et.china-embassy.org/eng/zagx/t282697.htm

Prestowitz, C. (2005) *Three Billion New Capitalists: the Great Shift of Wealth and Power to the East* (New York: Basic Books).

Priester, Karin (2007) *Populismus – historische und aktuelle Erscheinungsformen* (Frankfurt: Campus).

Putnam, R., R. Leonardi and R. Y. Nanetti (1993) *Making Democracy Work: Civic Traditions in Modern Italy* (Princeton: Princeton University Press).

Quijano, A. (2005) 'Colonialidade do poder, eurocentrismo e América Latina', in E. Lander (ed.) *A colonialidade do saber. Eurocentrismo e ciências sociais: perspectivas latino-americanas* (Buenos Aires: Clacso), pp. 227–78.

Quisumbing, A. (2007) 'Poverty Transitions, Shocks, and Consumption in Rural Bangladesh: Preliminary Results from a Longitudinal Household Survey', CPRC Working Paper 105 (Manchester: Chronic Poverty Research Centre).

Rai, S. (2006) 'India Becoming a Crucial Cog at the Machine at IBM', *New York Times*, 4 June.

Raijman, R. (2001) 'Mexican Immigrants and Informal Self-Employment in Chicago', *Human Organization* 60 (1), pp. 47–55.

Ramchandran, H. and S. L. Arora (2004) *Employment, Alternative Economic Survey* (New Delhi: Rainbow Publishers).

Ramo, J. C. (2004) *The Beijing Consensus* (London: The Foreign Policy Centre).

Rapley, J. (1996) *Understanding Development: Theory and Practice in the Third World* (Boulder: Lynne Rienner).

Rawski, T. and D. Perkins (2008) 'Forecasting China's Economic Growth to 2025', in L. Brandt and T. Rawski (eds) *China's Great Economic Transformation* (New York: Cambridge University Press), pp. 829–86.

Rehbein, B. (2007) *Globalization, Culture and Society in Laos* (London/New York: Routledge).

Rehbein, B. and H. Schwengel (2008) *Theorien der Globalisierung* (Constance: UVK (UTB)).

Reifer, T. E. (2005) 'Globalization, Democratization, and Global Elite Formation in Hegemonic Cycles: a Geopolitical Economy', in J. Friedman and C. Chase-Dunn (eds) *Hegemonic Declines: Past And Present* (Boulder: Paradigm), pp. 183–203.

Research Unit for Political Economy (2006) 'Why the United States Promotes India's Great Power Ambitions', *Monthly Review*, LVII (March), pp. 16–33

Reuters (2008) 'China Expands Credit Line to Oil-rich Angola', 4 July 2008. Sourced 16 July 2008 from www.alertnet.org/thenews/newsdesk/L0460226.htm

Roach, S. (2006) 'Globalization's New Underclass: China, the US, Japan and the Changing Face of Inequality', *Japan Focus*, retrieved 16 April, 2006, http://japanfocus.org/article.asp?id=575.

Robbins, R. H. (2004) *Global Problems and the Culture of Capitalism*, 3rd edition (Boston: Allyn & Bacon).

Rodrik, D. (2000) 'How Far Will International Economic Integration Go?', *Journal of Economic Perspectives*, 14 (1), pp. 177–86.

Rodrik, D. (2004) 'Globalization and Growth – Looking in the Wrong Places', *Journal of Policy Modeling*, 26, pp. 513–17.

Rodrik, Dani (2006) 'What's so Special about China's Exports' (Cambridge MA: Harvard University Press),

Rohter, L. (2005) 'Brazil Weighs Costs and Benefits of Alliance With China', *New York Times*, 20 November.

Rosenau, J. N. (1997) *Along the Domestic–Foreign Frontier: Exploring Governance in a Turbulent World* (Cambridge: Cambridge University Press).

Rosenau, J. N. (1999) 'The Future of Politics', *Futures*, 31 (9–10), pp. 1005–16.

Ross, A. (2006) *Fast Boat to China: Corporate Flight and the Consequences of Free Trade Lessons from Shanghai* (New York: Pantheon)

Sainath, P. (1996) *Everybody Loves a Good Drought* (New Delhi: Penguin).

Salmen, L. (1987) *Listen to the People: Participant-Observer Evaluation of Development Projects* (New York: Oxford University Press).

Samuel, H. (2008) 'African Leaders Revel in Largesse While People Live in Poverty', *Daily Telegraph*, 16 July, sourced on that day from www.telegraph. co.uk / news / worldnews /africaandindianocean/ 2303326/African-leaders-revel-in-largesse-while-people-live-in-poverty.html

Santos, B. S. (2002) 'Os processos da globalização', in B. S. Santos (ed.) *A globalização e as ciências sociais*, 2nd edition (São Paulo: Cortez).

Santos, B S. (ed.) (2003) *Reconhecer para libertar: os caminhos do cosmopolitismo multicultural* (Rio de Janeiro: Civilização Brasileira).

Sassen, S. (1995) 'On Concentration and Centrality in the Global City', in L. Knocks and J. Taylor (eds) *World Cities in a World System* (Cambridge: Cambridge University Press), pp. 63–78.

Sassen, S. (1998) *Globalization and its Discontents* (New York: New Press).

Sautman, B. and Yan Hairong (2008) 'Friends and Interests: China's Distinctive Links with Africa', in D. Grace Guerrero and Firoze Manji (eds) *China's New Role in Africa and the South. A Search for a New Perspective* (Cape Town, Nairobi and Oxford: Fahamu).

Savant, J.-C. (2005) 'China's Trade Safari in Africa', *Le Monde Diplomatique*, 11 May, at http://mondediplo.com/2005/05/11chinaafrica

Scalapino, R. A. (2005) 'China and the United States: Prevailing National Goals and Bilateral Relations.' Paper presented at the conference on 'China and the US Mutual Perceptions and Bilateral Relations', Center for American Studies, Fudan University, Shanghai, 27–28 May.

Schaeffer, R. K. (1997) *Understanding Globalization* (Lanham: Rowman & Littlefield).

Scherer-Warren, I. (1999) *Cidadania sem Fronteiras: Ações Coletivas na Era da Globalização* (São Paulo: Hucitec).

Schmidt, V. H. (2006) 'Multiple Modernities or Varieties of Modernity?', *Current Sociology*, 54 (1), pp. 77–97.

Schwengel, H. (2006a) 'Globalization with a European Face. Mediating Emerging Powers', in *Theory, Culture, and Society*, 23 (2–3), Special Issue on Problematizing Global Knowledge, pp. 414–16.

Schwengel, H. (2006b) 'The Public Sociology of Emerging Powers. The Machiavellian Moment for the Social Sciences.' Lecture at the Annual Meeting of the Indian Sociological Association in Chennai; Indian Sociological Association.

Schwengel, H. (2007) *Optimismus im Konjunktiv*. E-book at www.freidok.unifreiburg.de/volltexte/2008.

Scott, J. C. (1990) *Domination and the Arts of Resistance: Hidden Transcripts* (New Haven: Yale University Press).

Scruggs, L. and J. Allan. (2006) 'The Material Consequences of Welfare States: Benefit Generosity and Absolute Poverty in 16 OECD Countries', *Comparative Political Studies*, 39 (97), pp. 880–904.

Selden, M. (1997) 'China, Japan and the Regional Political Economy of East Asia, 1945–1995', in Peter Katzenstein and Takashi Shiraishi (eds) *Network Power: Japan and Asia* (Ithaca and London: Cornell University Press), pp. 306–40.

Sen, A. (2002) 'How to Judge Globalism', *The American Prospect*, 13 (1), available at www.prospect.org/print/V13/1/sen-a.html

Sen, A. (2006) *The Argumentative Indian: Writings on Indian Culture, History and Identity* (London: Penguin).

Sen, B. (2003) 'Drivers of Escape and Descent: Changing Household Fortunes in Rural Bangladesh', *World Development*, 31 (3), pp. 513–34.

Sen, G., A. Iyer and A. George. (2002) 'Structural Reforms and Health Equity: A Comparison of NSS Surveys, 1986–87 and 1995–96', *Economic and Political Weekly* (Mumbai), April 6.

Shanker, T. (2005) 'Rumsfeld Issues a Sharp Rebuke to China on Arms', *New York Times*, 4 June.

Shiva, V. and K. Jalees (2006) *Roti, kapda aur makaan* (New Delhi: Navdanya).

Shukai, Zhao (2000) 'Criminality and the Policing of Migrant Workers', *The China Journal*, 43, pp. 101–10.

Silva, Graziella Moraes Dias da (2006) 'Ações afirmativas no Brasil e na África do Sul', *Tempo Social*, 18 (2), pp. 131–65.

Silverman, G. (2005) 'Developing Countries Underpin Boom in Advertising Spending', *Financial Times*, 24 October

Singh, Manmohan, (2007a) 'We're off to a Good Start', *Times of India*, 25 October.

Singh, Manmohan (2007b) 'Ten Points Social Charter', *The Financial Express*, 25 May.

SIPRI—Stockholm International Peace Research Institute (2008) *Sipri Yearbook 2008: Armaments* (Stockholm: SIPRI).

Skinner, G. W. (1985) 'Rural Marketing in China: Repression and Revival', *The China Quarterly*, 103, pp. 393–413.

Slavin, B. (2007) 'US Support Key to Ethiopia's Invasion', *USA Today*. 1 August, sourced on 13 July 2008 from www.usatoday.com/news/world/2007-01-07-ethiopia_x.htm

Snow, P. (1995) 'China and Africa: Consensus and Camouflage', in T. Robinson and D. Shambaugh (eds) *Chinese Foreign Policy: Theory and Practice* (Oxford: Oxford University Press).

So, A. (2003) 'Introduction: Rethinking the Chinese Developmental Miracle', in A. So (ed.) *China's Developmental Miracle: Origins, Transformations, and Challenges* (New York and London: M.E. Sharpe), pp. 3–26.

Social Watch India (2007) *Citizens' Report on Governance and Development* (New Delhi: Sage).

Solinger, D. (1999) *Contesting Citizenship in Urban China: Peasant Migrants, the State, and the Logic of the Market* (Berkeley and London: University of California Press).

Solinger, D. (2003a) 'Chinese Urban Jobs and the WTO', *The China Journal*, 49, pp. 61–87.

Solinger, D. (2003b) 'State Transitions and Citizenship Shifts in China', Center for the Study of Democracy: University of California, Irvine, at http://repositories.cdlib.org/csd/03-12 (home page); accessed 1 July 2008.

Soros, G. (2002) *On Globalization* (New York: Public Affairs).

Souza, J. (2000) *A modernização seletiva: uma interpretação do dilema brasileiro* (Brasília: Universidade de Brasília).

Souza, J. (2003) *A Construção Social da Subcidadania. Para uma sociologia política da modernidade periférica* (Belo Horizonte: UFMG Press).

Souza, J. (ed.) (2006) *A invisibilidade da desigualdade brasileira* (Belo Horizonte: UFMG).

Souza, J. and F. Pinheiro (2003) 'Para a ralé, nada: entrevista com Jessé Souza', *No-mínimo*, 5, December. Available at: http://nominimo.ibest.com.br/ newstorm. notitia.presentation.Navigation Servlet?publicationCode=1&page Code=51; accessed 8 December 2003.

Steger, M. B. (2002) *Globalism: The New Market Ideology* (Lanham: Rowman & Littlefield).

Stein, G. J. (1999) *Rethinking World Systems. Diasporas, Colonies, and Interaction in Uruk, Mesopotamia* (Tucson: University of Arizona Press).

Stiglitz, J. (2002) *Globalization and its Discontents* (New York: Norton).

Stiglitz, Joseph E. (2006) *Making Globalization Work* (New York: Norton).

Stockholm International Peace Research Institute (SIPRI) (2004) *SIPRI Yearbook 2004*, Stockholm: SIPRI.

Storper, M. (2001) 'Lived Effects of the Contemporary Economy: Globalization, Inequality and Consumer Society', in J. Comaroff and J. L. Comaroff (eds) *Millennial Capitalism and the Culture of Neoliberalism* (Durham NC: Duke University Press), pp. 88–124.

Sun Zhe (2005) 'China's Peaceful Rise: Internal Debate and American Perception.' Paper presented at the conference on 'China and the US Mutual Perceptions and Bilateral Relations', Center for American Studies, Fudan University, Shanghai, 27–28 May.

Suri, K. C. (2006) 'Political Economy of Agrarian Distress', *Economic and Political Weekly*, 22 April.

Sztompka, P. (2006) 'Presidential Address', XVI World Congress of Sociology, Durban.

Taylor, I. (1998) 'China's Foreign Policy towards Africa in the 1990s', *Journal of Modern African Studies*, 36 (3), pp. 443–60.

Taylor, I. (2004) 'The "All-weather Friend"? Sino-African Interaction in the Twenty First Century', in I. Taylor and P. Williams (eds) *Africa in International Politics: External Involvement on Africa* (London: Routledge).

Taylor, I. (2006) *China and Africa: Engagement and Compromise* (London: Routledge).

Tejpal, Tarun J. (2006) 'India's Future, Beyond Dogma', *Tehelka, The People's Paper*, 25 November, p. 3.

The East African Standard (2006) 'Kenya Signs Exploration Contract', Nairobi, 18 April.

The Standard (2006) 'Oil Deals Likely as Angola Turns East', Beijing, 21 June.

Quoted in Ian Taylor, 'China's Oil Diplomacy', *International Affairs*, 82 (5), 2006, pp. 937–59.

Therborn, Göran, and Habibul Haque Khondker (eds) (2006) *Introduction to Asia and Europe in Globalization. Continents, Regions, and Nations* (Leiden and Boston: Brill).

Thompson, D. (1999) 'Skin Deep: Citizenship, Inclusion and Entitlements for the "Dark"-skinned Woman in Jamaica.' MA thesis, Institute of Social Studies, The Hague.

Thrift, N. (2004) *Knowing Capitalism* (London: Sage).

Timmons, H. (2006) 'Asia Finding Rich Partners in Middle East', *New York Times*, 1 December, pp. C1–5.

Trading Markets (2008) 'Anglo American to Invest Further US$400 m in Country', 26 June, sourced on 10 July 2008 from www.tradingmarkets.com/.site/news/Stock%20News/1715158/

Traub, J. (2006) 'The World According to China', *New York Times Magazine*, 3 September, pp. 24–9.

Trinh, T. and S. Voss (2006) 'China's Commodity Hunger: Implications for Africa and Latin America', *Deutsche Bank Report*, 13 June.

Truong, Thanh-Dam (1999) 'The Underbelly of the Tiger: Gender and the Demystification of the Asian Miracle', *Review of International Political Economy*, 6 (2), pp. 133–65.

Tucker, S. (2007) 'Asia Seeks Its Centre', *Financial Times*, 6 July, p. 7.

Tunon, M. (2006) *Internal Labor Migration in China: Features and Responses* (Beijing: International Labor Organization).

Tyrell, H. (2005) 'Singular or Plural – Preliminary Remarks on Globalization', in B. Heintz, R. Münch and H. Tyrell (eds.) *Weltgesellschaft*. Special Issue *Zeitschrift für Soziologie* (Stuttgart: Lucius & Lucius), pp. 1–50.

UN Country Team China (2004) *Common Country Assessment 2004: Balancing Development to Achieve an All-Round Xiaokang and Harmonious Society in China*, www.un.org.cn/public/resource (home page), accessed 15 June 2008.

UNDP (2005) *Human Development Report 2005: International Cooperation at a Crossroads: Aid, Trade, and Security in an Unequal World* (New York: UNDP).

United Nations (2007) *World Economic Situation and Prospects 2007* (New York: United Nations).

Urry, J. (2000) *Sociology Beyond Societies* (London: Routledge).

Van de Walle, N. (2001) *African Economies and the Politics of Permanent Crisis* (Cambridge: Cambridge University Press).

Van Luyn, F.-J. (2008) *A Floating City of Peasants: The Great Migration in Contemporary China* (New York and London: The New Press).

Vanguard (2005) 'Nigeria to Supply China 30,000 B/D of Crude Oil . . . Corporation to make $800 m.' Lagos, 12 July.

Vatikiotis, M. (2005) 'Why the Middle East is Turning to Asia', *International Herald Tribune*, 24 June.

Vianna, L. W. and M. A. Rezende de Carvalho (2000) *República e Civilização Brasileira*, in *Gramsci e o Brasil*. Available at www.artnet.com.br/gramsci/arquiv 119.htm. Accessed 20 January 2001.

Wade, R. (1996) 'Japan, the World Bank and the Art of Paradigm Maintenance: the East Asian Miracle in Political Perspective', *New Left Review*, 217, pp. 3–36.

Wade, R. H. (2001) 'The Rising Inequality of World Income Distribution', *Finance and Development*, 38 (4), pp. 34–9.

Wade, R. H. (2004) 'Is Globalization Reducing Poverty and Inequality?', *World Development*, 32 (4), pp. 567–89.

Wade, R. H. (2005) 'Bringing the State Back In: Lessons from East Asia's Development Experience', *Internationale Politik und Gesellschaft*, IPG, 2, pp. 98–115.

Wallerstein, I. (1979) 'Dependence in an Interdependent World: the Limited Possibilities of Transformation within the Capitalist World-economy', in I. Wallerstein, *The Capitalist World-Economy* (New York: Cambridge University Press), pp. 66–94.

Wallerstein, I. (1993) *Historical Capitalism* (London: Verso).

Wallerstein, I. (1999) 'The Rise of East Asia, or The World-System in the Twenty-First Century', in Immanuel Wallerstein (1999) *The End of the World As We Know It* (Minneapolis: University of Minnesota Press), pp. 34–48.

Wang Yong (2000) 'China's Domestic WTO Debate', *China Business Review*, 27 (1) (January–February), pp. 54–62.

Wang Zhengyi (2004) 'Conceptualizing Economic Security and Governance: China Confronts Globalization', *Pacific Review*, 17 (4) (December), pp. 523–45.

Watts, J. and A. Clark (2007) 'China Flexes Financial Muscle with $3bn Stake in US Private Equity Firm', *The Guardian*, 22 May.

Weisbrot, M. (2002) 'The Mirage of Progress', *The American Prospect*, 13 (1), January, avaliable at www.prospect.org/print/V13/1/weisbrot-m.html.

Weil, Robert (2006) 'Conditions of the Working Classes in China', *Monthly Review*, LVIII (June), pp. 25–48.

Weitzman, H. (2005) 'Peru Takes Faltering Steps in Bid to Win China Prize', *Financial Times*, 30 May.

Whalley, J. and X. Yue. (2006) 'Rural Income Volatility and Inequality in China', National Bureau of Economic Research Working Paper 12779 (Cambridge MA: NBER)

Whelan, C. (2004) 'Developing Countries' Economic Clout Grows', *International Herald Tribune*, 10–11 July, p. 15.

White, D., A. England, T. Hawkins, D. Mahtani, J. Reed and A. Yeh (2006) 'Friend or Forager? How China is Winning the Resources and the Loyalties of Africa', *Financial Times*, 23 February.

Whitehead, M., G. Dahlgren and T. Evans (2001) 'Equity and Health Sector Reforms: Can Low-Income Countries Escape the Medical Poverty Trap?', *The Lancet*, 358, pp. 833–36.

Williams, Ian (2004) 'The Real National Security Threat: the Bush Economy', *AlterNet*, 13 January.

Wilson, D. (2007) *Cities and Race: America's New Black Ghettos* (London: Routledge).

Winn, N. (ed.) (2004) *Neo-medievalism and Civil Wars* (London: Frank Cass).

Wolf, M. (2005) 'On the Move: Asia's Giants Take Different Routes in Pursuit of Economic Greatness', *Financial Times*, 23 February.

Wolfe, A. (2005) The 'Great Game' Heats Up in Central Asia, *Power and Interest News Report*, 3 August.

Wong, J. and S. Chang (2006) 'China's Outward Direct Investment: Expanding Worldwide', *China: An International Journal*, 1 (2), pp. 273–301.

Woon, Yuen-Fong (1999) 'Labor Migration in the 1990s: Homeward Orientation of Migrants in the Pearl River Delta and Its Implications for Interior China', *Modern China*, Vol. 25 (4), pp. 475–512.

World Bank (1998) 'The Initiative on Defining, Monitoring and Measuring Social Capital', Social Capital Initiative Working Paper 1 (Washington DC: World Bank).

World Bank (2006) *World Development Report* (New York: Oxford University Press).

Xia Liping (2004) 'The New Security Concept in China's New Thinking on International Strategy', *International Review*, 34 (Spring), pp. 29–42.

Xin, Chen (2003) 'New Development of Consumerism in Chinese Society in the Late 1990s', in Lau Kin Chi and Huang Pin (eds) *China Reflected*, special issues of *Asian Exchange*, 18 (2) and 19 (1), pp. 162–75.

Xinhua (2006) 'China Provides Assistance to Africa Without Political Strings', 23 June, sourced on 16 July 2008 from www1.china.org.cn/english/features/wenjiabaoafrica/172485.htm

Xinhua (2007) 'Roundup: China-Zambia Ties Cemented through Assistance, Investment', 2 March, sourced on p July 2008 from http://news.xinhuanet.com/english/2007-02/03/content_5690521.htm

Xinhua Domestic Service (1990) March 12. Cited in *FBHIS-CHI*, 12 March 1990. Quoted in Taylor (2004).

Xu, K., D. Evans, K. Kawabata, R. Zeramdini, J. Klavus and C. Murray (2003) 'Household Catastrophic Health Expenditure: A Multi-country Analysis', *The Lancet*, 362, pp. 111–17.

Ye Jiang (2002) 'Will China Be a "Threat" to Its Neighbors and the World in the Twenty-first Century?', *Ritstumeikan Annual Review of International Studies*, 1 (December), pp. 55–68.

Yu Xintian (2004) 'Understanding and Preventing New Conflicts and Wars: China's Peaceful Rise as a Strategic Choice', *International Review*, 35 (Summer), pp. 1–16.

Yu, G. T. (1991) 'Chinese Foreign Policy since Tiananmen: The Search for Friends and Influence', in T. Lee (ed.) *China and World Political Development and International Issues* (Taipei: Cheng).

Yúdice, G. (2004) The *Expediency of Culture: Uses of Culture in the Global Era* (Durham NC: Duke University Press).

Zhang, Li (2001) *Strangers in the City: Reconfigurations of Space, Power, and Social Networks Within China's Floating Population* (Stanford: Stanford University Press).

Zhao Quansheng (2005) 'Beijing's Dilemma with Taiwan: War or Peace?', *The Pacific Review*, 18 (2), pp. 217–42.

Zhou, Kate Xiao (1996) *How The Farmers Changed China: Power of the People* (Boulder: Westview Press).

Zong He (2005) 'Helping NGOs Develop Strength', *China Daily*, 28–29 May.

Zoubir, L. S. (2004) 'Not Just the World's Workshop', *Le Monde diplomatique* (English edition), October.

Zysman, J. and S. Cohen (1987) *Manufacturing Matters: the Myth of the Post-industrial Economy* (New York: Basic Books).

Index